Work, Consumption and Culture

Affluence and Social Change in the Twenty-first Century

Work, Consumption and Culture

Affluence and Social Change in the
Twenty-first Century

Work, Consumption and Culture

Affluence and Social Change in the Twenty-first Century

Paul Ransome

SAGE Publications
London ● Thousand Oaks ● New Delhi

First published 2005

SAGE Publications Ltd
1 Oliver's Yard
55 City Road
London EC1Y 1SP

SAGE Publications Inc
2455 Teller Road
Thousand Oaks, California 91320

SAGE Publications India Pvt Ltd
B-42 Panchsheel Enclave
Post Box 4109
New Delhi 110 017

British Library Cataloguing in Publication data

A catalogue record for this book is available from the British Library

ISBN 0 7619 5984 X
     0-7619 5985 8

Library of Congress control number available

Typeset by C&M Digitals (P) Ltd., Chennai, India
Printed in Great Britain by Athenaeum Press, Gateshead

For Willow (aged two), Alfred (aged four) and Harriet
(aged thirty-something)

Contents

Preface and acknowledgements

The discussion presented in the chapters which follow runs a considerable risk of error and omission not least because of the breadth of the subject matter it grapples with. A more concise discussion of work or of consumption or of culture would have saved some of the author's embarrassment, but this would have meant sacrificing one of the main objectives of the study, which is to look at the relationships between work, consumption and culture. We have made arguments about these relationships and the importance of affluence as a driving force in their constitution. We have drawn support from the substantial corpus of theoretical work already available. We have looked at statistical evidence on incomes and patterns of consumption. We have developed secondary analyses of previous empirical work, and we have brought forward new ethnographic data on perceptions of occupational roles and gender. Ultimately however, it is up to the reader to decide whether these arguments are persuasive.

I am especially grateful to the publishers for their forbearance in supporting a project which was longer in the making than intended. I am also grateful for support from the Economic and Social Research Council who funded the research (award number L2122520120) which yielded the data referred to in Chapter 7. I also had the pleasure of presenting the basic arguments to undergraduates in the Department of Sociology and Anthropology, University of Wales, Swansea. The current audit regime in higher education sometimes inhibits the production of extended pieces of work, but the performance and banter of the lecture theatre and seminar room still provide a highly stimulating environment in which to test one's ideas.

In the end however, writing requires a place to concentrate and it is my family who have played the leading role in providing this. In being completed the book is already a success for us and signifies just how much I am indebted to them.

1 *Introduction: the affluence hypothesis*

The key elements in this book are work, consumption and culture. The purpose is to look again at the increasingly popular idea that the lives of people now living in the industrialised West are determined much more by the way they consume things than by how they produce them. That consumption has displaced production as the leading factor in shaping the kind of society people are now living in.

So why would it matter if the realm of consumption had displaced the realm of production or work as the dominant realm of activity from which people construct their lives and why might such a change be of interest to sociologists? The short answer is that since the production side of human activity provides the foundation of human activity in general, it is no small matter to suggest either that production is no longer as important as it once was, let alone that some other realm has become more important even than work. If consumption has become emphatic in determining how people live their lives, how they relate to others and how they express their identity, this would mean that a pretty major shift has taken place in the character of modern society (for example: Campbell, 1987; Featherstone, 1991; and Millar, 1995). An apparent decline in the importance of work for people and for society re-opens fundamental questions about why people do the activities they do and the purposes or goals they hope to fulfil through doing them (Slater, 1997a and 1997b). In proposing that production-side activities no longer have the priority they once had, it is not so much a matter of showing that work is no longer important, since clearly human activity in general still depends on the satisfactory discharge of production-side responsibilities, but of saying clearly why the activities of consumption have become more important, how has it come about that 'the figure of the consumer and the experience of consumerism is both exemplary of the new world and integral to its making' (Slater, 1997b: 9)?

Production versus consumption

In arguing the case for the rise of consumption then, we need to explain why people now seek the outcomes of consumption-type activities more vigorously than the outcomes of production-type activities. Compared with other kinds of activity, the meaning and purpose of working activities and the reason why they are given priority is clear, since work is the primary means of satisfying our survival needs. The meaning of work is a largely practical matter and so are the consequences of it for a person's social and economic position, and their status in society more generally. To the extent that consumption is a necessary corollary of production we can explain acts of simple consumption wholly or partly in terms of the same motivations and expectations which we refer to in explaining acts of production – in order to achieve this or that outcome, I need to produce and consume this or that commodity. And if this is the limit of our analysis there would be no need to invoke the idea of a transition from a work-based to a consumption-based social type since limited consumption is part and parcel of production.

Many acts of consumption however, are much more complex than this and administer to desires and expectations which are not always clear and which often vary from one individual to another. In order to support the case for the rise of consumption one would have to show that people seek outcomes through consumption which are somehow outside or beyond what they can achieve through work and that people really do believe in the meaning and purpose of consumption and in a measure which surpasses that attributed to working activities. If these developments had taken place, then a reasonably strong case could be made for describing a type of society, a way of living, in which people give priority to the outcomes of consumption rather than of production. A consumption-based society would be one in which people's lives are largely structured by consumption, and where the activities of consumption are seen as carrying the highest levels of meaning and purpose. As Cross expresses it: 'Consumerism is not only the basis of both the modern economic order and public culture, but it defines how most people organise their time around working and spending' (Cross, 1993: 184).

Sociology and consumption

In answer to the second question, if one accepts that sociology is all about trying to understand the forms and meanings of human social action,[1] then sociologists are bound to be interested in the boundaries which lie between one realm of activity and another. If the realm of activities we call work, a realm which is believed by many to dominate human social action, has been superseded by its apparent opposite, this is bound to attract a good deal of attention (Warde, 1990a: 1990b). Whether as sociologists or not, we are able to make pretty accurate judgements about where people stand in society and how we should interact with them, along the various ribs which lead off from the spine which working life provides. It represents a considerable departure from all conventional sociological accounts of modern society to suggest that something *other than* work and production gives society its basic character and structure (Featherstone, 1990). Modern societies are so-called because of their position in the historical sequence, but what makes them 'modern' is the fact that they are characterised by a particular way of *producing things*. What we are trying to do in this book is to see not only if modernity is also characterised by a particular way or *consuming things*, but whether a point has been reached where the consumption side has become dominant.

Actions speak louder than words

As one might expect then, much of the discussion in the following chapters will be taken up with an account of differences in the types of things people do when they are producing things and when they are consuming them. Continuity from one phase of social development to another is a consequence of the fact that people keep on doing many of the same things, and in this instance, that means work. This must be the case since certain of our actions are unavoidable if we want to keep ourselves alive. Basic needs are not negotiable and so neither are the basic survival-making or, in our kind of society, income-getting, activities. Continuity is also maintained because the same people are involved in production and in consumption; these activities are not carried out by different sets of people who only ever meet at the moment of exchange. Unless one holds to the idea that people living in these societies are suffering from mass schizophrenia, it follows that the needs and desires which motivate one part of their activities are going to have an impact on other parts of it. Another of the arguments we will be making is that understanding the relationship between work-based and consumption-based society means that we have to understand how production and consumption are interrelated. More often than not they are two parts or phases of a larger single whole and so consequently, 'production and consumption must be analysed as a unity rather than as a simple opposition' (Fine and Leopold, 1993: 253).

The meaning of it all

Although we will need to spend some time describing and evaluating physical similarities and contrasts in the activities of the two realms, we are also interested in similarities and contrasts in the ways which people understand and justify their activities as producers and as consumers.

Differences in the ways which such understandings are arrived at, and in the contents of those understandings, tell us a good deal about whether, and how, consumption-based society might differ from work-based society. We will work from the premise that the understanding people have of their activities is made up partly of practical meaning in the sense that some physical outcome emerges, an outcome which confirms or validates that activity, but that it is also made up of a cognitive or ideational meaning in the sense that intellectually, we try to justify or legitimate our actions by reference to our value system.[2]

The search for meaning is carried out on a number of fronts and often at the same time. One of the fronts in which this volume is particularly interested is the front along which people struggle to understand the meaning of activity as it affects their sense of personal and social identity. Accepting that an important aspect of the meaning people find in or give to their activities is how it enables them to express their sense of self, it follows that one of the key respects in which the activities of work and of consumption might be thought to differ one from the other is in terms of their impact on how people develop a sense of identity. If it is the case that '[modern] identity is best understood through the image of consumption', that the resources 'through which we produce and sustain identities increasingly take the form of consumer goods and activities ...' (Slater, 1997b: 85), then it is important to know whether such a change really is taking place and what may have become of the identity-meanings associated with production.

THE AFFLUENCE HYPOTHESIS

Not only are we interested in the kinds of activities and experiences which we take to be constitutive of work-based and consumption-based social types, we are also interested in the mechanism by which one type might develop into the other type. Many factors are implicated in such a change (and many of them have been discussed at length),[3] but in this account we want to single out the decisive role played by 'affluence' defined in the first instance, and quite simply, as ready access to surplus income. The basic argument we hope to support is that affluence – a capacity and expectation to spend freely – increases the range and variety of people's experiences because surplus income gives people choice over the commodities and services they consume. Choice signifies autonomy and autonomy signifies an awareness that things do not have to remain as they are. If we accept that choice and autonomy are universally desirable features of human social life, the prospect of living in an affluent society will be regarded by many as 'a good thing', as 'better than' living in one where freedom to spend has yet to be achieved. (Affluent) consumption becomes '... the privileged site of autonomy, meaning, subjectivity, privacy and freedom' (Slater, 1997b: 31). Both in terms of the kind of activity it is (at the level of formal rationality), and in terms of the meanings people attribute to consumption as they try to understand and justify their activities as affluent consumers (as a form of substantive rationality), affluence is an enabling force in social development.

In order to argue convincingly that affluence influences social development in this way one would need to show not only that there is such a thing as affluence and that it is has become a general characteristic of the way of life of people living in that kind of society, but also that it has materially altered the balance between work and consumption as the primary influence over people's lives. The basic argument here is that as people are more easily able to satisfy their basic survival needs, they have devoted an increasing proportion of their disposable income to consumption and leisure activities, and have consequently come to regard work as of secondary rather than primary importance. Rather than living in a society in which our orientation to self and other is largely determined by activities carried out in the realm of work, we are now living in one in which these orientations are largely determined by activities in the realm of consumption: a society wherein 'consumption now comprises the labour by which we appropriate goods and prise them out of the anonymous and oppressive conditions under which they are manufactured and exchanged ...' (Millar (ed.), 2001a, Vol. I: 7). The significant thing about affluence and choice is that under conditions of affluence we are able to consume things because they bring pleasure and satisfaction in and of themselves without always being tied to the satisfaction of basic needs. Affluence allows consumption for purposes other than simple subsistence. As a result 'the meaningful or cultural aspect of consumption comes to predominate, and people become more concerned with the meanings of goods than with their functional use to meet a basic or "real" need' (Slater, 1997b: 133).

Whilst recognising that the analysis of needs and wants, of survival and satisfaction deserves close attention (standard points of departure are Soper, 1981; Doyal and Gough, 1991) and may be something which should be central to a critical evaluation of 'how we live in consumer society' (Slater, 1997a and 1997b) we will simply state two things which guide the discussion in this book. One is that particular actions, whether of production or consumption, can provide more than one type or aspect of satisfaction or pleasure and often at the same time. For example, eating *tapas* in a trendy wine bar satisfies private as well as social needs; nutritional as well as symbolic ones and, even if in different measures, simultaneously. Second, that the desire for satisfaction is very often something which is constantly renewed because many needs are only ever temporarily fulfilled. However completely I satisfy my hunger at breakfast time, I will have to do so all over again at supper time. In saying that such-and-such an action satisfies this-or-that need we have to accept the multi-faceted nature of satisfaction and the rarity of needs which can actually be satisfied once and for all.

A counter argument would be that even if an increasing proportion of the population can afford to spend more of its resources on consumption-type activities this does not mean that everyone is able so to do. Affluence is a fortunate circumstance for the minority but is not universally achievable. In addition, it is logical to assert that a consumer ethic has to be based on a work ethic of some kind, since people still have to earn enough money to support their consumer lifestyle. Maintaining high levels of disposable income might actually reinforce the work ethic, and motivate people to work more rather than less energetically. As we shall see in the following chapter, there is strong support for this view amongst economists and sociologists. Reviewing explanations of why hours of work have tended to increase rather than decrease during the twentieth century despite increases in the efficiency of production, Voth concludes for example that this was because 'of the lure of new and increasingly affordable consumer goods' (Voth, 1998: 157). Similarly, Cross concludes that consumer society is characterised by a preference for goods rather than for free time such that people prefer to work the same hours (or more) in return for the capacity to buy more consumer goods: 'The triumph of consumerism meant a rejection of the progressive reduction of worktime and of "democratic leisure". It realised instead the dominance of a work-and-spend culture' (Cross, 1993: 5). As far as economic position, social status and identity are concerned, whilst these are undoubtedly affected by our behaviour as consumers, they are also and already affected by participation in the realm of working activities. To the extent that consumption is one of the ends to which work is the means, work must retain a primary rather than subordinate role in people's lives.

PLAN OF CHAPTERS

The discussion roughly divides between Chapters 2, 3, 4 and 5 which describe the basic differences between our two proposed types of society, and three further chapters (6, 7 and 8) which attempt to understand how these differences might affect particular aspects of life and society. If these consequences are sufficiently large – if a turn to consumption really does alter the basis of social and personal identity and give rise to a different kind of culture – then this would support the argument that a general change is taking place in the nature of society: that the social form based on work is being superseded by one based on consumption.

Work-based society

In considering whether the position of work in the hierarchy of activities has changed, whether the realm of working activities is as important as it used to be, we need to know what position it used to hold and why, and to what extent it has slipped and why. We need to say clearly what the principal characteristics of work-based society are. What is it about this society that allows us to designate it as a particular type we have called work-based?

We will say that a work-based society is one in which the ends to which work is the means are given clear priority over the ends of activities performed in all other realms. One would have to show that people regard work as their central life interest in the sense that they attribute great significance to the benefits which come from working, that their lives are somehow saturated by work. Quantitatively, we can look at data on working hours and other measures of work dependency and work intensity to see what the patterns of time use and distribution are within a work-dominated society. Qualitatively, we can briefly review evidence of the intrinsic benefits people expect to be able to fulfil through working. Adopting a Weberian style of analysis, the main contention of this chapter will be that the realm of working activities has become dominant because it is accepted as being both formally rational in terms of the means it employs, and substantively rational in terms of ends to which those means are directed. Moving outside or beyond the realm of work is difficult because this would mean resisting these rationalities and developing new ones.

Whilst one would have to accept that not all work-based societies, or societies passing through a work-dominant phase, will exhibit each of these features in their most extreme or purest form, these elements would certainly need to be there in some concentration or we would not be justified in categorising such a society as work-based. When we discuss the idea of consumption-based society, we will take this as our base line for judging whether the activities of consumption have come to provide an alternative means of achieving the ends listed here, and/or whether consumption-based society is characterised by different kinds of priorities and expectations.

Consumption-based society – a theory of the new consumption

Having identified the key characteristics of work-based society in Chapters 2 and 3, we will follow the same procedure in Chapters 4 and 5 and identify the key characteristics of consumption-based society. Invoking the affluence hypothesis described above, we will assert that consumption-based society is characterised by a particular kind of consumption which we will call 'the new consumption'. In developing a theory of the new consumption (its key characteristics, how it interlocks with other realms of activity, the way it affects people's behaviour), we will make a basic distinction between two different types of consumption. Simple consumption which can be further divided into necessary, elaborated and indulgent consumption, will be distinguished from complex consumption which includes the categories affluent, conspicuous and symbolic consumption. Our basic argument is that people undertake different kinds of consumption in order to find different kinds of pleasure or satisfaction. For analytical purposes, these pleasures and satisfactions can be understood as forming a continuum of utility. At one end utility is sought in terms of the basic satisfaction of day-to-day needs and desires, and at the other end utility is sought in terms of more elaborate, sometimes quite abstract even symbolic kinds of satisfactions.

What distinguishes one type of consumption from another is that different types of consumption activities are aimed at achieving particular kinds of utility. Whilst it is obvious that all types of human society offer opportunities for simple and complex types of consumption (we have already noted that plenty of consumption goes on in work-based society), it will be argued here that for a society to be classified as consumption-based, there must be clear evidence that increasing amounts of time and other resources are being shifted towards complex types of consumption. This would indicate that the kinds of pleasures and satisfactions which people increasingly expect to be able to fulfil are very much at the complex and abstract end of the scale of utility. A desire to achieve these kinds of satisfaction, and society-wide access to the means of so doing, is a defining characteristic of consumption-based society. We will use statistical data to assess what type of consumption activity and utility is typically being enjoyed by the UK population at the outset of the twenty-first century. Assuming that affluent consumption has something to do with levels of disposable income, we will look at data on incomes and income distribution. Emphasising that affluence has as much to do with *the types* of consumption activity people engage in as it does with absolute levels of such activity, we will go on to consider recent trends and patterns of consumption and consumption activities.

Social identity and activism – workers versus consumers

In Chapters 6 and 7 we look at the implications of a transition from work-based to consumption-based society in terms of how it might affect the way people form a sense of social and personal identity. What factors does each social type bring to bear on the formation of identity? If we define identity formation as the process by which a person acquires a sense of themselves as a unique being in the world, a perception that is fundamentally shaped by the circumstances of their biography (Craib, 1998) then such a significant transition in those circumstances is bound to have far-reaching implications for social and personal identity. Starting with the formation of social identity, given that occupational role (some might say 'position in the means of production') provides people with the most important measure of where they stand in society relative to other people (their 'class' position), the idea that these markers could be assessed more accurately by looking at where people stand in the hierarchy of consumers is certainly very challenging. Fundamental questions would have to be answered about how effectively people can understand their economic position and social status as consequences of their activities as consumers rather than as workers. Do the hierarchies of consumption provide an effective alternative to work as the key regulatory device in the character of social experience and social interaction? (Saunders, 1984, 1986 and 1988; Pakulski and Waters, 1996).

A further important consideration is how the factors which shape social identity also determine the way that people subsequently express their identity through various kinds of social *activism*. Position in the occupational hierarchy for example, is assumed to provide a very reliable indicator of the kinds of social activism a person is likely to get involved with, the causes a person or group might be prepared to fight for, and the likely make-up of their allies and adversaries in these struggles. One is bound to consider whether a shift away from worker identity towards consumer identity means that old struggles have been resolved and/or will be replaced by new ones. What form is social activism likely to take in a consumption-based social type (Crow, 2002)?

Personal identity – proletarian or sovereign consumer

Turning from social identity towards the formation and expression of personal identity, we need to consider how readily people will give up elements of their sense of self which have for so long been crafted out of the experiences of work. People invest a great deal of themselves in work as a source of personal identity, and it is likely that many would be very reluctant to relinquish them (Du Gay, 1996). This might be the case particularly for men since perceptions of what it means to be a man are heavily bound up with assumptions about differences between the roles of income-getter and home-maker. In work-based society, 'gender' is constructed and maintained by being principally involved with particular kinds of activity, and paid occupation is certainly one of the most important (Charles, 2002). On the other hand, to the extent that the realm of consumption might be thought to provide an expanded realm within which people can develop and express their sense of personal identity and/or to develop entirely new ways of expressing their sense of self, perhaps the importance of work in this regard will diminish. Might it be that the turn to consumption is actually a response to the fact that people are becoming less and less willing to accept the limits to identity which the paid occupational role tends to set (Hall and Du Gay (eds), 1996)?

The cultures of work and consumption

We have already noted that people strive to understand their activities (understanding and motivation are obviously linked), and that that understanding is made up partly of practical meaning (a desired outcome is achieved) and partly of a cognitive or ideational meaning in the sense that intellectually, we try to justify or legitimate our actions by reference to our value system (social cohesion depends on there being alignment between individual value systems and the general value system which prevails in society at that time). If we accept that people understand and justify their activities in a society which is dominated by work by reference to a distinctly work-based value system, it seems probable that social transition would entail considerable modification of this value system. One might say that the degree to which the prevailing value system has been displaced provides a reliable measure of the extent of social transition.

If culture is a realm in which people debate various meanings and understandings of the reality in which they live, one would expect that conflict between established and emergent value systems would be reflected in culture. Whatever else they might have to say on the matter, most academics would agree that the culture of the late-modern period is certainly characterised by considerable turbulence and upheaval: 'In modernity, the individual casts off from the traditional society only to be cast adrift in a turbulent sea of sociability without paddle or anchor' (Slater, 1997b: 88). Some have gone so far as to suggest that the cultural realm has become the primary site of debate and conflict between competing value systems (rather than simply reflecting events which are occurring in other bits of the society) (for something modern see Raymond Williams 1985, and for something postmodern see Featherstone, 1991). If one believes that social progress depends on the resolution of these conflicts, and that such a resolution will have to take place in the cultural realm, then 'culture' becomes more important than 'economy' or 'politics': 'the tendency towards cultural disorder and de-classification ... is bringing cultural questions to the fore and has wider implications for our conceptualisation of the relationship between culture, economy and society' (Featherstone, 1990: 6). Although the discussion in Chapter 8 rejects the strong version of the culturalist perspective, this does not mean that a transition towards consumption-based society will not be reflected in significant changes in the contents and role of the cultural realm. One might say that such a transition has a great deal to do with cultural change.

The affluence hypothesis revisited

In the final Chapter (9) we return to the question of whether to accept or reject the argument that a work-based social type has been displaced by one based on consumption and what part affluence plays in this relationship. There are three basic conclusions which could emerge here. First, that a full-blown consumption-based social type has emerged in the United Kingdom and elsewhere at the outset of the twenty-first century, a development which is closely associated with the attributes of affluence, most important amongst which is disposable income. Second, that notwithstanding the fact that average standards of living/levels of disposable income have certainly been maintained at historically high levels, that work has become more rather than less important as the basis of social life and experience. Third, that a modified social type can be observed, one which is characterised by the coexistence of work and consumption but where the balance between the two has altered not least because of increasing affluence. This latter possibility is perhaps the most attractive as it would allow us the common-sense conclusion that people assemble their personal and social identities by engaging in action in both realms of activity, without either having a truly dominant role. The pluralist outcome is often the most reassuring if least exciting.

THE FLY IN THE OINTMENT

Throughout the discussion which follows we must be wary not to get carried away with the idea that just because some change or other has taken place in the conditions which surround people's lives (and it would be truly remarkable if none had occurred), that this inevitably provides evidence of a fundamental shift in the character of modern Western industrial society. Knowing that work-based society at the outset of the twenty-first century is not the same thing as it was mid-twentieth century does not necessarily mean that everything about that kind of society has changed. In considering the extent to which the changes which have occurred relate to the emergence of the new consumption, we must also be careful not to confuse changes which can be corroborated by controlled investigation, with changes which might or might not have taken place in the real world, but which are *believed* to have taken place by theorists who have already invested heavily in the idea of social change. Changes in the lives of the observed may or may not be the same as changes which are ascribed to them by those doing the observing. To the extent that the angle of view of the observer affects the impression they have of what might be happening in social development (as Hanson puts it: 'there is more to seeing than meets the eyeball' (Hanson, 1958: cited in Phillips, 1987: 9), changes in the perspective of the observer and/or differences in the perspectives of different observers, are bound to generate different interpretations of change and its consequences.[4]

For the purposes of abstract discussion and debate this separating of the phenomenon we are interested in (what people do at work, what impact consumption has on identity, etc.) from our examination of it (the ideas and theories we develop to understand what is going on) is not necessarily a problem since by definition academics develop thoughts which are lifted away from the actual object and context to which they apply. At a more mundane level however, we must avoid the temptation of applying to the real world, conclusions about changes which have themselves been developed from largely or wholly theoretical origins and/or largely for the purposes of theoretical exposition. These conclusions are actually conclusions about changes in the theory rather than conclusions about changes in concrete observable reality. For example, in his critical review of accounts of the (alleged) 'communicative intent' (Baudrillard, 2001) which may or may not lie behind consumption (itself part of ongoing debates over the 'consumption as communication thesis'), Campbell warns that 'it is one thing for academics to "discover" symbolic meanings attached to products: it is another to assume that the conduct of consumers should be understood in terms of such meanings' (Campbell, 1997: 350). It is one thing for Sherlock Holmes to sift fragments of evidence and then test a hypothesis based upon them, but quite another for him to hallucinate an entire crime without any concrete evidence at all. The two stories generated by these two methods might be equally interesting and dramatic, but only the former will result in actual criminal proceedings. The latter is truly fictitious.

Although the academic community is generally smart enough not to be taken in by these manoeuvreings (although see Mouzellis, 1995 and Callinicos, 1999), one of the factors we do have to take into account when considering arguments about a change in the balance between work and consumption is that there has been a change of direction in the interests and thus perspective of the sociological and cultural studies communities. If a sufficient proportion of this community is predisposed to investigate consumption rather than work, to see identity as something which people acquire as consumers rather than as workers, then expectations have already been raised that evidence can be found to substantiate claims about these kinds of changes (standard points of departure are taken to be Saunders, 1988 and Warde, 1990a). In the production versus consumption debate for example, Fine and Leopold have noted that in the headlong rush 'to put consumption forward as a substitute for production to serve as an explanatory category in sociology', not only has the continuing importance of production been somewhat overlooked but ironically, 'this has come about despite an earlier attempt to eschew the reductionism associated with exclusive dependence on class relations of production'. At least up until the early 1990s then:

> consumption in the new analysis has displaced production in name alone ... There are insuperable problems in constructing an opposi-tion between production and consumption ... The result has been the failure to develop, and a hostility towards, theoretical structures that unite production and consumption'. (Fine and Leopold, 1993: 247, 250, 253, 255)[5]

Regarding the theoretical/empirical pitch of this volume, the hope is to develop a largely conceptual framework within which to grasp key aspects of the debate over whether something called work-based society has been, or might be displaced by something called consumption-based society. The model I have in mind is Durkheim's text *The Division of Labour in Society* where he famously compares key elements of pre-modern and modern society. The language and concepts should be familiar to the reader. Whereas Durkheim deploys the concept of social solidarity as the primary *mechanism* by which different social types develop (the mechanical solidarity characteristic of pre-modern or traditional society is contrasted with the organic solidarity characteristic of modern society), the key mechanism explored here is affluence.

Conscious of distinctions drawn (following Althusser (1969)) by Mouzellis (1995), and heeding Fine and Leopold's (1993) warning that it is all too easy to get stuck in the 'middle-range' between 'unified' grand theory on one side and 'working hypotheses' on the other side – something which has blighted attempts to develop a satisfactory theory of consumer behaviour, the bulk of this text could best be classified as 'conceptual'. Efforts have been made however, to 'take in the slack' by rigging with secondary analysis of empirical work carried out by others, fresh analysis of statistical data on hours of work, levels of income, and on patterns of consumption and leisure activities, and, to further the discussion of personal identity in Chapter 7, presentation of new data from a recently-conducted study into gender and job insecurity in South Wales (ESRC award number L2122520120, Nickie Charles and Paul Ransome). Where possible, the propositions made here have been framed in such a way as to make them amenable to empirical testing, that is, to see if sufficient evidence can be assembled behind them to convince the interested reader that they are 'true'.

NOTES

[1] 'Sociology is a science which attempts the interpretive understanding of social action in order to arrive at a causal explanation of its course and effects. In action is included all human behaviour when and insofar as the acting individual attaches a subjective meaning to it ... . Action is social insofar as, by virtue of the subjective meaning attached to it by the acting individual, it takes account of the behaviour of others and is thereby oriented in its course' (Weber, *Economy and Society*, 1978: ; quoted in Morrison, 1995: 274).

> [2] 'Formal rationality is a matter of fact, substantive rationality is a matter of value. Formal rationality refers primarily to the *calculability of means and procedures*, substantive rationality primarily to the *value* (from some explicitly defined standpoint) of ends or results .... The formal rationality of the modern social order is a matter of fact; whether or not this social order is substantively rational, in contrast, depends on one's point to view – i.e. on the ends, values or beliefs one takes as a standard of rationality.' (Brubaker, 1984: 36–7)

[3] For example, if we characterise the transition from work-based to consumption-based social types in terms of a transition from mass production to mass consumption, factors such as technological advance in commodities, developments in retailing and distribution, the growth of advertising and marketing, the spread of urban living, the emergence of fashion and leisure and so on, all require close attention. For a discussion see Fine and Leopold (1993), also Voth (1998). The now standard point of departure is McKendrick et al. (1982).

[4] Of the evidence presented in a recently published research monograph, the author reflected: 'My eventual analysis will have involved reconstructing previously existing constructions. And the reconstructions of mine will inevitably be informed by my own intellectual formation ... [which includes] the stock of knowledge and frames of analysis acquired from the sociological tradition ...' (Glucksmann, 2000: 49).

[5] Fine and Leopold are particularly critical of the approaches adopted by Castells (1977) and by Saunders (1988) both of whom develop theories in urban sociology which require fairly autonomous concepts of consumption.

2 *Work-based Society*

Our basic strategy will be to set up an opposition between an ideal-typical work-based society on the one hand and a consumption-based society on the other. This will allow us to examine the characteristics of one type in direct contrast with the characteristics of the other. In deploying this dualism we are not suggesting that either social type has ever existed in its purest form, or that these are the only ways of categorising the leading features of societies which currently exist in the industrialised West. Nor are we claiming that one type will always and inevitably give way to the other in faithful historical sequence. What we are hoping to do however, is to develop some closer sociological understanding of the mechanisms of social transition, specifically as they may relate to increasing levels of affluent consumption. Although it would be most satisfying to reach firm conclusions about whether and how one manifestation of the status quo is or is not giving way to another, our initial expectation is to find that production and consumption are complimentary realms of activity – in the language of social theory, a duality – and thus that all advanced industrial societies currently display elements of both ideal types. It is also noted however, that there is a growing tendency (not least in the minds of many sociologists) to take work-based activities so much for granted that other realms of activity appear to have become dominant. Whether the essence matches up with the appearance is one of the things we hope to discover.

Defining the work-based society

We should begin by elaborating our ideas about what constitutes a work-based society. Essentially we are suggesting that in this social type people regard work – defined here simply as formal paid employment[1] – as their central life interest in the sense that they attribute greater significance to the benefits which come from this realm of activity than they do from any other realm. Although paid work, and especially work performed in the shadow of capital accumulation always involves a degree of compulsion, we are also interested in the way that people are somehow content or reassured that working activities saturate their lives. Whether this sometimes reluctant consent is built to last is one of the questions we will be addressing shortly, but it seems reasonable to accept that the idea of work-centredness found in work-based society is something about which people have positive expectations. In Gramscian terms, work is hegemonic to the extent that people continue to be prepared to participate in it despite the inconveniences it involves. Work is also hegemonic in that this realm provides a common core of experience for people, a core which is itself crucial to social stability and growth. To adopt a postmodern hermeneutic for a moment, work in work-based society is not simply a burden and a necessity, a means of putting bread on the family table, but a performance of the whole individual which defines through action what the relationship is between worker, bread, table and family.

We will compile evidence of the concreteness of work-based society from three main sources. First, we can look at measures of *work intensity* meaning essentially how many of the population are involved in paid employment, and the number of hours they typically work. Second, we can look at *work-centredness* meaning the extent to which individuals orient their lives and expectations around working activities. Third, we can look at the attitude of mind, the world view, the ideational envelope of the *productivist work ethic* and consider why it has become so dominant. This will pave the way for our discussion in the following chapter of the role and nature of affluence in work-based society. The main point we will want to make is that within capitalism at least, generating financial income (and for most people today this means what they can earn through paid employment) is fundamental. At its simplest, affluence depends on how much income one has and how freely one is able to spend it.

WORK INTENSITY IN WORK-BASED SOCIETY

The simplest measure of the degree to which a society is work-based is the proportion of people's lives it occupies. It would be difficult to argue convincingly that a society was not work-based, or was becoming progressively less work-based, unless it could be shown that the proportion of the population's time and energy it typically occupies is low or is reducing (as we shall see in Chapter 4, one of the assumptions often associated with consumption-based society is the notion that work-time decreases and leisure time increases). Taking economic activity (the proportion of the population of working age who are employed, self-employed or actively looking for work) as a fair reflection of work-intensity, and using the United Kingdom as a case in point, government statistics show that rates of economic activity are not only high but in some categories such as part-time working, are increasing. In Spring 2002 'there were 27.7 million people in employment' which was 'the highest number … since the series began in 1959'. Between 1987 and 2002 'the total number of people in employment has risen by 3 million as more people are working and fewer people are unemployed' (*Social Trends*, 2003: 78). The writers of the report conclude that in the United Kingdom 'there are more people in employment than at any time [since 1945]' and that nearly 60 per cent of households in 2002 can be described as 'work rich' in that all members of that household who are of working age, are working (*Social Trends*, 2003: 76 and Table 4.6).

The enthusiasm for paid employment has also remained strong amongst women, and especially for part-time paid employment (25 per cent of employees work part-time and 82 per cent of part-time workers are female). Following Hakim we can note that 'Women's full-time employment rates have been virtually stable since 1881', and that: '*All* the increase in employment in Britain in the post-War period … consisted of growth in female part-time jobs …' (Hakim, 1996: 61–63) The evidence developed by Hakim clearly shows that even if rates of increase are disputed (Gershuny concludes for example, that during the 1980s and 1990s; 'for both men and women, hours of work have been rising pretty steadily' Gershuny, 2000: 53), there has been no significant *decrease* in rates of economic activity.[2] If there is any actuality in the notion that people in the United Kingdom are working less intensely than in previous decades, there is little evidence that these people are female. It will not be long before rates of economic activity for males and females are the same or before there will be equal numbers of males and females in the United Kingdom workforce. We might add that these developments show that, even if it were at least partly true in the past, work-based society is no longer a place where income-getting is the sole preserve of male household members.[3]

As one would expect, if rates of economic activity are high, rates of unemployment are relatively low. Using the International Labour Office (ILO) measure, in 2002 in the United Kingdom, the unemployment rate for all females aged over 16 was 4.6 per cent and for males was 5.8 per cent (*Social Trends*, 2003: Table 4.19). As if having one job were not enough, this report also notes that 'around 4 per cent of those in employment' (employee or self-employed) in the United Kingdom 'had a second job … 5 per cent of women and 3 per cent of men' (*Social Trends*, 2003: 81).

Time for work

Of course work-intensity is not just about whether or how many people have a paid job (or even how many paid jobs people have) but how many hours they spend doing those jobs. If everyone aged 16 to 75 had a paid job it might not follow that the total quantity of paid work done had increased if they all only worked two days per week. This simple point plays an important part in Hakim's arguments, one of which is that official statistics fail to distinguish within the category of part-time working, between a marginal worker doing only a few hours' causal work per week, and someone working up to 29 hours per week. Although both are counted as 'employed' there is clearly a very significant difference in the contributions they make (Hakim, 1996). Beginning with an informal calculation of our own, if we assume an average waking day of 17 hours, and deduct a further 1 hour of waking time for keeping our bodies clean and 2 hours for keeping ourselves fed[4], we could say that as a broad approximation we have 14 waking hours available per day or 98 per week. In an average working week with five days at work and two days not (and leaving aside for a moment the complexities of flexible working arrangements – for a discussion see Felstead and Jewson (eds) (1999)), this means that in 2004 somebody with a typical 37-hour full-time job spends nearly 38 per cent of their available waking time per week actually at work (37 hours as percentage of the 98 available). Over an average year in which 48 weeks are spent working this amounts to around 35 per cent of waking hours (48 × 37 hours as percentage of 5,096 total waking hours) and over an average lifetime of 75 years, 37 of which are typically spent working, work accounts for 17.2 per cent of the entire waking lifetime (1,776 × 37 years as percentage of 382,200 total waking hours).

Current UK government data suggest that although the nominal number of hours of those working 'full-time' is between 35 and 40 hours per week (The European 'working time directive' – implemented 1 October 1998 – seeks to limit working so that including overtime, 'working time shall not exceed an average of 48 hours for each seven days'; for commentary see McMullen, 2000), many full-time employees and especially men are working a good deal more than this: 'around 25 per cent of working men and 11 per cent of working women aged 25 to 49 years were working more than 50 hours per week' and 'nearly 1.4 million men and 0.25 million women are working in excess of 60 hours per week' (*Social Trends*, 2003: 88 and Table 4.26).[5] This report does however draw attention to the fact that as many as 18 per cent of male and 33 per cent of female full-timers aged 25 to 49 are not happy with this situation and regard themselves as 'overemployed' in the sense that they would prefer 'to work fewer hours for less pay'. Against this however, must be set the 10 per cent of male and 9 per cent of female full-timers who regard themselves as 'underemployed' in the sense that they 'want to work more hours' (around 40 per cent of part-timers feel underemployed) (*Social Trends*, 2003: Tables 4.28 and 4.29).

Around the margins of working time strictly measured we should add other time spent in preparing for work. These are bits-and-pieces of time which are soaked up by work. This temporal collateral damage of work includes such things as being suitably turned out, having appropriate clothing and other equipment, and arguably being sufficiently well fed to cope with the working day. Even if one allows that a deduction should be made for non-work periods at work such as rest and meal breaks, any gains here are easily off-set by time spent travelling to and from work. Compared with the routines of localised working around the mills, mines, steel works and docks of the early to mid-years of the twentieth century when the majority of the working population walked to work, the contemporary regimes of often long-distance commuting certainly seem more rather than less intense. Whether the burden of servicing the work-related needs of household income-getters is carried out by income-getters themselves or by other household members, the true extent to which the domestic activity of households is directly related to the demands of paid work should certainly be included in our measure of time spent in work-related activity (Hakim, 1996; Bradley et al., 2000; Gershuny, 2000).

A little more obliquely, we could also consider including in our audit of work and directly-work-related time an allowance for the time we have invested in gaining the qualifications necessary to work at all. Whilst basic literacy and numeracy are obviously part-and-parcel of the general learning process, there are other kinds of qualifications which have very little use outside their field of application. A redundant or retired engineer for example might never again have to set a lathe or make calculations about clearances and tolerances. As we know from studies of the experience of unemployment, one of the losses which people feel most keenly is of a sense of purpose and satisfaction.[6] As and when one leaves a job for the last time the question of why she or he bothered to spend so much of their lives doing that particular thing hangs in the air like a guilty conscience especially if one has no further use for the skills and experiences the job required (Sayers, 1998). Like work itself, doing the training and gaining the qualifications are largely means to an end rather than ends in themselves. Continuous messages from employers' organisations about skills shortages and the need to retrain, the whole managerial philosophy which travels under the banner 'investing in people', and even messages from the social-sciences funding councils about increasing the training component of doctoral programmes, constantly reiterate the expectation that the work of learning to work is never done.

One could argue that assessing work-intensity only in terms of official measures of the economic activity rates and hours of work of those currently and directly participating in paid employment (bodies that the data are actually able to record), underestimates the extent of work-related activity across the population as a whole. For example, many of the activities of those falling into categories such as people in full-time education or training, the unemployed, the sick, the disabled, the retired, and those under working age, are oriented towards the demands of work, past present or future. The clearest factor mitigating economic activity is the number and age of dependent children within the household, and especially if it is a lone-parent household. In 2002, the economic activity rates of lone mothers was 57 per cent compared with 73 per cent for the female working-age population as a whole (this figure falls to 39 per cent if the dependent child/children are aged under five years) (*Social Trends*, 2003: Table 4.3). We might also want to include in this category forms of market and non-market work which tend to be undercounted in, or to fall outside, official measures of economic activity. In her review for example, Hakim includes people engaged in 'marginal market work' (less than ten hours per week) such as family workers, those in the informal economy, seasonal and temporary workers. In the non-market category she includes voluntary work, domestic, reproductive and caring work. According to Hakim however, we should not overestimate the contribution of these 4 million or so marginal workers in the informal economy because 'the number of *hours worked* are too trivial to make a great difference to the conventional measures of the size of the labour force and the *earnings* involved are too small to dramatically alter their financial dependence on others' (Hakim, 1996: 40).

We should also note that work-intensity is not evenly spread across the population as economic activity rates are mitigated by differences in cultural expectations and in levels of education and qualifications. United Kingdom data for 2001–2 show for example, that employment rates are very much higher for those with higher qualifications than for those without, and amongst White, Indian or Pakistani people than amongst Black or Black British people (*Social Trends*, 2003: Table 4.10). Rates of self-employment are also much higher amongst members of the Pakistani or Chinese community than amongst members of the White, Black Caribbean or Black African communities (*Social Trends*, 2003: Table 4.16). Differential access to employment opportunities has also been noted as one of the major constituents of 'polarisation' between different groups or classes of women. Bradley et al., conclude for example, that 'young middle-class women with higher degrees can grasp the opportunities on offer, while those without qualifications from working-class backgrounds may find themselves facing the same restricted labour market choices as their mothers ...' (Bradley et al., 2000: 89).[7]

Whilst it is certainly true that not every member of the household works (although as we have seen the proportion of work-rich households in Britain is increasing), we are all dependent on those that do (we do not have to stretch this point too far in order to include dependency on the state as a kind of society-wide household responsibility). It is the high degree of dependency on that proportion of the population which is actively in work which is one of the characteristics of work-based society. As is frequently observed, the ageing of the population in the United Kingdom and other Western economies amounts to an increased burdening of those that are in work. Government statisticians reported in 2003 for example, that 'the number of people aged 65 and over will exceed the numbers aged under 16 by 2014'. Between 1970 and 2001, the proportion of the European population aged over 65 years increased from 12 to 17 per cent (*Social Trends*, 2003: 31–2).

As many studies of the experiences of unemployment and job insecurity have shown (see for example Heery and Salmon (eds) (2000)), being without work, or excluded from work is not at all the same thing as being free of the needs and expectations which work is normally and habitually performed in order to fulfil. To preview a point we will be discussing shortly, the fundamental essence of the productivist ethic is that work provides the most appropriate, some would say 'rational' means, of putting us in touch with the resources we need to satisfy our various needs. Leaving aside the complex (and somewhat rare) possibility that work can itself become an end (an end-in-itself or wertrational action in Weber's terms), it is typically regarded as just a means to an end (a zweckrational action). If one loses access to what have become the conventional means of achieving these ends, the ends are still there and still need to be satisfied. Hunger, cold, lack of creative and social opportunity are not caused by lack of work; they are part of the amalgam of expectations and needs which work was invented to satisfy. If one is not satisfied with the means currently available for satisfying one's needs and expectations, then one only has three alternatives: (a) minimise one's needs, (b) find alternative means of satisfying them, or (c) give oneself over to mortality.

WORK-CENTREDNESS IN WORK-BASED SOCIETY

We have already alluded to the idea that work dominates the lives of people in work-based society because they somehow expect it to do so. Few people express much surprise at the fact that they will ordinarily spend over a third of their weekly waking time during the middle years of their lives working. It is also generally accepted that a good deal of one's time before entering the workforce will be devoted to preparing for that happy day, and that the manner of one's retirement will largely depend on how successful one's working years have been. In trying to account for this general acceptance of the dominance of work (an acceptance which renders it dominant) we need to do two things. In the following section we will consider the kinds of justificatory devices people use to square the demands and burdens of work with a willingness to continue being involved in it. How do we legitimise the fact that 17 out of every 100 of our waking hours throughout our lives will be spent doing something which we might very well prefer not to do? This means looking at the work ethic of productivism, the ideology which surrounds work in a work-based society and binds people to it. First though, and before we look at the substantive rationality of work-based society, we need to look briefly at the relationship between work and the expectations people have about what it provides.

The need to work

In terms of the formal rationality of work in work-based society there is no need to belabour the point that work provides the central mechanism in society through which people can gain access to resources necessary to fulfil various categories of needs (Ransome, 1996; Slater, 1997b). Following the largely unambiguous findings of empirical research into these matters we can simply state that the principal expectations which people have of work are for material and psychological security (principally through income and continuity of employment), opportunities for creativity (i.e. having interesting and challenging work), and opportunities for social contact (Ransome, 1996). The prevailing organisation of work is believed to be, and for all practical purposes actually is, the only way currently available of enabling people to meet these needs.

If work is accepted as being a means to an end, then the dominance of a particular set of working arrangements depends on how well it enables us to meet those ends: are current working arrangements properly functional, are they fit for purpose? If we are imagining a society in which work dominates all other realms of activity, then logically the ends to which work are the means must also dominate all other ends. The idea of work-based society makes no sense at all if (a) the working arrangements it contains fail to provide a mechanism through which people can adequately satisfy their needs, or (b) the needs it enables people to satisfy are not actually very important to them. A work-based society is precisely one in which that category of activities we label work provides the only currently available and realistic means of satisfying our most urgent needs.

Given the amount of time and other resources which are given over to working it is truly remarkable how few alternative conceptions there are about work and how it could be organised in the industrialised West. Indeed when alternative concepts are proposed they are usually given very little serious consideration (Frankel, 1987, refers for example, to the 'post-industrial utopianism' of writers such as Illich, 1971, 1973, 1975; Bahro, 1984, 1985; Toffler, 1970, 1980, and Gorz, 1982, 1985). Clearly other conceptions of work have been deployed in the past, and despite suggestions of a global convergence towards the Western model (Arrighi, 1994; Waters, 1995; Castells, 1996), other societies today operate successfully with quite different conceptions of work. So how are we to account for the fact that our particular conception has become so dominant?

The answer is simple if one looks in the right place. It is not so much that everyone agrees that the current Western concept and thus organisation of work is superior to all other possible conceptualisations and organisations (although it has been pretty successful), but that the underlying needs which people have are seen as universal, and current working arrangements are seen as allowing, at least in principle, adequate if not equal means of satisfaction for all. There is society-wide (and indeed industrial-society-wide) agreement that work is the dominant realm of activity because current working arrangements are accepted as being the best way for people to meet their needs. Even if one argues that capitalism has manipulated people's perception of needs and how they can best be satisfied so that they fit neatly with its particular way of administering to them (Lee, 1993; Lodziak, 1995; Slater, 1997b), the fact remains that the current work paradigm does provide people with an effective means of satisfying their needs. Arguments over particular techniques for getting people into work, organising and paying them (all detailed and for many rather boring aspects of the formal rationality of paid employment) are somehow seen as less important than, or are subsidiary to, a more fundamental acceptance that everyone has the same basic needs. It is agreement over ends which takes priority and there is very little room for manoeuvre over which needs and in what order we choose to try to satisfy them. There are no people who do not need food, shelter and opportunities for creativity, and thus no category of persons for whom the category of activities we label work has no application. This also accounts for why the contents of the category 'work' tend to be quite similar across societies who have followed the same historical trajectory. Other than in nuance and detail the manner and pattern of paid employment found in North America is very much the same as that found in Europe and Australasia. Why are they the same? Because there is agreement that they are the best, the most practical and rational way, of enabling people to satisfy their needs. Which needs? The needs we all have in common and are familiar with. It is only when current arrangements fail to allow people to meet their needs (for example during periods of job insecurity) that the mechanism of employment comes under fresh scrutiny, and even then it is only the details which may alter not the underlying structure of employment.

THE PRODUCTIVIST WORK ETHIC

Compared with alternative concepts of work,[8] the Western concept has become dominant because it draws a great deal of support from an underlying acceptance, even enthusiasm, for a highly productivistic conception of human activity and nature. This conception is reflected in what Belk (following Sartre, 1943) refers to as 'the basic states of our existence; having, doing, being' (Belk, 1988 in Millar, 2001, Vol. III: 193). The extraordinary vitality of the productivist ethic comes from the fact that it nourishes all three of these roots of human existence, and very often simultaneously. Whether we express ourselves primarily through our actions, our possessions or through what Fromm refers to as a 'being mode of existence' (Fromm, 1976 in Belk, 1988), productivism is key to all of them.

Furthermore, and highly significant for our definition of affluence in terms of standard of living (which is itself dependent on income), in modern *capitalist* society, not only has all productive activity become 'work', but work has become 'work for economic ends': 'If a single criterion of the possessive market society is wanted, it is that man's labour is a commodity, that is, that man's energy and skill are his own yet are regarded not as integral parts of his personality, but as possessions, the use of which he is free to hand over to others for a price' (Macpherson, 1962: 47). As Gorz has put it more recently, in modern (and postmodern) society work is 'work done with payment in mind. Here *commodity exchange*, is the principal goal. One works first of all to "earn a living" ...' (Gorz, 1989: 221 original emphasis). Given the overwhelming emphasis on 'rationality' in the conduct of economic affairs in modern societies (capitalist and non-capitalist alike) the rewarding of work by wages means, as Schwimmer (1979: 287) puts it, that 'all economically useful activities are fully comparable by a yardstick transcending their diversity'.

Not only then, does paid work dominate other realms of activity but a particular definition of work has come to dominate the concept of work itself. We are confident in describing the societies of the industrialised West as work-based, not simply because they are dominated by productive activity, since this is a prerequisite of all human societies and throughout history, but because of the particularly productivistic, the particularly workerly conception of work around which such assertively work-based societies have oriented themselves. Because of the very close association it conjures between the innovation of systems of production, and people's perception of the needs they have, Western productivism makes particularly aggressive and demanding assumptions about the level at which various needs could or should be met: '… unlimited need – the constant desire for more and the constant production of more desires – is widely taken to be not only normal … but essential for socio-economic order and progress' (Slater, 1997b: 28–9). Notwithstanding powerful arguments from the Green lobby (see Chapter 6), we will continue to have highly ambitious expectations about the satisfaction of needs as long as the advanced industrial infrastructure has the capacity to 'deliver the goods'. Only when this capacity has been overreached will we actually consider the possibility that we have reached the limits of our needs. As Baudrillard puts it: 'The system only sustains itself by producing wealth and poverty, by producing as many dissatisfactions as satisfactions, as much nuisance as "progress". Its only logic is to survive and its strategy in this regard is to keep human society in perpetual deficit' (Baudrillard, 1998: 55).

Adopting the perspective of an aggressive productivism means giving paid work top position in the hierarchy of activity. The things people do outside the realm of work simply do not have the same kind of status or utility as those done in work. This distinction between real needs and trivia, between worthwhile activity and frivolity, establishes in the mind a whole series of dualisms, between for example, work and play, or work and leisure, between the high-status public paid activity of men and the low-status private unpaid activity of women. Within hard-core productivism, the alleged exclusivity of work as a means to satisfying specific and urgent needs, the particularly ambitious interpretation of the levels to which they can be satisfied, and the non-negotiability of them leaves very little room for alternatives to develop and grow. It is an all-enveloping conception of work which smothers competitor conceptions almost before they see the light of day. In terms of challenging the core status of paid work in work-based society, it is a relatively trivial matter to argue for flatter organisational hierarchies or just-in-time methods of manufacture, when compared with the extremely daunting task of challenging the assumptions about human nature upon which productivism bases itself.

The rationalities of the work paradigm in work-based society

Adopting Weberian terminology, we can say that the productivist conception of work has become dominant because it is accepted as being formally rational in terms of the means it employs (i.e. industrialism), and substantively rational in terms of the ends to which those means are directed (i.e. the satisfaction of needs). Making a convincing case either that there are alternative means and ends within the realm of work, or that there are worthwhile alternative realms of activity outside or beyond the realm of work itself is difficult because this means resisting these aggressive and fully-established rationalities and developing new ones.

Although the fact it has repeatedly been 'called in evidence' in wider discussions about the existence of otherwise of post-something society, gives the impression that it involves something more radical and substantive, arguments over post-Fordism, flexible specialisation and so on, represent a much more limited debate about the formal rationality of *the means and techniques* employed to produce goods and provide services (Amin (ed.), 1994; Kumar, 1995; Ransome, 1999). Changes in how things are produced, in what way and by whom, clearly do impact upon people's working lives (although it must be said that it is only sociologists of work who take much interest in other people's working arrangements), but discussion of them adds very little to our knowledge of the substantive rationality of contemporary production: 'Utility ... is the core of a formal concern with how we calculate in pursuing our interests rather than a substantive concern with what those interests are or how they came about' (Slater, 1997b: 44).

As Weber has so usefully pointed out, describing and assessing the technical merits of a particular piece of action is much more straight forward than trying to understand *why* it takes place. What the debates over Fordism and post-Fordism do illustrate is that relatively significant changes can take place in the day-to-day business of working *without* there being any consequent reconsideration of the substantive rationality of productivism. The fact that the productive system has the capacity to innovate is evidence of just how firmly established it has become, not of its imminent decline.

The essential characteristic of work-based society then, is that a particularly robust and resilient work paradigm has become the primary and principal object of people's activity. As I have argued extensively elsewhere (Ransome, 1996 and 1999), this paradigm is hegemonic in the sense that it articulates a set of shared ideas and beliefs about what work is and what its purposes are. In terms of its own function within the social structure, the productivist work ethic aides hegemony by uniting in the mind what is already united in action. If people willingly act together in the same labour process, and if, as we have argued, work is a means to an end, then the work ethic provides a means of articulating in an intellectual or ideational way, the shared purposes of work. In this sense, the work ethic is part of what Durkheim called the 'collective or common consciousness', 'the totality of beliefs and sentiments common to the average citizens of the same society [having] specific characteristics that make it a distinctive reality' (Durkheim, 1933: 79–80). In making an essential contribution to the overall belief system of work-based society, the productivist work ethic aids social stability. Following Gramsci, Williams has defined this as a 'socio-political situation' in which 'the philosophy and practice of a society fuse or are in equilibrium: an order in which a certain way of life and thought is dominant, in which one concept of reality is diffused throughout society' (G. Williams, 1960: 587; see also Ransome, 1992).

The importance of an hegemonising ideology of productivism within work-based society also plays a leading role in the 'regulationist' model developed by left-thinking economists to explain important aspects of the transition from Fordism to post-Fordism during the 1980s (aspects which include the wider political and cultural context). Again following Gramsci, Lipietz suggests for example, that 'the struggles, armistices and compromises' which surround the emergence of a reliable 'mode of regulation' in the political sphere, are equivalent to struggles over 'competition, labour conflict and the regime of accumulation in the economic sphere' (Lipietz, 1994: 339). (See also Aglietta, 1979.)

In terms of the basic content of the substantive rationality of the work ethic of productivism in the West, we need look no further than Weber's classic account in *The Protestant Ethic and the Spirit of Capitalism* (1976). Although some refinements have been made and some of the religious gloss has faded, the principles of economic conduct he describes for the sixteenth and seventeenth centuries of hard work and industriousness, diligence, thrift, and frugality, and the combination of (spiritual) soul-saving and the (pragmatic) saving of capital continues to provide an essential point of departure (Marshall, 1982; Ransome, 1996). The persistence of these principles of economic conduct owes a good deal to the fact, as indicated by Weber and subsequently by others, that they sanction limitless accumulation and presume that needs are boundless and can never therefore be fully satisfied. Neither one's soul nor one's capital can be saved too much. The very last thing the productivist needs is to be told that there is no longer any need to go on producing. If your whole concept of self is based on the presumption of purposive action, and if you believe that this can only be achieved by means of activities which have been categorised as work, then the prospect of being deprived of the opportunity to produce through work would be a complete nightmare. The productivist work ethic thus becomes self-reliant and self- justifying in that it defines for itself the ends to which it is directed. In Weberian terms, and following Lowith, the substantive rationality of productivism 'becomes itself an end or an end in itself' (Lowith, 1982: 47).

SUMMARY

In summary then, we can say that the key characteristic of work-based society is that work, in the form of paid employment, has become the dominant realm of activity. Work dominates people's lives both practically and ideationally. Practically, it overshadows all other realms of activity in terms of the proportion of our lives and energy it takes up. Whether one measures work intensity in terms of levels of economic activity, hours spent at or preparing for work, or the extent of direct or indirect dependency on those who are involved in paid work, it is difficult not to reach the conclusion that people in work-based society today are at least as highly work-centred and work-oriented as they have been since the emergence of industrialism. Taking the United Kingdom as a case in point, moderate shifts in patterns of working between men and women, or between full- and non-full-time employment have actually had very little impact on the sum of work being done. If anything, this sum is increasing rather than decreasing. Convincing evidence of any weakening of the work-based character of that society is difficult to find.

Ideationally, people in work-based society accept that work is the only means available through which they can satisfy their needs and expectations. These needs and expectations are themselves a product of what can be achieved if one whole-heartedly applies the (formally rational) techniques of modern economic production. Such achievements are only limited by what the techniques of production allow. This often willing acceptance of work survives any suggestion that there might be better or simply different ways of achieving these ends because it invokes intellectual, emotional and even moral support from a fully-established productivist world-view. In work-based society, all creative urges, all imagination and sociability, can be convincingly represented as reflecting the essential productivism which lies at the core of human nature. The productivist philosophy of having, being and doing, and the industrial work-ethic virtually become one and the same thing. Work in work-based society is truly paradigmatic because we are prepared to accept that both as a concept and as a practice, productivism provides an adequate means of interpreting the motivations and meanings of our actions, and therefore of justifying and legitimating them; the market 'is seen as a mechanism which automatically secures the substantive values of liberty, progress and justice' (Slater, 1997a: 52).

NOTES

[1]Hakim offers a more formal definition:

> *Work* is any productive activity, any activity that produces goods or services. *Employment* is any work done for pay or profit, any work producing goods or services that are traded in the market economy. The key distinction is between *market* work and *non-market* work … . The substitution rule or third-person criterion is used to distinguish between activities in the fuzzy borderline area between work and non-work. If an activity would lose its value (utility) if a substitute did the task, it is not work … studying is not work, because the value of it would be lost if the task was performed by a substitute. (Hakim, 1996: 22–3)

[2]In challenging what she regards as a mistaken assumption underlying many accounts of 'the feminisation of work' of dramatic increases in employment amongst women during the twentieth century, Hakim argues that: '*The only increase in female employment since the 1950s, and indeed since 1851 or before, is the massive expansion of part-time jobs*', (Hakim, 1996: 63, emphasis added). She presses this point by emphasising that when full consideration is given to the fact that 'it takes 2.4 part-time employees to provide the same number of work hours as one full-time employee … the real contribution of part-timers to the workforce is much smaller than the headcount suggests'. She concludes that although by the mid-1990s 'part-time employment accounted for 22 per cent of all jobs … [they] still only accounted for 10 per cent of all hours worked … full-time employee jobs … still account for three-quarters of total work hours …' (Hakim, 1996: 67).

[3]For discussions of women's participation in income-getting before and during the twentieth century see: Pahl, 1984; Walby, 1986; Finc, 1992; Charles, 1993; Hakim, 1995.

[4]'The UK 2000 Time Use Survey' showed that both men and women spend around 8 hours sleeping, just under two hours eating and two hours travelling. Women spent up to 5 hours a day on 'household and family care', 'shopping and services', and 'childcare' compared with around 2 hours 40 minutes for men, reported in *Social Trends*, 2003: Table 13.1. For a comprehensive analysis of time use within and outside the home see Gershuny, 2000.

[5]Data from the *New Earnings Survey* show that for all employees in the United Kingdom in 2002, overtime accounted for over 4 per cent of gross weekly earnings. This ranged from 11.8 per cent for male manual workers to 1.5 per cent for female non-manual workers (*Social Trends*, 2003: Table 5.10).

[6]Sayers has commented for example that research shows: 'the great majority want work and feel a need for work, even when they find it unsatisfying in all sorts of ways: dull, repetitive, meaningless.' These aspects are reflected by research into the negative effects of unemployment which 'have shown a lowering of self-esteem and morale, and increases in the suicide rate and the incidence of psychiatric treatment' (Sayers, 1987: 18).

[7]Developing the notion of polarisation between women more generally, Hakim concludes: 'The polarisation process that started in the 1980s has produced a sharp divide between these home-centred women and the minority of career-oriented women for whom employment is just as central to their lives as it is for men' (Hakim, 1996: 215). We will be discussing the impact of work on identity in Chapter 7.

[8]For points of departure see Wallman (ed.), 1979; Godelier, 1980; Pahl (ed.), 1988. For a full discussion see Ransome, 1996.

3　Affluence

DEFINING AFFLUENCE

In all societies affluence is understood in terms of standard of living, and, in societies operating with a capitalist philosophy standard of living depends directly on the amount of money a person has control over; 'the possession of wealth presently assumes the character of an independent and definitive basis of esteem … a conventional basis of reputability' (Veblen, 1994: 29). (We should say 'control over' rather than 'has' because people often and increasingly use credit to spend money which, in effect, 'they don't yet have'. Heavy borrowing for household consumption might be one of the criteria of consumption-based society).[1] Following Shammas (1993), we will take 'standard of living' to include features of 'utility' (defined in terms of desire, satisfaction and pleasure); 'opulence' (excess commodities) and 'freedom' the capacity for autonomy – 'to be free to do this or be that'. Overall, 'what is valued is the capacity to live well'.[2] If, as measured against the conventional expectations of people living at a particular time and in a particular place, household income routinely exceeds that which is necessary for satisfying the expected range of typical needs of members of that household, then we can describe that household and its members as *affluent*.

Affluence is relative

Whilst recognising the hazard of circularity in this definition, since one might argue that what is regarded as 'conventional', 'expected' or 'typical' will include an assessment of standards of living or affluence which have already been achieved (affluence is in some respects an aspirational concept), it remains useful because it emphasises that affluence is always and everywhere a relative thing: 'social position depends to a very large extent on being able to meet "the demands of pecuniary emulation", to live up to "the normal pecuniary standard of the community"' (Veblen, 1994: 30). If affluence is ultimately about the satisfaction of needs it makes good sense to follow the logic of arguments put forward by Doyal and Gough (1991), and more recently by Slater (1997b), and embrace the idea that perceptions of affluence *must be relative* because the needs against which they are judged are socially constructed and profoundly cultural; that they are: '... the way in which particular real people and communities formulate their values, identities, commitments in terms of what they "need" in order to live the kind of life they deem good' (Slater, 1997: 57).

Affluence means choice

As we have said, in contemporary capitalist society, the meeting of needs, whether ordinary or sophisticated, immediate or deferred, moral or material, is mediated by the earning and spending of money (pre- and non-capitalist systems have other ways of doing it, but this is how it is done in the industrialised West): 'before production can be translated into consumption, income has to be generated and distributed across different socioeconomic groups ...' (Fine and Leopold, 1993: 72). 'The consumer's access to consumption is largely structured by the distribution of material and cultural resources (money and taste), which itself is determined in crucial ways by market relations – above all the wage relation and social class .... Access to commodities is restricted by access to money.' (Slater, 1997b: 25–7). Since we do not earn loaves of bread or pints of milk but dollars, pounds and euros, everyone understands that (after taxes) a person has the right to choose what to spend his or her income on. The greater the income, the greater the choice, and in theory at least, the greater the choice the happier a person will be (we will be looking in detail at 'the joy' of owning things in the following chapter).

Affluent individuals and affluent societies

A further consideration in applying the label 'affluent' is to distinguish between an affluent individual or class of people, and an affluent *society* since clearly the fact that there are one or two of the former does not mean that society as a whole is affluent. Given that 'objective' statistical assessments of 'economic well-being' or 'prosperity' tend to measure and compare the circumstances of households rather than of individual people (or at least assess individual disposable income in terms of their share of previously-calculated household income), there is quite a strong case for taking 'household' as the unit of assessment for measuring the degree and extent of affluence in society. This does not cover all possibilities however as there may be generally non-affluent households which contain an affluent household member – for example, a childless employed adult living in the same household with his or her pensioner-parents. The aggregation of individuals into households (a household can be made up of a single person although it would not constitute a 'family' even if it does contain a cat and a dog),[3] for the purposes of assessing affluence also suits our current approach since, looking at things sociologically, we are much more interested in affluence as a society-wide phenomenon than as an individual one. Associating a society-wide transition towards consumption-based society with increases in affluence or affluent consumption, requires a concept of affluence which is already quite highly collectivised.

This approach is well-established and is reflected in earlier discussions of affluent society by, for example, Bell and Galbraith during the 1970s and 1980s. Their analysis assumes a connection between mass production and mass consumption, and between mass consumption and mass affluence: '… the generalisation of commodity consumption to the entire population … to any individual anywhere …' (Slater, 1997b: 26). If the broad mass of the population can be described by sociologists and more importantly by its members as affluent, then it seems fair enough to describe the society in which they live, work and consume as affluent society. This is helpful to the present discussion as it indicates that first, we need to consider how well-off or prosperous an individual or household needs to be in order to be classified as affluent, and second, how many such individuals or households are sufficient to describe the whole society as affluent.

The unevenness of affluence

These considerations alert us to the fact that affluence is always unevenly distributed across individuals and households within a particular society. Even if one could imagine a society where everyone is objectively affluent in the sense that they exceed some numerical measure of income or expenditure, and is subjectively affluent in the sense that they believe themselves to be so (we will be looking at the subjective aspects of affluence in some detail in the following chapter), it would not be long before some would begin to pull clear of the field. The general state of affluence would no longer be perfect and new criteria of 'super-affluence' would have to be added. Bearing all these variations in mind, it would be sensible to see affluence in terms of a series of levels or strata to reflect the fact that people often assess their own standard of living relative to those amongst whom they live (who might incidentally, have the same level of income, and even have the same kinds of occupation) rather than relative to the whole of society. Even if they regard themselves as affluent in this local context they are also able to recognise that compared with other groups in society they may not be affluent at all.

Table 3.1   Average individual earnings, GB 1990–2002

	Private sector (£)	Public sector (£)	Whole economy (£)	% increase on previous period
1990	75.9	75.9	75.9	–
1992	88.5	90.8	89.0	19.6
1994	94.9	97.0	95.3	6.9
1996	101.6	101.5	101.6	4.6
1998	112.1	106.9	111.1	5.3
2000	124.5	116.2	122.9	9.4
2002	133.3	125.8	132.0	8.3

Source: Adapted from *Economic Trends*, HMSO 2002, Table 3.7.

Note: Figures as at January each year, seasonally adjusted, 1995=100.

AFFLUENCE AND INCOME

So what are the levels of income typically enjoyed in the United Kingdom in 2004, where do they come from and what level of income renders a person or household 'affluent'? Since around 80 per cent of income for two-adult, working-age private households comes from wages and salaries (although savings is a source of income particularly for older people, recent data show that in 2001 80 per cent of the United Kingdom population had less than £10,000 in savings – 57 per cent had less than £1,500, and 34 per cent none at all – *Social Trends*, 2003: Table 5.27),[4] some understanding of the level of individual earnings and household income is a useful place to begin. It is also a relatively 'objective' if somewhat aggregated way of looking at things.

Average earnings in affluent Britain

Looking at Table 3.1 it can be seen that data on average individual gross earnings (based on information from employers) show that between January 1990 and January 2002, average individual earnings for the whole of the British economy increased by nearly 74 per cent from £75.90 to £132.00. Average earnings in the 'private sector' were a little above, and in the 'public sector' a little below this figure. Figures recorded in the right-hand column show that there has been a steady increase in earnings year-on-year throughout this period.

Looking at standard of living in terms of net *household* disposable income (i.e. after taxes and other deductions) from all sources (earnings, investments benefits, pensions and so on) United Kingdom data for 2001 show that 'household disposable income per head, adjusted for inflation, increased one-and-a-quarter times between 1971 and 2001' (*Social Trends*, 2003: 92). (Differences in the rates of change in household as distinct from individual income depend on other factors such as changes in the composition of the household itself.) On the face of it, such increases might be taken as evidence of increasing prosperity and thus affluence.

Economic well-being obviously depends on the price of goods and services, since gains in income mean very little if the cost of living rises at the same rate. Data on changes in the retail prices index show that in the United Kingdom, 'inflation rates were generally below 5 per cent ... during the 1990s .... Between January and September 2002 inflation rates were consistently below 2 per cent ...' (*Social Trends*, 2003: 124 and Figure 6.13). The fact that incomes increased much more sharply than retail prices during this period indicates that at least in terms of the amount of income coming into the average household, purchasing power was rising thus creating the right circumstances for improvements in standards of living. It seems entirely reasonable to conclude that for the average individual and household, the sustained and relatively substantial increase in income which took place especially during the last ten years or so in the United Kingdom indicates increasing affluence.

We should also note however that since 1971, the rate of increase in household disposable income has been much stronger amongst those in the higher income bracket than amongst those in the lower income bracket. This means that whilst individuals in modern Britain are generally affluent, those falling into the top quarter and especially into the top 10 per cent of the population divided according to earnings, have enjoyed an appreciably greater rise in income, and thus in prospects for affluence than those in the bottom 10 per cent. Measured in terms of rising incomes, affluence, or at least the potential for being affluent is unevenly distributed. Those in the higher income bracket are proportionately more affluent compared with others in society than they were 30 years ago (*Social Trends*, 2003: Table 5.14). In this sense, increases in income leading to improvements in standards of living and possibly affluence are not very democratic. Those at the top of the heap are even more affluent compared with those in the middle or at the bottom of the heap. The fact that those at the bottom are undoubtedly far better off in 2003 than were those at the bottom in 1903 is not considered at all. The clearest illustration of this inequality is given by data on 'personal wealth' which is a measure of the value of assets held by individual adults. Although marketable personal wealth in the United Kingdom increased substantially between 1976 and 2000 (from £280 million to nearly £3 billion) which might itself be seen as an indication of increasing affluence, 64 per cent of it was owned by just 6 per cent of the population. The least wealthy 50 per cent owned just a single per cent of personal wealth in 2000 (*Social Trends*, 2003: Table 5.6).[5]

Clearly level of income depends in part on source of income, and this in turn depends on the composition of the household. The income of two working-age adults for example, is likely to be greater than that of a pensioner. As we have already noted, in two-adult households (which, with 'no children', and with 'dependent'/'non-dependent' children each made up 29 per cent of British households in 2002 *Social Trends*, 2003: Table 2.2), between 75 and 78 per cent of income comes from wages and salaries. In single-adult no-children households (which under pension age make up 15 per cent and over pension age 14 per cent of households) the proportion is also around 75 per cent. In two-pensioner households around 70 per cent comes from retirement (state) and private pensions and other benefits. In single-adult households with dependent children (which make up 6 per cent of households), 60 per cent of income comes from 'other benefits' and tax credits, and only 33 per cent from wages and salaries (*Social Trends*, 2003: Table 5.3) (Data reproduced in Table 3.3 below show that nearly half of the final disposable income of households in the bottom quintile income group comes from 'benefits in kind').

If the household is substantially dependent on the earned income of household members (rather than on savings, investments or pensions for example) then its prospects will also be affected by circumstances in the labour market (which incidentally, is a simple if rather crude way of emphasising that consumption depends directly upon a person's involvement in the production side). We can note for example, that women tend to be paid less than men, that earnings are higher in Central and South-Eastern Britain, that jobs in financial services pay better than those in agriculture and hotels and restaurants, that professional and managerial occupations pay better than retail occupations (*Social Trends*, 2003: 98). It is important to bear these and other labour-market variations in mind when trying to envisage differences in economic prospects or affluence between one household and another.

In terms of actual figures, the *New Earnings Survey* shows that in 2002 the average gross weekly earnings of male and female manual workers were £366 and £250 respectively and for non-manual workers £608 and £404 respectively (*Social Trends*, 2002: Table 5.10). Data from the *General Household Survey* on families with dependent children in 2000 (see Table 3.2) indicate that 59 per cent of married-couple households had a typical gross household income of over £500 per week. A further 21 per cent of families of this type had incomes of between £300 and £500 per week. Of cohabiting-couple families, 29 per cent had weekly incomes of between £300 and £500, and a further 43 per cent of over £500. Lone-parent households (which, with dependent children, accounted for around 6 per cent of all households in 2002) were generally less well off (and especially if the parent had

Table 3.2 Usual gross weekly household income (£s) by family type, GB 2000, as percentage of all GB families falling into each category

	0–100	100–200	200–300	300–400	400–500	Over 500
Married couple	6	7	6	10	11	59
Cohabiting couple	9	11	9	17	12	43
Lone mother	20	39	14	12	4	10
Lone father	16	22	9	13	22	19
All lone parents	20	37	13	12	6	11

Source: Adapted from *Living in Britain 2000, Results from The General Household Survey*, London: HMSO, 2001, Table 3.11.
Note: Data are for families with dependent children.

little or no earned income) with 57 per cent having an income of less than £200 per week. Households headed by a lone father tended to be better off than those headed by a lone mother with much greater proportions of the former having incomes of £400 or more. According to this survey, 20 per cent of lone-parent households in Britain in 2000 had an income of less than £100 per week.[6]

Sorting all the households in the United Kingdom into five strata according to household income, and taking account of differences in size of household (a statistical technique called 'equivalisation', for an explanation see *Social Trends*, 2003: 101), data reproduced in Table 3.3 show that after all deductions and additions have been made for direct and indirect taxes, and for direct and indirect benefits from the state, the average final household income in 2000–1 was £20,460 per year or £394 per week. The top fifth of households had an average income of £39,080 (£752 per week) and the bottom fifth £9,670 (£186 per week): 'the ratio of average final income in the top quintile group to that in the bottom quintile group is 4:1' (*Social Trends*, 2003: 105).

With a final income of at least £250 for every household above the bottom 20 per cent of households by income, it seems reasonable to conclude that at least 80 per cent of households in modern Britain are able to meet their immediate needs and 'maintain an acceptable standard of living given the norms of society' (*Social Trends*, 2003: 106). If affluence is defined as standard of living relative to those on the lowest incomes, we might again conclude that 80 per cent of households in modern Britain are relatively affluent. Every household in the top 60 per cent of households by income has an average income of at least £336 per week.

Table 3.3   Distribution of households by final annual average income (£s), quintile groups, UK 2000–1

	Bottom quintile	Next quintile	Middle quintile	Next quintile	Top quintile	All households
Gross income including benefits	8,420	14,290	22,080	32,000	56,850	26,730
Disposable income after taxes	4,970	9,100	13,730	19,770	36,690	16,850
Plus benefits in kind	4,690	4,080	3,720	3,080	2,390	3,590
Final income	9,670	13,190	17,460	22,870	39,080	20,460
Weekly final income	*185.96*	*253.65*	*335.77*	*440.00*	*751.53*	*393.46*

Source: Adapted from *Social Trends*, HMSO 2003, Table 5.17.

Low-income, non-affluent households

An established means of assessing the general state of economic well-being or prosperity is to look at the proportion of households having a 'low income': 'The threshold generally adopted is 60 per cent of median equivalised household disposable income' (*Social Trends*, 2003: 106) (taking 60 per cent of the 2000–1 average of £20,460 just mentioned this suggests a 'low income' of less than £12,276 per year or around £236 per week). Data for the United Kingdom show that until the mid-1980s between 10 and 15 per cent of households fell into this category. In the early 1990s however, this proportion rose to as high as 20 per cent although it had fallen back to around 17 per cent in 2001. Measured in terms of individuals rather than households the percentage of people living in low-income households rose from 13 per cent in 1981 to 23 per cent in 2001 (*Social Trends*: Tables 5.18 and 5.19). It seems reasonable for our purposes to accept that such households and individuals are non-affluent.

One does have to be cautious here however, since arguably, if the average income in society is particularly high, then even those with less than 60 per cent of that average could still be categorised as affluent and especially if 'affluence' was measured only in terms of passing a particular income threshold. Similarly, since we are discussing averages, there will be a number of people even in the low-income category whose income is well above the average for that category. We have seen from Table 3.2 for example, that 11 per cent of lone parent families (who make up around 6 per cent of all families) have a weekly income of more than £500. Adult members of these households might regard themselves as affluent compared with others in what is generally regarded as the non-affluent lone-parent category, and would certainly be regarded as such by the 11 per cent of cohabiting-couple families with incomes of less than £100 per week.

Summary

To summarise these points, the simplest 'objective' way of measuring affluence is to compare directly the levels of income of individuals and households, and declare that if household disposable income exceeds a particular amount it can be categorised as an affluent household and its members as affluent individuals. A suitable and simple figure would be the average household disposable income of society at that time. To the extent that individual and household incomes are rising and faster than taxes or retail prices, contemporary Britain can accurately be described as an affluent society. At the level of particular households and individuals affluence and the capacity to be affluent, is unevenly distributed with perhaps 20 per cent of households having an income which is less than 60 per cent of the national average. Households falling into this low-income category are more likely to be those composed of retired pensioners or lone parents than of married or cohabiting couples with dependent children. The employment status of adult members will very often be a decisive factor. To the extent that even for the 20 per cent of households having a low income of around £236 per week (60 per cent of the average United Kingdom income in 2001 of £20,460), members of these households are able to meet their basic needs, and to have an acceptable if sometimes minimal standard of living, it still seems realistic to describe modern Britain as an affluent society. In terms of average incomes at least, and for a large majority of households, it is certainly not a non-affluent or poor society. At the base of society however, there are households with incomes of less than the average even for low-income non-affluent households. Pensioners depending wholly on state pensions, lone parents reliant on state benefits, and households with or without dependent children where adults have no earned income feature prominently in this category. The fact that even a small minority of the population are living not only in non-affluent, but in poor circumstances when so many others are at or above the average, points to some of the moral dilemmas of affluence.

Whilst as we have shown in this chapter, actual possession of cash (earned income plus savings and investments) provides one kind of yard-stick, and might be indicative of the likely level of affluence or the capacity to become affluent, it is imperfect because different households have different levels of expenditure – some are much more costly to run than others, and clearly standard of living and the capacity to be affluent, depends on how thinly the jam has to be spread. Although as we have noted, equivalence scales can be used to take account of these important variations when comparing the incomes of individuals from different types and sizes of household (*Social Trends*, 2003: 271), there are other ways of comparing the relative standard of living of households. The simplest is to look at households in terms of *how they spend* their income. Patterns of expenditure provide tangible and often conspicuous evidence of purchasing power and income, and thus of affluence. Although such a comparison is still objective in the sense that a household either has a washing machine or it does not, it also has an element of subjectivity since patterns of expenditure and consumption reflect the choices of household members. We will be discussing these assessments of affluence in the following chapter.

The level of income a person or household can control is the basic measure of how successfully they are participating in work-based society. Although 'affluence' and the various sub-divisions which can be described within it are socially constructed all members of a particular society have a pretty clear idea of who is affluent and who is not. The desire to achieve affluence, to live within the affluent strata of society, to enjoy the pleasures and satisfactions which affluence makes possible, ranks very highly in the hierarchy of motivations. It is right up there with the urge to survive and the urge to reproduce. And it is by no means a coincidence that in modern industrial capitalist societies both survival and reproduction are greatly facilitated once one has crossed the threshold of affluence. In societies like ours, where cash is the mechanism of transmission, the gearbox and clutch, between productive activity on the one hand and satisfying consumption on the other, social position is inescapably measured in terms of the volume or amount of cash one has control over.

Whilst these expectations are reinforced by the ideology (substantive rationality) of productivism (advertising sells us the idea, the image, the propaganda of material success as the path to happiness), these expectations are assuredly rational in a formal practical sense since affluence actually does make it easier to survive and reproduce. The membership of a club whose participants had found it easier to meet their needs with less rather than more income, would be very exclusive indeed. Like it or not, capitalist economies invariably produce forms of society where survival and reproduction become very difficult unless people do interpret autonomy, success and freedom in terms of income, and income means paid employment. Those who advocate alternative ways of living, who choose not to participate in the mainstream, to reject the rat race, to get off the gravy train, to slide down the greasy pole, may wish that it were otherwise but they have yet to establish any popular alternative to the work-based, income-getting, affluence-flavoured hegemony. In the following chapter we turn our attention to 'the other side of the coin', which is that in modern society, knowing how to spend income is almost more important than having it in the first place. Nobody gets credit any more for cash under the bed, or boxes of gold in the basement. Modern consumption-based society is a place where the spending of money has itself become a major preoccupation.

NOTES

[1]In their analysis of contemporary processes of class formation, Savage et al. (1992: 17), emphasise the importance of the possession of 'assets' which go beyond actual cash. These are 'property assets, organisational assets and cultural assets'. We will be discussing these in more detail in Chapter 4.

[2]We can note in passing that in trying to explain the apparent incompatibility between the hedonistic desire to enjoy and the ascetic compulsion to save which might have hindered the development of modern rational capitalism, Campbell (1987) argues that within the notion of utility, a distinction should be made between satisfaction and pleasure. He argues that pleasure signifies indulgence in a way that simple satisfaction does not, and that conceptions of 'pleasure as a synonym for utility' (economistic definitions) rather miss the point that one can aim for satisfaction without any intention to gaining pleasure. The position taken here, is that 'pleasure' is generally included within 'satisfaction'; that to be satisfied also means to be pleasured, even if this is simply a drop of water for a thirsty child. 'Utility' signifies pleasure *and* satisfaction.

[3]The definition currently used by the United Kingdom government in conducting the *General Household Survey* or national census, is that a household is 'a single person or group of people who have the address as their only or main residence and who either share one meal a day or share the living accommodation' (*Living in Britain*, 2001: 168).

[4]Data on 'household income' which are derived from United Kingdom national accounts (rather than household surveys) show this proportion as only 50 per cent. The aggregated data do however include non-profit making institutions where 'operating income' and 'property income' are likely to be much higher (*Social Trends*, 2003: 93).

[5]… the impassioned biographies of heroes of production are everywhere giving way to biographies of heroes of consumption … movie stars, sporting or gambling heroes, and a handful of gilded princesses or globe-trotting barons – in a word, the

lives of *great wastrels* ...' (Baudrillard, 1998: 45–6). For commentary on '"The leisure class" today' see Rojek (2000).

[6]Data from the *Expenditure and Food Survey* for 2001–2, which are based on responses from around 7,000 households, suggest that households in the lowest 20 per cent of households divided according to gross income group, had a gross income of £114 per week, and that households in the highest 20 per cent had a gross weekly income of £1,314, *Family Spending*, 2003: Table 8.3.

4 *Consumption-based society*

If the analysis put forward in the previous chapters is substantially correct, then the proposition that work-based society is being displaced by something we wish to call consumption-based society ultimately depends on whether significant changes are taking place in the rationalities which underpin the kinds of activities which are typical of work-based society. In trying to distinguish a work-based from a consumption-based social type, we need to specify with reasonable precision what the differences are between acts of production and acts of consumption. How do these two kinds of activities and their underlying rationalities differ one from the other?

RELATIONS OF PRODUCTION AND CONSUMPTION

We will consider the types of activities associated with consumption, the extent to which people engage in them, and whether all of this is decisively associated with increasing affluence in the following chapter. First though it is necessary to address a number of issues concerning the sometimes complex nature of the relationship between production and consumption. Unless one is prepared to operate with a highly segmented notion of the individual and their actions, that the activities of work and of consumption are entirely distinct in both intent and realisation, one has to accept that production and consumption are both part of the overall activity of the individual and of society.[1] Janet Brown has an identity as a worker and as a consumer. In looking at her overall identity it would be ridiculous to disregard the effect that one aspect has upon another. As with individuals so with society. The consumption side makes little sense without the production side and vice versa.

The advantage of recognising that, in the broadest sense, acts of consumption have essentially the same motivations and purposes as acts of production, is that we can examine consumption/consumptivism in the same terms as we have already examined production/productivism. Becoming more interested in acts of consumption does not mean that we have to provide an entirely new or distinct understanding of the causes of social activity (or incidentally, to invent an entirely new kind of society where such things might go on). We can comfortably move our focus away from work and towards consumption without abandoning productive activity as the core component of our understanding of human nature and its motivations. It is the very closeness of the relationship between production and consumption which compels us to consider their similarities and differences very much in terms of the contribution each makes to the overall activity of the individual and of society. Or, to express the same thought slightly differently, what differences are there in the contributions each makes to the overall activity of the individual? Theories of consumption, or theories of the behaviour of consumers, will be left wanting unless they develop as part of a more general theory of action. We can repeat our earlier reference to Belk (1988: 193), that along with production, consumption also allows people to articulate 'the basic states of our existence; having, doing, being'.[2]

Secondly we must acknowledge not only that there is a relationship between acts of production and acts of consumption but that this relationship is a particularly close one. To anyone approaching these debates with a background in economics, it might seem ridiculous that the point still needs making since arguably the entire edifice of post-Benthamite utilitarian economics, and almost all of its neo-classical and liberal variants, make the basic assumption that utility is made manifest at the point where what has been produced is finally consumed. Since the measurement of utility, conventionally defined as pleasure or satisfaction, is what economics does, there can be no question of the intimacy of production (supply) and consumption (demand). As Langlois and Cosgel put it: '... neoclassical consumer theory (Lancaster, 1971; Strigler and Becker, 1977) has already absorbed the simile of consumption as production ...' (1977: 107, see also Lane (1991). Fine and Leopold go so far as to suggest that one of the reasons why there is no satisfactory theory of consumer behaviour is because of the 'deficiencies in conceptually distinguishing the theory of consumption (treated as demand) from the theory of production (treated as supply). For between the two, there is an exact parallel; the demand theory is essentially identical to the axiomatic theory of supply' (Fine and Leopold, 1993: 51).

We can briefly illustrate some of the issues involved here by considering the apparently simple act of eating a fresh apple. The picking of the apple from the tree is an act of production as would be the act of climbing the tree if the apple had not already been picked or of picking the apple up from the ground if it had fallen without being picked at all. Any other preparation for eating such as cleaning, peeling, coring, slicing, etc., would also be acts of production. Only the actual eating of the apple would be an act of consumption strictly speaking, although one could argue that biting and chewing the apple before actually tasting and swallowing it are in some sense productive rather than consumptive acts. At the same time however, each of the various acts of production we have mentioned could be seen as involving some elements of consumption, if for example, a ladder were used to climb the tree or a basket to carry the fruit away. If one were looking at the consumption of apples in some processed form, then clearly we would have to consider many intervening sequences of production/consumption. Even in our example, one could debate whether to include acts involved in cultivating the orchard and all the years of effort and experimentation that this might entail.

Although a full account would take us too far away from our main task, this example helps illustrate the importance of distinguishing between what Marx called 'productive consumption' and 'final consumption' (Marx *Capital I*: XXIII). The former refers to the consumption of various resources, including raw materials and labour power, which routinely takes place as production proceeds. Within capitalism, the value of these inputs remains within the process of production – and this is what makes them productive forms of consumption for the capitalist. Final consumption however, consumption which is productive for the private consumer, is seen as 'lying outside the realm of the circulation of value, and [as] no longer participating directly within it' (Fine and Leopold, 1993: 259). Fine and Leopold are at pains to point out that most theories of consumption (in economics but also in sociology) are seriously weakened because they tend to treat all kinds of consumption as if they were instances of final consumption. Although the consumption of apples in the pie factory and by the private citizen are ostensibly instances of the same kind of process in which commodities are exchanged for money and consumed, clearly the value of the processed apples remains within the production process and has yet to be finally realised, whilst the value of the apple eaten for lunch has been finally consumed.[3]

Five general aspects of the relationship between production and consumption are indicated by this kind of example:

1   Acts of consumption can only take place once something has been produced. Even fallen apples are the result of some kind of labour process.
2   All acts of production presume that an act of consumption will follow. Even if a product remains unconsumed, the assumption that it will be, or ordinarily would be consumed, is certainly in the mind of the producer at the time that production takes place and thus forms part of the idea of producing it.
3   In as much as they are a manifestation of creativity and intent, many acts of consumption are themselves forms of production. The consumption

of apple nutrients produces the body, the consumption of other kinds of desirables produces sensations of pleasure and satisfaction in the consumer.

4   Conversely, once one moves beyond the most elementary acts, production invariably requires some form of (production–) consumption in the sense that in hitting a nail with a hammer, the actor is 'consuming' the hammer and the nail, or at least the purpose for which the hammer and nail were themselves produced.

5   When considered in terms of the intended outcomes or purposes of the activity, many acts of consumption are almost indistinguishable from the acts of production with which they are associated; they are simply a culminatory act which occurs at the end of a sequence of actions which began with the process of production. Some of these sequences might be cyclical in the sense that the initial act of production might very well have been inspired by some previous act of consumption.

Seeing consumption and production as aspects of the same activity rather than as quite distinct and separate bits of activity suggests several useful lines of enquiry. We can consider their similarities and differences in terms of the basic motivations which underpin them. Are acts of production and acts of consumption both aimed at satisfying the same needs? We can also consider differences which arise from the position that consumption occupies in the strings or sequences of action which people undertake. Why is it that intrinsically, as actions-in-themselves, acts of consumption are more satisfying than acts of production? Finally, and corresponding to our discussion of the work ethic of Protestantism in Chapter 2, we can consider the ways in which the new consumption is articulated and legitimated ideationally through a burgeoning ethic of consumption.

Motivation: the need to consume

Beginning with motivation, and consistent with our position that production and consumption are two parts of the larger and more inclusive whole of the activity of the individual, we can provisionally say that both are motivated by a desire to obtain rewards which are prized for the sensation of satisfaction or pleasure they enable the actor to experience. Production and consumption are thus united in that they are both measured in terms of utility defined as satisfaction and pleasure. If, as in our apple-eating example, both the act of production and the act of consumption are motivated by the expected pleasure of eating an apple, then motivationally they are not separate acts but two phases or constituents of the same act.

Whilst the motivational similarities are fairly obvious in instances of simple consumption where the producer and the consumer are one-and-the-same person, and where consumption follows production more-or-less immediately, the question of motivation and need is somewhat more oblique where the two acts (or two constituents of the same act) take place at different times and/or are performed by different actors. As has often been observed, it is the separation of production from consumption in terms both of the doer and when the two are done which marks the beginning of modern forms of production. Adam Smith's 'division of labour', Marx's 'modern industry' and Weber's 'modern rational enterprise' all emphasise the fundamental importance of this development and the risks it entails for people's sense of well being. Much of Marx's critique of the capitalist labour process for example, is based on his early analysis of how the separation of conception and execution, a prerequisite for the detailed division of labour, causes profound alienation:

> The object labour produces, its product, stands opposed to [labour] as *something alien*, as a *power independent* of the producer .... In the sphere of political economy this realisation of labour appears as a *loss of reality* for the worker, objectification as *loss of and bondage to the object*, and the appropriation as estrangement, as alienation [Entausserung] .... (Marx, 1975: 324, original emphasis)[4]

Whether one accepts or rejects these critiques, the dislocations required by modern production obviously have implications for the way that people understand their various needs and how they seek out the means of satisfying them. The needs which producers have and seek to satisfy through productive consumption are not always the same as the needs which consumers have and seek to fulfil through final consumption. Acts of final consumption might be regarded as ends-in-themselves rather than as means to a further end. Acts of final consumption are performed in response to a wide range of needs which vary between different people and for the same people but at different times and on different occasions. The durability (utility even) of any theory of consumption will depend on how well it can accommodate and reconcile these kinds of distinctions.

A determination to understand human action in terms of the different types or categories of needs we hope to satisfy is of course well-established in the human and social sciences (Maslow, 1943, 1968; Marcuse, 1964; Fromm, 1976; Soper, 1981; Doyal and Gough, 1991; Slater, 1997b). To take just two examples from the humanist genre, the French psychologist Lucien Sève distinguishes between concrete activity and abstract activity, suggesting that whilst the latter administers to social production outside the individual, concrete activity includes activity which 'relates to the individual himself, for example, acts directly satisfying personal needs, learning of new capacities unconnected with the carrying out of any requirements of social labour' (Sève, 1978: 337). A similar contrast has been developed by Gorz who distinguishes between heteronomous activity which is 'made up of socially predetermined and relatively impersonal tasks' tasks 'which individuals have to accomplish as functions co-ordinated from outside by a pre-established organization' (Gorz, 1982: 102 and 1989: 32), and auto-nomous activity which is activity 'in which the individual is the sovereign author of actions carried out without recourse to necessity, alibis or excuses' (Gorz, 1982: 93–8):

> I refer to those activities which are themselves their own end as autonomous activities. They are valued for and in themselves not because they have no other objective than the satisfaction and plea-sure they procure, but because the *action which achieves the goal is as much a source of satisfaction as the achievement of the goal itself*: the end is reflected in the means and vice versa; I may will the end by virtue of the intrinsic value of the activity which achieves it and the activity by virtue of the value of the end it is pursuing. (Gorz, 1989: 165, original emphasis)

In searching for a theory of consumption which embraces the similarities and interdependencies between the realms of production and consump-tion, whilst also accommodating the differences between them, we can usefully borrow these distinctions between abstract/heteronomous activity on the one hand, and concrete/autonomous activity on the other, and say that generally speaking, the kinds of activities which go on in the realm of production are of the former type while those in the realm of consumption are of the latter type.

Intrinsic satisfaction – the holy grail of action

In looking for similarities and differences in the kinds of actions which are performed in the realms of production and consumption, these accounts suggest that a good deal depends on *the position* that a particu-lar piece of activity has in the string or sequence of actions which sur-round it. Whether concrete or abstract, autonomous or heteronymous, action does not simply happen but is determined by the actions which came before it, and in its turn will affect the actions which occur later in the sequence. What distinguishes acts of production from acts of con-sumption here, is that typically, the more abstract or heteronymous kinds of outputs associated with production (and one might add, the act of production itself) tend to be incomplete since they presume that further actions will follow. Acts of consumption on the other hand, tend to be terminal or conclusive in the sense that they are the moment at which the actor achieves satisfaction or pleasure. Acts of production are a means to a further or consequent end, whilst acts of consumption entail no presumption that a further or subsequent action is required. One has to allow here that although most acts of private consumption fall into Marx's category of 'final consumption' as discussed above, it is quite probable that they will set in train a further sequence of production/consumption. The modern consumer ethic propagates the fundamental belief that the desire to consume will never be truly satisfied. The point is, that within what might be an endless cycle of actions, there has to be a moment when *we feel* that we have reached some conclusion, some end point, even if we accept that it remains temporary.[5]

If it is the case that acts of consumption are terminal or conclusive in terms of their proximity to the actor's dividend of satisfaction (acts of consumption constitute 'the moment of return' at the culmination of the sequence of action-investments which come before), we can go a little further and argue that acts of consumption also differ from acts of production not just because of important differences in the outcomes they produce, but because of differences in the levels of intrinsic satisfaction they offer as actions-in-themselves. Acts of consumption not only coincide with the actual moment of satisfaction (the bite of chocolate, the swallowing of beer, the scent of the rose), they are often actions which are self-satisfying in that no subsequent or further action is required (reading a book, listening to music, viewing a film). Acts of work performed in the realm of production are generally not very satisfying in themselves, not least because they are a means to an end, whereas acts of final consumption generally are pleasurable because they are an end.

The rationalities of production and consumption

These distinctions help considerably in our comparison of production and consumption because they point to the fact that different rationalities of action are in play. Adopting a Weberian typology we can say that typically, being means to other ends, acts of production (and actions in the realm of production) are stamped with purpose-rationality (zweckrationality) while acts of consumption (actions in the realm of consumption) predominantly display value-rationality (wertrationality) since the action is satisfying in and of itself; it is itself an end rather than a means to-an end. Acts of consumption are considered more desirable than acts of production because they produce high levels of intrinsic, spontaneous and immediate satisfaction. It is the immediacy of satisfaction which makes acts of consumption seem concrete and real to the actor and is in marked contrast to the more abstract and detached character of actions in the realm of production. If it is sufficiently pleasurable in itself and/or as a means to satisfaction, the desire to repeat that action provides both the motivation and the justification for so doing. Whilst actions in the realm of production sometimes fall into this category (what we might call instances of the 'William Morris effect' they are much more commonplace in the realm of consumption.

Recap

To recap the argument so far, we have suggested that the relationship between acts of production and acts of consumption is particularly close, so close in fact that there are many instances where in terms of basic motivation, the two are virtually indistinguishable. This happy state of affairs is however dramatically altered under circumstances where techniques of production require a much greater separation of conception from execution. In this new situation, production and consumption become more and more separated as fewer and fewer people finally consume the commodities they directly produce. In theorising the differences which have been identified between acts of production and acts of consumption we have noted the importance of the sequence in which these different actions occur. Most importantly that acts of production are almost always intermediate and not conclusive or terminal. Both as actions in themselves and in terms of the things they produce, the levels of satisfaction and pleasure which acts of production yield (their utility) are much more limited than is the case in acts of consumption which, as terminal acts, constitute the moment of return for the actor. Typically, the realm of production is one where actions are directed outwards or away from the actor in the sense that the ends to which such actions are the means are often abstract and difficult to determine. It is the immediacy of pleasure and satisfaction, the positive sensation which arises at the moment when desired ends are achieved which constitutes the concreteness and autonomy of the activities of consumption. Characteristics which make them much more desirable (and in this sense at least, *more necessary*) to the actor.

THE ETHIC OF MODERN CONSUMPTION – PLEASURE, LEISURE AND ENJOYMENT

Having looked at issues of need and motivation, we have arrived at a point where we can usefully consider differences and similarities in the belief systems, the principles of justification, the substantive rationalities which underpin the ethics of modern production and modern consumption.[6] Given what we have already said about the complexity of the relationship between production and consumption it is certainly worth considering whether the roots of the ethic of modern consumption can also be found in the Protestant work ethic which has provided much of the legitimating rationale of Western productivism. Although this might initially seem a rather idiotic suggestion, since early Protestantism sought to control and limit, rather than encourage, the pleasures and satisfactions of consumption, a reasonable and interesting case can be made.

Although the Protestant ethic provided a very powerful means of promoting and justifying particular kinds of behaviour in the conduct of economic affairs, it also, and just as important from the point of view of the accumulation of capital, had a very powerful role in placing limitations upon what was or was not allowed in the realm of consumption. As Weber puts it: 'the old leisurely and comfortable attitude towards life gave way to a hard frugality in which some participated and came to the top, because they did not wish to consume but to earn, while others who wished to keep on with the old ways were forced to curtail their consumption' (Weber, 1976: 68). The substantive rationality of the modern period is thus Janus-faced. Expressed through the protocol of the Protestant work ethic, the same credo offers justifying principles for work *and* for consumption, for how one should conduct oneself both as producer *and* as consumer. This ethic gave rise to a variety of culture in which such values were highly placed and thus tended to hold a dominant position. As Weber points out, exponents of this ethic were obsessed with saving capital gains for investment (rational behaviour) rather than wasting them on pleasure (irrational behaviour).

Whilst this provides a clear and widely accepted explanation (although see Tawney, 1982 and Marshall, 1982) of how capital was accumulated during the seventeenth and eighteenth centuries in certain key districts of Northern and Western society, it is also quite a good explanation of why the forms of indulgent consumption we are familiar with today did not really get going until the mid-twentieth century. In Britain for example, the Victorian approach to spending and enjoyment, certainly adopted many of the principles of abstemiousness and asceticism as set out in the Protestant ethic (for example Smiles's, 1859 classic *Self-Help*). Of the 1920s, and albeit 'harvesting a much longer revolution' beginning in the 1880s (Richards, 1991), Slater suggests that this was '… probably the first decade to proclaim a generalised ideology of affluence …. It promoted a powerful link between everyday consumption and modernization' (Slater, 1997b: 12). Or as Horowitz puts it: 'From 1880 through 1920 the shift from a producer to a consumer culture gained new momentum …. This change from sanctions of religion to those of personality involved the increasing identification of happiness with pleasure' (Horowitz, 1985: 67).[7]

Similarly, with the experience of many people in the twentieth century who having tolerated the economic uncertainties of the 1920s and then suffered the tedium of shortage and rationing in the 1940s, finally let themselves go with the mass consumption (in all its senses) of the 1960s and 1970s. It was as if people finally got fed up with the ideology of restraint and moderation and decided instead to invest directly in the here-and-now, in immediate pleasure and instant gratification. 'Forget the heavenly hereafter, I'll take a chance on having my reward now'. Referring to the work of Daniel Bell (1974) and J.K. Galbraith (1969), Slater suggests that 'the affluent society was a consumer society in which economic prosperity brought insatiable and morally dubious wants, a crisis in values over the work ethic ... and hedonistic, amoral, non-familial consumption' (Slater, 1997b: 12).[8]

From elite to mass consumption

For many commentators, the feature which most clearly distinguishes modern consumption from earlier forms is that it is *mass* consumption (Katona, 1964; Westley and Westley, 1971; Hudson, 1983 cited in Fine and Leopold, 1993).[9] The main reason for this is of course that mass consumption is assumed to be an inevitable corollary of mass production: 'consumer society is perceived to be the consequence of mass production (of uniform goods through the factory system) in the twentieth century' (Fine and Leopold, 1993: 65). Although other commentators prefer to argue that 'the consumer revolution of the eighteenth century [should be] considered as *complementary and equal* to the supply side transformations of the Industrial Revolution' (ibid.: emphasis added. Standard points of departure are McKendrick et al., 1982 and Brewer and Porter (eds), 1993), it seems quite impossible not to characterise twentieth-century consumerism in terms of mass consumption, and this would not be possible without mass production.

A second important reason for considering the role of mass consumption in consumption-based society is because some have argued that in the late modern period, the leading edge of consumer demand is for bespoke and individualised commodities rather than for commodities which are the same as everyone else has got. Feeding into debates over the alleged transition towards 'post-Fordism' which dominated the sociology of work for much of the 1980s, one of the originators of ideas about 'the second industrial divide' suggested that: 'Consumers will be increasingly willing to pay a premium for a variant of the good whose possession sets them off from the mass; and as the number of variants competing for attention and encouraging further differentiation of tastes increases, it becomes harder and harder to consolidate production of a standard product' (Sabel, 1984: 199): See also Piore and Sabel (1984). For commentary see Pollert (ed.) (1991) Gilbert et al. (1992); and Amin (ed.) (1994). More recently Langlois and Cosgel have concluded that producers and consumers are equally involved:

> Consumers are active, not only because they may seek novelty or choose in an existential context, but also because they are in effect producers, who must actively organise their own consumption using the skills and routines they possess or can acquire. The boundaries between consumers and producers are permeable. They shift in response to entrepreneurial possibilities seized by consumers, producers, or both; and the pattern of change will be governed by the historical distribution of capabilities among consumers and producers and by the technological characteristics of the products involved. (Langlois and Cosgel, 1998: 118–9)

Although these debates pretty much petered out during the 1990s it seems clear enough that with advanced production technologies it is perfectly possible to offer the consumer a decent range of variations of what is essentially the same basic commodity. In this context, the term 'mass consumption' in consumption-based societies in the late modern period actually refers to the good economies of scale that can be achieved by making things in relatively large batches, but without implying that everyone is consuming identical items. The range of choices does not actually have to be that great for consumers to be happy that they are not always copying the Joneses. It is not at all the same as the mass consumption of the early and mid-modern period where large economies of scale could only be achieved if the commodities were identical (as Henry Ford famously said 'you can have any color as long as its black!').[10]

The third reason why we need to talk about mass consumption is to distinguish it from elite consumption. Mass consumption is not just about the scale on which things are produced and consumed, it is also about perceptions of the social location and status of those that are doing the consuming. In this sense, mass or 'popular' consumption is understood to be vulgar and common, as distinct from elite consumption which is understood to be refined and exclusive. These distinctions have been used by sociologists to understand the differences between one class and another (or as making manifest the differences between classes) and so we will defer further discussion of them until Chapter 6. At this point we can note however, that one important aspect of the transition towards a fully formed consumption-based society, is that one important constituent of elite consumption, namely leisure consumption, ceases to be associated only with a social elite and becomes much more widely available right across the social spectrum

(Rojek, 1995 and 2000). Social exclusivity is no longer defined in terms of access to leisure-consumption, and thus by the mid-twentieth century, leisure consumption has fallen out of the category of elite consumption where it used to comfortably reside: 'differences that were once expressed in terms of time allocation [between work and leisure] are perhaps now expressed in terms ... of the possession or use of special commodities or services whose particular function is to denote wealth' (Gershuny, 2000: 31–2). Leisure-consumption thus becomes an important part of what mass consumption is. In the late modern period, leisure has ceased to be a kind of refined idleness and has developed into a new range of activities and entertainments. Leisure time contains very little in the way of idle relaxation and contemplation but a great deal of activity. The field of leisure-consumption in consumption-based society is a busy domain filled with meaning-rich artefacts all clamouring for attention. The mass affluent consumers of late modern society expect to be entertained, not just relieved temporarily of the burden of work-saturated time.[11]

We can note one further additional and recent constituent of 'mass' consumption, and one which has developed particularly in the field of entertainment. 'Simultaneous mass consumption' has become possible as a result of the availability of cheap forms of mass communications technologies and is made up of events which literally involve masses of people in some form of simultaneous consumption. Leading examples would be coverage of global sporting events such as the football World Cup or the Olympic Games which, although mediated are enjoyed simultaneously by millions of consumers at the same time (Rowe, 1999).

Outside the field of entertainment, the destruction of the twin towers in New York in September 2001 and its aftermath was a massively globalised event. The cultural and sometimes globalising effect of such events should not be underestimated (Bradley and Greenberg (eds), 1991; Morley and Robins, 1995; Leslie (ed.), 1997).

To the extent that leisure consumption is typically not a survival-type activity (although the respite all of us require from our daily toil could be classified as 'leisure'), we can note a clear association between mass consumption/leisure-consumption and affluence. Even without invoking Veblen's characterisation of 'the leisure class' as a class having the capacity always to be at leisure, to actively and deliberately fritter time away – 'the abiding test of good breeding is the requirement of a substantial and patent waste of time' (Veblen, 1994: 51) – the levels of pleasure, leisure and entertainment which now form part of our ordinary expectations as mass consumers obviously require quite high levels of disposable income. (We will be addressing these issues in more detail when we look at data on patterns of consumption and expenditure in the following chapter.)

Live now pay later

A simple but highly suggestive proof of this new-found sense of freedom can be seen in the emergence of a new attitude towards debt. From the pawnbrokers of the nineteenth and early twentieth century, through hire purchase agreements of the 1950s and 1960s, to credit and store cards of the late modern period, the pressure to 'spend now pay later' has continuously increased. Through my own letter box in the past few days for example, I received offers of unsecured personal loans from commercial lenders claiming 'Big Loans. Small rates'. 'Its easy … It makes sense … It's affordable' 'You could afford to really treat yourself now and spread the cost'. 'Turn your dreams into reality'. 'Easy to arrange over the phone.' 'Worry free borrowing'. 'It takes just one short phone call to apply'. 'Need to borrow some money? It's no big deal … need it right now? No problem'. 'We can agree your loan in minutes and have the money in your account within the hour'. Contemporary consumption-based societies are places where heavy borrowing for household consumption is pretty much the norm (Ritzer, 2001).

What we have here is a switch away from saving and towards debt. We noted in our discussion of household incomes in the previous chapter that apart from some more affluent pensioner households, very little domestic income comes from savings and investments. The reason of course is that most people do not have any savings or investments from which they can draw an income. Recent data show that in 2001 only 20 per cent of the United Kingdom population had savings of more than £10,000, 23 per cent had less than £1,500, and 34 per cent none at all (*Social Trends*, 2003: Table 5.27). As one would expect, households with members aged over 60 years are more likely to have savings, and those with unemployed, sick or disabled members a lot less likely. Looking at things from the spending side, the corollary to savings is borrowing, or more accurately, spending on credit. In order to sustain such high levels of consumption, many households have turned towards various kinds of credit. Government data record for example, that of all adults aged 16 years and over in 2001, 62 per cent had a credit or charge card, and 35 per cent had a store card (*Social Trends*, 2001: Table 6.10). As a result, annual net consumer borrowing in the United Kingdom (excluding mortgages) 'was the highest level ever in 2001 at £17.6 billion' (*Social Trends*, 2003: 123). The number of bankruptcies, which provides a fair indication of the extent to which people are unable to repay their debts, has been between 20,000 and 25,000 each year since the mid-1990s (*Social Trends*, 2003: Figure 6.12).

During the twentieth century then, and reaching a peak in the affluent postwar 1950s and 1960s, the productivist ethic of ascetic enjoyment and abstemiousness finally collapsed as the capacity for creating ever-more expectations of satisfaction continued to expand. A capacity which was itself a response to increasing demand from novelty-seeking consumers:

> The spirit of modern consumerism [is a] ... self-illusory hedonism characterised by a longing to experience in reality those pleasures created and enjoyed in imagination, a longing which results in the ceaseless consumption of novelty .... The romantic ethic can be seen to possess a basic congruence, or 'elective affinity', with this spirit, and to have given rise to a character type and ethical conduct highly conducive to the adoption of such attitudes. In particular, romantic teachings concerning the good, the true and the beautiful, provide both the legitimation and the motivation necessary for modern consumer behaviour to become prevalent throughout the contemporary industrial world. (Campbell, 1987: 205/6)

The ethic of productivism is still in play but it is now geared to providing satisfaction for needs, wants and desires which have less and less to do with basic survival, and more and more with pleasure, leisure and enjoyment. The new ethic of consumption decisively breaks the constraints imposed by the self-disciplines of hard work, diligence and thrift, of saving and moderation, and offers instead a new set of legitimations based on the self-indulgences of enjoyment. As a style or cultural form, postmodernism emerges from the shell of modernism as the adult butterfly emerges from the chrysalis. What could be more counter- or postmodernist than if the challenge to the productivist hegemony were based upon its very inverse, spending and excess? At the core of the substantive rationality of consumption-based society is a rejection of saving and moderation (although not of work), and a celebration of spending and enjoyment. Affluent consumers have trumped the work ethic with the ethic of consumption by demanding now what has been promised for so long.

Given the closeness of the relationship between production and consumption this is exactly what one would expect to find since essentially productivism and consumptivism are both children of the same basic form of substantive rationality. If, and particularly in the context of simple consumption, the motivations which underlie these strings or sequences of production/consumption are often indistinguishable, then the logic of the arguments used to justify one's actions as a consumer are very likely to be the same as, or very similar to, those used to justify one's actions as a producer – 'any non-evaluative approach to consumer culture is therefore wonderfully in tune with a market society' (Slater, 1997a: 52). We have what seems to be an unlimited capacity for producing the means of pleasure and satisfaction so why should we not put them to their intended use? Modernity is all about realising the pleasures and returns that our productive capacity has created.

The legitimacy of modern consumption

In order to preserve this aura of legitimacy (that it is substantively rational) the ethic of modern consumption adopts the same strategy as the ethic of modern production in that it also skirts around uncomfortable questions about what and where are the limits of consumption. It does this by invoking the familiar assumption that utility is mainly about pleasure and satisfaction. If someone gains pleasure or satisfaction from a particular act of consumption, then they are experiencing a proper need and are thus fully justified in acting to fulfil it. Attempts to assess degrees of need and levels of satisfaction (the equivalent of realm-or-production dilemmas over what and how much to produce) are evaded by always referring back to the desire of the individual. As Slater puts it: 'Needs and wants ... are unchallengeable: they may be described or explained to be understood, but they cannot be subjected to any critical yardstick in relation to which they can be found false, or wrong, or irrational or regressive .... Needs are reduced to preferences, and are therefore effectively arbitrary' (Slater, 1997b: 51–2). Defining needs in terms of meaning, Baudrillard reaches a similar conclusion: '... if one admits that need is never so much the need for a particular object as the "need" for difference (*the desire for the* social *meaning*), then it will be clear that there can never be any achieved satisfaction, or therefore any definition of need' (Baudrillard, 1998: 77–8).

Modern consumption is also legitimated by making a virtue out of the fact that some needs can never be satisfied. Consumers should not be embarrassed by the fact that their hunger and thirst need to be sated and slaked over and over again. Repetition of satisfaction does not indicate uncontrollable appetite, gluttony and indulgence, but a pragmatic acceptance that many of our needs really do require endless satisfaction. Much the same approach is adopted in developing ideas about *the extent to which* needs and desires should be satisfied. Whereas the Protestant work ethic strongly promoted the idea of restraint in the satisfaction of needs and desires (dressed up as morally commendable but in practical terms to ensure the accumulation of investment capital), the ethic of the new consumption promotes the idea that it is virtuous to go on wanting to be satisfied and if possible, to ever higher levels. As Veblen observed:

> [In] order to [uphold] his own peace of mind ... an individual should
> possess as large a portion of goods as others with whom he is
> accustomed to class himself; ... but as fast as a person makes new

acquisitions, and becomes accustomed to the resulting new standard
of wealth, the new standard forthwith ceases to afford appreciably
greater satisfaction than the earlier standard did ... . The tendency ...
is constantly to make the present pecuniary standard the point of
departure for a fresh increase in wealth. (Veblen, 1994: 31)

To the extent that the Protestant ethic operated as a kind of psychological
constraint on the behaviour of the individual, an internally-imposed
restriction on what was acceptable (Weber, 1976), or that it provided an
essential moral platform for what Durkheim referred to as the capacity
for 'self regulation',[12] these devices are radically deactivated in modern
consumption. It is the incapacity of individuals to set reasonable limits
upon their behaviour as consumers which liberates consumption from
any further discussion of what its limits might be.

Whilst this notion of limitlessness is adopted in the assessment of utility
(as pleasure and satisfaction) across the full range of consumption-type
activities – for a bigger and better house, more toys, clothes and holidays,
etc., it applies especially to one of the most demanding of the new domains
of consumption, namely the formation and presentation of identity.
Modern consumption provides one of the most important realms through
which we construct and express our sense of identity, and quite naturally,
any suggestion that there are limits to consumption is tantamount to suggesting that there are limits to the amount of identity a person can reasonably expect to have. And no free-thinking autonomous sentient being
is going to accept that kind of nonsense! (We will be discussing identity in
detail in the following chapters.)

Time to consume

The simplicity and directness of these means of justifying and legitimating acts of consumption, and the continuity they have with the ideology of productivism, gives them an aura of rational authority that is
difficult to resist. After all, if people demand more things, in greater
quantity and with more variety ('smaller, faster, cheaper, better'), this
stimulates production, and, notwithstanding arguments over whether
or not supply proceeds demand, production is what makes the world go
round. Although the demands that consumers make in late-modern
society are less for basic commodities and services and more for consumption-type commodities often directed towards leisure and entertainment, they still create demand in the economy (Gershuny, 2000: 134).
If it were not for the demands of consumers, innovation would slow
down, production would stagnate and the barbarians would soon be
crossing the frontiers!

This aura of legitimacy also helps people to overcome the apparent irony, as Cross puts it, 'that productivity has led to increased consumption but not to a parallel growth of free time. While some commentators ... have regretted the time famine which has spread with the two-income family, few make the obvious linkage between worktime and the dominant culture of consumption' (Cross, 1993: 2). A key feature of consumption-based society is that people prefer having more goods to having more free time. They are prepared to work the same hours (or more) in return for the capacity to buy more consumer goods. Pleasure, leisure and enjoyment are not seen in terms of increasing amounts of non-work time, but in terms of an improving capacity to consume: 'The triumph of consumerism meant a rejection of the progressive reduction of worktime and of "democratic leisure". It realised instead the dominance of a work-and-spend culture' (Cross, 1993: 4). Further still, and reviewing ideas about 'self-provisioning' discussed by Pahl, Gershuny and Offe during the mid-1980s, Cross notes that as 'manufactured goods have become cheaper relative to services ... households have an incentive to purchase domestic "capital goods" and to do their own domestic jobs and improvements' (Cross, 1993: 201). Here we have an example of how production consumption (as distinct from final consumption) has been brought within the home.

Although these authors have suggested that it is increases in the productivity of consumer goods and services, and what Voth (1998) calls the 'increased productivity of leisure' rather than further increases in the efficiency of production, which might result in a reduction in working time, what has actually happened is that people continue to be more interested in acquiring more consumer goods ('capital' or otherwise) than in working fewer hours. If leisure commodities and services provide higher levels of satisfaction at the moment of final consumption than earlier versions, consumers will want more rather than less of them: '... it might be rational for high-wage earners to work longer hours in order to buy more intensely pleasurable consumption experiences' (Gershuny, 2000: 8). The utility of consumer commodities – measured in terms of satisfaction – has been increasing, not just the levels of efficiency with which such commodities can be produced.

A related point is made by Becker (1965, 1976, 1981, and 1985) who argues that when measured in terms of the amount of time they save on doing domestic chores, it is the increased utility of consumer durables (washing machines, dishwashers, microwave ovens and so on) which partly explains why there has actually been relatively little reduction in working hours during the twentieth century – paid work expands to fill the time which is increasingly available (and one might add, there is no limit to the amount of time which could be spent on domestic chores rather than on leisure).[13] Gershuny (2000) also refers to the apparently paradoxical nature of some of these trends in developing his thesis that three convergences are taking place 'in time-use patterns: by nation, gender and "class"' (Gershuny, 2000: 5). 'The twenty countries we shall be discussing in this book show overall a general increase in leisure (i.e. a decline in the total of paid plus unpaid work)' significantly however, and despite this being the period when one would have expected that labour-saving durables would have resulted in a reduction in the time spent on unpaid domestic activities, 'some of the richer countries, towards the end of the century, show a small decline in leisure time'.[14]

A second convergence discussed by Gershuny, is 'a gender convergence' wherein 'the women come to do absolutely more paid, and absolutely less unpaid work. The men do generally less paid and increase their unpaid'. The third, and 'slightly more complex' convergence is 'in time use across the different *status groups*'. Again the interesting supposition from our point of view is that 'those of higher status previously had more leisure, and subsequently had less of it, than those of lower social status' (ibid.: 5–7), meaning that the association of 'the leisure class' with 'idle' or 'free' time made by Veblen and others at the turn of the twentieth century has been significantly reversed at the turn of twenty-first: 'once leisure signified status, but no longer, now the most important people are the busiest … we now demonstrate our status by our *lack of leisure*' (Gershuny, 2000: 9, emphasis added).

Materially, the logic of the post-materialist argument rests on the assumption that as production becomes ever more efficient, people will prefer to have (even 'need') fewer goods, but more 'free' or leisure-time. As we have already seen however in our discussion of work-intensity, there is no evidence of any dramatic decrease in economic activity. Increases in the availability of leisure or non-work time (which are made up partly from reducing hours of paid work and less time being spent on unpaid domestic tasks) stimulate demand for pleasure-, leisure- and enjoyment-oriented forms of consumption. Consumption-based society in the late modern period is a leisure society 'but a profoundly materialist one, in which the increase in leisure time plays a central role in maintaining and promoting economic growth … far from being an indicator of a post-materialist society, increasing leisure time may well be the mechanism for maintaining the stability of an ever more materialist society' (Gershuny, 2000: 134–5).

And so we return to the discussion of needs with which we began this chapter. The urge to consume continuously stimulates the need to produce. An essential and common element in the productivist ethic *and* in the ethic of modern consumption, is to make a virtue out of the never-ending quest for needs-novelty:

[T]he industrial system itself, which presupposes the growth of needs, also presupposes a perpetual excess of needs over the supply of goods ... the system does however, verge on a contradiction in that growth not only implies the growth of needs and a certain disequilibrium between goods and needs, but further implies *the growth of that very disequilibrium* between the growth of needs and the growth of productivity .... There are no limits to man's "needs" as a social being (i.e. as a being productive of *meaning* and relative to others in *value*). The quantitative intake of food is limited, the digestive system is limited, but the cultural system of food is, for its part, indefinite. (Baudrillard, 1998: 64, original emphasis)

SUMMARY

To summarise the definition of consumption-based society developed in this chapter, we can say that this is a type of society in which the pleasures and satisfactions of acts of consumption come to be seen as more desirable than the pleasures and satisfactions which come from production-side activities. Through consumption, the activities of production are revealed for what they are; a means of achieving some act of final consumption. As actions in themselves and as the moment when anticipated satisfaction is achieved, acts of consumption are qualitatively different from acts of production. Positioned at the end of sequences of action, they are experienced as more concrete, more autonomous and thus more satisfying than acts of production. Even though any rational account of the production–consumption relationship must acknowledge that the two are inseparably linked, that they are actually two aspects, two moments of the same 'event', the more favourable association of pleasure and satisfaction with the consumption part of the event greatly enhances people's perceptions of their desirability and thus importance. Consumption-based society is a place where priority is given to the benefits of consuming things despite a fairly open acknowledgement that necessary production must be completed first.

Inevitably these developments have run parallel with changes in the nature of consumption itself. We will be discussing these in more detail in the following chapter, but for now we can note that during the twentieth century, consumption has increasingly come to be seen as a realm of pleasure not just of necessity. Whereas consumption-as-leisure used to be the preserve of a privileged minority it has now become available to all. Whether in the form of mass consumption of mass-produced commodities, of individual consumption of bespoke goods which have been mass-manufactured, or of leisure activities which are experienced simultaneously with others, consumption-based society is a place where everyone is a mass consumer for purposes of pleasure and enjoyment.

In terms of prevailing values and beliefs about the relative virtues of production and consumption, the desire to maximise satisfaction through consumption now sits very comfortably alongside the productivist ethic. So long as it provides fairly direct opportunities for satisfaction through consumption, production is embraced as the bearer of all things good. Having settled earlier concerns about the morality of increased consumption – not least by arguing that consumption virtuously stimulates production and thus requires more not less dedication to one's working life – the limitlessness of consumption is reconciled with the limitlessness of pleasure and satisfaction. In consumption-based society, the rationalities of consumption are seen as providing a natural extension to the rationalities of production.

NOTES

[1]The intimacy of the relationship between production and consumption is something which has been widely acknowledged in sociology, cultural studies and economics. See for example: Lee, 1993; Uusitalo, 1998: 215, Langlois and Cosgel, 1998: 119 and Fine and Leopold, 1993.

[2]Although his own account of needs as things which 'arise from core values of historically and collectively evolving ways of life' (Slater, 1997a: 57), is sometimes unsatisfactory because it tends to discount the fact that some needs are only ever satisfied temporarily, Slater usefully underscores this point by arguing that there is always an intersection between production and consumption and this invariably constitutes the expression of some kind of 'need'.

[3]Additionally we can also note that these distinctions have also made it difficult to evaluate the quantity and share of effort which goes into domestic work within the household. Hakim notes for example: 'In industrial society most domestic work is consumption work, with goods and services produced for immediate consumption within the household, so that productive work in the household context is less easily identified' (Hakim, 1996: 23). Although these activities clearly have an 'economic' benefit to household members, this benefit is not easily measured by economics as monetary exchange does not take place.

[4]The theme of alienation has provided the basic motif of all Marxist and Marxian accounts of the capitalist labour process virtually uninterrupted from the original in the 1840s. See for example Blauner, 1964; Braverman, 1974; Wood (ed.), 1982 and Lee, 1993.

[5]The principal exception to this rule would be an act of suicide. By deliberately and knowingly performing an action which will permanently end the sequence of one's actions, suicide may be the only action which is truly 'final'.

[6]We emphasise *modern* consumption since clearly, like production, there are many instances of pre-modern forms. As should be clear already, in this discussion, 'modern' refers to the historical period and modes of life which developed from about 1750 in what was about to become the industrialised West. For discussions of consumption in the pre-modern period see Stuard, 1985; Thirsk, 1978; and McCracken, 1987 all of whom are cited in Fine and Leopold, 1993.

[7]Slater provides a useful account of the historical sequence of the coming of 'consumer culture', and by slightly redefining it by invoking the idea of the 'commercial revolution' based on the ethic of 'trade and commerce', he traces this back towards the seventeenth century.

[8]For introductions to 'the sociology of consumption' which emerged during the 1980 particularly in Britain, to explore these new happenings see: Douglas and Isherwood, 1979; D. Millar (ed.), 1995; Keat et al. (ed.), 1994; Warde, 1990a; Gabriel and Lang, 1995; and Mort, 1997.

> [9]For an item to be considered a mass-consumed commodity in any given place, two things must happen. It must be bought by people of varied income levels and they must be buying it on a more or less regular basis .... Between about 1650 and 1750, tobacco, sugar products and caffeine drinks became items of mass consumption, meaning 25 per cent or more of the adult population [those aged 15 years or over] regularly used them. (Shammas, 1993: 181–99)

[10]The more technical aspect of these debates is about whether product innovation originates with producers (process and product innovation) or with consumers (new tastes, appetites and expectations). For an introduction to debates over 'long waves' and 'paradigm shifts' in economic development see: Kondratiev, 1935; Schumpeter, 1989; Aglietta, 1979; Freeman et al., 1982 and Ransome, 1996. A more distinctly sociological critique of the way that consumption (demand) is manipulated by production (supply) in 'affluent society' is put forward by Galbraith, 1969 and 1972.

[11]In his analysis of changing time-use patterns Gershuny argues that it is actually part of the 'logic of development' of industrialised societies that: 'as the number of high-valued-added workers increases, the market for their products must continually widen. A modern high-value-added society must provide for mass consumption not elite consumption' (Gershuny, 2000: 32). 'Superordinate' or 'higher' class or social positions in late-modernity are expressed through possession or use of commodities and services rather than through having lots of free or leisure time as was the case during the pre- and early-modern period. We will be discussing the impact of such developments on social or 'class' differentiation in Chapter 6.

> [12]A regulative force must play the same role for moral needs which the organism plays for physical needs. This means that the force can only be moral. The awakening of conscience interrupted the state of equilibrium of the animal's dormant existence; only conscience, therefore, can furnish the means to re-establish it. (Durkheim, 1968: 247–8)

[13]Becker's ideas have been influential within sociology as well as in economics. Following Hakim, we can note that 'rational choice theory' sometimes called 'rational action theory' or 'exchange theory', has given rise to the 'new home economics' and 'human capital theory', 'which studies non-economic aspects of the family, including the sexual division of labour in households, the supply of wives' labour to the market economy, decisions about investments in children, decisions about marriage and divorce' (Hakim, 1996: 13).

[14]This paradox is explained by trends in the amount of unpaid domestic work being done by households moving in opposite directions for different classes, and between men and women. Working-class households are doing a lot less, and middle-class households a lot more domestic work.

5   *Acts of consumption*

Having explored some the similarities and differences between acts of production and consumption in terms of motivations, needs, values and rationalities, we now turn our attention to exploring the specific types of activity which preoccupy people in consumption-based society. What does a society in which most people are involved in the activities of consumption look like? How are people spending their time (and money)? In this discussion we are focusing squarely on things which go on within the consumption side, specifically the activities of final consumption performed by private individuals (we are not in other words, going to say very much about productive consumption and the production-side of things).

A TYPOLOGY OF SIMPLE AND COMPLEX CONSUMPTION

As is the case when studying acts of work, it is useful when studying consumption to make distinctions between one type of consumption and another, and to accept that different levels of priority might be assigned to them. Priorities which lie at various points along the continuum of utility ranging from the basic satisfaction of day-to-day needs and desires at one end through to more elaborate, sometimes quite abstract even symbolic kinds of satisfactions at the other. In the same way that Fromm, Marcuse, Herzberg, Maslow, Soper and Gough felt able to distinguish between one category of needs and another, it is also sensible, since acts of consumption are obviously oriented towards the satisfaction of needs, to imagine that there are also different types of consumption. We will approach this potentially daunting task by making a rudimentary distinction between simple consumption and complex consumption. Within these two broad groupings we can devise a number of further categories as shown in Figure 5.1.

Simple consumption

In the category simple consumption, and bearing in mind what we have already said about how acts of production and consumption of this type

	Necessary Consumption
Simple consumption	Elaborated consumption
	Indulgent consumption
Complex consumption	Affluent consumption
	Conspicuous consumption
	Symbolic consumption

Figure 5.1   Typology of consumption

tend to form pairs, we can place acts which are most closely associated with maintaining our basic survival. These acts of consumption are strictly *necessary* in the sense that we cannot avoid them; we have no choice but to consume food, drink, and the materials required for clothing, housing and protection from predators and other sometimes hostile human beings. All forms of human society must consume at this level in order to maintain any kind of material existence. These are constituents of what Marx and Engels called 'the first historical act … the production of material life itself' (Marx and Engels, 1970: 48). Building upon this foundation, we next encounter a category of *elaborated consumption* which refers to acts of consumption associated with advances in productive capacity and sophistication. Materials used in making tools and machines, in organising agriculture and industry, in building the economic infrastructure and our expanding use of raw materials. These acts of consumption are still governed by straightforward necessity, but represent advances in the means by which we aim to achieve and maintain satisfaction of these basic requirements. These developments could be regarded as advances in the *range and capacity* of productive consumption, in the sense that as the techniques of production become more advanced, so too do the commodities which are used within it.

Beyond acts of elaborated consumption, and moving a little away from the strictures of bare necessity, are acts of *indulgent consumption*. The emphasis here is on acts which are preformed in anticipation of some pleasurable benefit or effect which cannot be justified solely on the grounds of simple necessity (other perhaps than the necessity of doing it because one has the capacity so to do). Indulgent consumption includes bits-and-pieces of consumption – (in modern society) the luxury chocolate after a meal, the slightly more exotic house furnishing or frivolous garment. It might also include other occasional treats such as a meal in a smart restaurant or family outing to the local adventure park. Indulgent consumption is relative in the sense that what one person might regard as an occasional luxury, another might expect to consume more frequently. It tends to be local and individual in orientation because not everyone in society ordinarily has access to these items and activities. It is a type of consumption which characterises a society with elites not a society of the masses.

Complex consumption

This notion of relativity, of how one person's idea of indulgence and luxury is another person's standard expectation, highlights one of the crucial characteristics of those types of consumption which fall into our other broad category which we have labelled complex consumption. That is, that people increasingly make choices about many of their acts of consumption. Choice of consumption suggests a loosening of the link between consumption and bare necessity and a corresponding strengthening of the link between consumption and what we might call non-essential or elective necessity. In this sense the satisfactions which the consumer seeks to satisfy are more and more chosen by them rather than being imposed by the non-negotiable demands of the body. They are, as we have already said, autonomous rather than heteronymous activities.

This category is therefore largely made up of acts of consumption which are deemed by the actor to provide satisfaction of something more than basic needs. Unlike acts of simple consumption which can relatively easily be paired off with corresponding acts of production (growing the corn to make the flour to make the dough to make the loaf to eat), the satisfactions and pleasures produced through complex consumption can be achieved by a variety of means. This partial disassociation of means from ends thus allows the creation of much more complex ways of finding satisfaction. Beyond keeping the body safe and stocked with sufficient calories and fluids, this kind of consumption aims to give expression to more complex needs for cerebral stimulation, for the pleasure which comes from solving the puzzles of the sign and what it is supposed to signify. Comparison, interpretation, imagination are all typical attributes of acts in this category since as Baudrillard and others have pointed out, complex consumption in the modern world has become very much a matter of consuming meanings and significances: the process of consumption becomes 'a process of signification and communication [and] a process of classification and social differentiation ... in which the sign/objects are ordered ... as status values in a hierarchy' (Baudrillard, 1998: 60–1).

Breaking the category of complex consumption down a little, we can identify *affluent consumption* which implies a way of acting, a lifestyle, which does not restrict itself to occasional indulgence but assumes more-or-less continuous opportunities for consuming beyond necessity. Affluent consumption implies an elastic realm of pleasure-seeking where things previously regarded as luxuries are continuously added to the stock of things which one expects as a matter of course. An easy way of understanding this realm is to think of examples of non-essential (in the sense that physical survival does not depend on them) consumption which we take for granted but which our parents, and certainly our grandparents would have regarded as occasional or rare luxuries (for, them, examples of indulgent consumption). The English fable of receiving nothing more than an orange and a few walnuts in one's Christmas stocking comes to mind! (We will be looking at the association of affluence with consumption shortly.)

The category *conspicuous consumption* is intended to capture the way in which knowledge of what a person consumes becomes a simple and immediate means of comparing one person with another. One of the things we increasingly consume are the very comparisons that acts of consumption allow us to make. Knowing that we judge others by looking at what they consume, we soon come to seek out forms and means of consumption for ourselves which send particular kinds of messages to those observing our own behaviour. We take notice of the fact that consumption becomes a mirror of who and what we are socially. We also consume conspicuously because the ethic of modern consumption sanctions and even promotes such behaviour.

The association of conspicuous consumption with wealth, invokes the idea of luxury consumption. As Veblen puts it, one of the things which renders luxury consumption conspicuous, is the fact that such items are conspicuously lacking in practical use; the consumption of unproductive goods, and the 'unproductive consumption of goods', provides 'a marker of prowess and a perquisite of human dignity ... it becomes substantially honourable in itself, especially the consumption of the more desirable things ... [such as] choice articles of food, and frequently rare articles of adornment' (Veblen, 1994: 69). What Veblen is arguing here, is that one of the most socially praiseworthy uses of otherwise idle time is to acquire a knowledge of workmanship, provenance, aesthetics and so on, thus making gentlefolk even more discerning in their tastes and purchases. Conspicuous consumption is about constantly upgrading the quality of the items which one consumes. The gentleman of leisure 'not only consumes beyond the minimum required for subsistence and physical efficiency' (a level and type of consumption which is available even to members of 'the labouring classes'), 'but his consumption also undergoes a specialisation as regards the quality of the goods consumed. He consumes freely and of the best in food, drink, weapons and accoutrements, amusements, amulets and idols or divinities … He becomes a connoisseur' (Veblen, 1994: 73–4). This capacity for selective consumption provides conspicuous evidence of superiority in other respects also: 'Refined tastes, manners, and habits of life are a useful evidence of gentility, because good breeding requires time, application, and expense, and can therefore not be compassed by those whose time and energy are taken up with work' (Veblen, 1994: 48).

Consistent with the thoroughgoing rejection of deferred gratification and self-restraint, the complex consumer requires the world to witness their capacity for affluent consumption. The tingle of gratification a person feels when a friend or neighbour or work colleague expresses a sense of surprise and envy at their latest purchase becomes a vital aspect of the utility of consumption. Again we find a repetition of the protocol of ostentation which lies at the root of frenetic productivism, only this time we crave acknowledgement of how well we are consuming rather than how well we are producing.[1]

For Baudrillard, conspicuousness becomes a defining characteristic of consumption in late modern society because public recognition of our consumption by others is one of the principal mechanisms through which we are able to express 'difference' or 'distinction' between ourselves and those others. Consumption is 'a process of signification and communication', 'a process of classification and social differentiation', and by participating in it we are able either to 'affiliate' to our own group or to mark ourselves off from it 'by reference to a group of higher status' (Baudrillard, 1998: 61).

Symbolic consumption

At the most abstract end of our typology we find acts of what we will call 'symbolic consumption'. In this category we include forms of consumption whose utility is measured primarily in terms of the particular kinds of satisfactions and pleasures which come from consuming 'meanings' in their disembodied or intangible form. We emphasise primarily, because potentially at least, all types of consumption have a symbolic aspect to them. The apparently simple act of eating bread might have a highly charged symbolic aspect if, for example, it forms part of the Christian Communion or marks the end of the Jewish Sabbath or Muslim Ramadan. Within our typology then, complex consumption includes acts of consumption which operate directly and explicitly at the level of meanings and significances, but *also includes* the quest for the 'meaning' aspect of bits of consumption which might be classified elsewhere in our typology. 'Ordinary' consumption always has the potential to produce utility in terms of the enjoyment of its 'symbolic' meanings although habitually, it is not seen in this

Period	Pre-modern	Modern	Late-modern
Dates	Before 1760	1850–1950	1980 onwards
Type of society	Predominantly production-based	Production-consumption balance	Increasingly consumption-based
Type of utility	Simple	Simple	Simple and complex
Type of consumption	Simple	Elaborated/ indulgent/ affluent	Affluent/ conspicuous/ symbolic
Mode of consumption	Pre-modern	Modern	Late-modern
Scale	Local/family/ individual	Mass	Global
Style of consumption	'Primitive'	Modernist	Modernist/ postmodernist
Content of consumption	Rudimentary/ traditional	Traditional/ modern	Modern/ postmodern

Figure 5.2   The progress of consumption

light. The extent to which a particular piece of consumption is explicitly meaning-oriented, or simply has this capacity, might sometimes be quite arbitrary.

Symbolic consumption and/or the symbolic aspects of consumption have been most vigorously associated with consumption in the late- or postmodern period, with the consumption of postmodern ideas, artefacts and activities, and with postmodern styles of consumption.[2] As Figure 5.2 illustrates, progress from one type, style or level of consumption to another can be associated with the historical progression from pre-modern, through modern and towards late modern society.

Leaving a discussion of articles and activities which might be classified by art historians and culturalists as 'postmodern' in style or aesthetic form (in the sense for example, that there is a difference between the modern style and the post-modern style of architecture) to one side,[3] one of the main features of consumption in the late modern period is the emergence of an attitude of mind, a 'postmodern' orientation towards consuming things which tends to highlight meaning and interpretation above the other facets which acts/activities of consumption might make available to us. One of the leading advocates of this approach is Jean Baudrillard who argues that 'the order of consumption' in 'the growth society' of the mid-twentieth century is saturated with meaning, significance and symbolic values:

> [This society lives] *off signs and under the protection of signs.* More and more aspects of our contemporary societies fall under a logic of significations, an analysis of codes and symbolic systems …. the system of consumption is in the last instance based not on need and enjoyment but on [an arbitrary classificatory arrangement] a code of signs (signs/objects) and differences. (Baudrillard, 1998: 32–3,79, original emphasis)

Our participation in, or submission to, this sign-system may sometimes reach a point where the tangible reality of actual objects and physical activities is overwhelmed by the loss of reality of the sign-system: 'So we live, sheltered by signs, in the denial of the real …. The image, the sign, the message – all these things we "consume" – represent our tranquillity consecrated by distance from the world, a distance more comforted by the allusion to the real … than compromised by it' (Baudrillard, 1998: 34).

Although Baudrillard's description of the mode and function of (post)modern consumption in the (late) modern period can be critically interpreted as implying that real needs have been entirely displaced by abstract ones, that actual fleshy reality has been imagined or dissolved away as the sign-system becomes all-powerful,[4] it is quite plausible to interpret him as simply wanting to emphasise that the symbolic aspect or 'sign-value' of needs, desires, wants and so on, has come much more to the fore. Correspondingly, and at least in terms of what mostly preoccupies us as postmodern consumers in late modern society, the more rudimentary purposes which our consumption is aimed at satisfying (their use-values) have indeed fallen somewhat into the background. Complex consumption is 'complex' because the business of making and manipulating and consuming meanings, ideas and interpretations is more involved, more 'of the mind' or 'in the head' than gathering and eating fallen apples.[5]

It should be clear from these examples, that we have moved some way beyond the direct and localised circuits of production/consumption generally associated with simple types of final consumption in work-based society, and towards a type of society where at least in terms of how the meaning of things is interpreted, there are many more instances where there is no longer any necessary relationship between a particular act of production and a particular act of consumption. Meaning-bearing objects and activities still have to be produced for people to enjoy, but there is much greater fluidity and variety in consumption. One could even suggest, and despite Baudrillard's insistence that as a modern day consumer 'one is permanently governed by a code whose rules and meaning-constraints – like those of language – are, for the most part, beyond the grasp of individuals' (Baudrillard, 1998: 61), that in its more extreme form, the new consumption is all about experimenting with the categories into which different instances of consumption fall. To the extent that there are variations within the sign-system between a sign and what it signifies (conventionally 'cat' signifies 'not dog' but there are very many other things which a cat is 'not'), and that the pleasure of significa-tion is not tied uniquely to any particular instance of signification (it is not just Picasso which pleasures my mind but Van Gogh also), the possibili-ties of complex consumption would seem almost infinite. It may be that contemporary consumption is an '… endless circuit of superfluous "signs" leading to a superficial postmodern existence that has lost authenticity and roots …' (Millar (ed.), 2001: 9, 'introduction' to Vol. I), but there really could be more to it than that!

CONSUMPTION-INTENSITY AND CONSUMPTION-CENTREDNESS

In order to claim that modern work-based society is being challenged by a social form which is decisively stamped with the mark of consumption, one has to demonstrate not merely the presence, but the widespread availability of consumption in all its forms. As we have been at pains to point out in our discussion of work-based society, it is the extent and degree of penetration of consumption which is decisive not just the fact that people routinely consume things since this is a basic feature of all human social groups. When describing modern or late modern societies as consumption-based societies, what we are really suggesting is that the broad mass of the population are habitually able to participate in the different types of complex consumption we have just been discussing. At a minimum, this is taken to mean mass affluent consumption. In this way, these advanced or high-order consumption-based societies can be distinguished from less developed societies where consumption is mostly restricted to forms of simple consumption.

Being affluent: spending money

We noted in Chapter 3 that income provides one way of assessing the extent of affluence in society. In light of the fact that individual and house-hold incomes are rising, and faster than taxes or the prices of consumer goods and services, it was suggested that contemporary Britain can accu-rately be described as an affluent society. At the level of particular house-holds and individuals however, we also noted that affluence and the capacity to be affluent, is unevenly distributed with perhaps 20 per cent of households having an income which is less than 60 per cent of the national average. To the extent that at around £236 per week, this still allows household members to meet their basic needs, we still feel justified in saying that as a whole, modern Britain is affluent. In terms of average incomes it is certainly not a non-affluent or poor society.

Although actual possession of cash (earned income plus savings and investments) provides a useful and accessible yardstick, and might be indicative of the likely level of affluence or the capacity to become affluent, it only tells part of the story. As we argued throughout the previous chapter, people in consumption-based society are much more interested in the spending of money than they are in how it has been earned. The basic assumption here is that patterns and levels of household expenditure provide tangible and often conspicuous evidence of the purchasing power and thus standard of living of that household: the more you are able to consume, the higher the standard of living you can enjoy. Affluence is strongly implicated in this process of social structuring and interpretation because of a simple tautology: expanding patterns of household consumption demonstrate increased spending power and spending power is one of the main characteristics of affluence. At the same time, 'affluence' is defined as the ability to purchase those items. I am affluent because I am able to consume these items, and because I do, I am affluent. (As we have already noted, the fly in the ointment here is that increases in purchasing power might come from increased household borrowing rather than from increases in earned income. See for example Rowlinson and Kempson, 1994; Ritzer, 2001.) Following the distinctions we have been making in this chapter between simple and complex consumption, the gist of our argument will be that in the same way that a particular level of income suggests affluence, so also does a particular level and kind of consumption.

Divisions of consumption

In developing a picture of what we can usefully call the divisions of consumption in modern Britain (which may or may not reflect divisions in levels of household income on the one hand, and produce 'class' divisions on the other), we will use government statistical information to compare patterns of consumption between one household and another and over time. Beginning with trends in the overall quantity of consumption which goes on in society, there is no doubt that household expenditure in the United Kingdom has risen very considerably during the last 50 years. Data on households' final consumption expenditure (which is 'expenditure on goods and services used for the direct satisfaction of individual or collective needs and wants', although rather confusingly, these data also include 'non-profit institutions serving households') at 2002 prices, show that the total amount of household expenditure in the United Kingdom has risen from around £10 million in 1951 to £655 billion in 2001 (*Economic Trends*, 2002: Table 1.6). Survey data for this period show that 'annual household expenditure in the United Kingdom has more than doubled over the last 30 years ... in 2001, household expenditure grew at an annual rate of 4.1 per cent' (*Social Trends*, 2003: 118). If affluence is defined in terms of a sheer increase in the amount of stuff that is consumed by households, the volume of consumption behaviour, Britain has certainly been exhibiting signs of affluence for at least the past 50 years. We can also note in passing, that the rate at which households have been able to increase their levels of consumption has been more rapid in the last two decades than in previous decades. If affluence is defined in terms of an *increased* capacity to consume goods and services, then the general trajectory of rising consumption certainly implies increasing affluence. A society in which the capacity to consume more is slowing or even decreasing, would certainly not feel like an affluent society but like one in recession.

Beyond this very general level however, and perhaps a little disappointingly for those who would expect to find a direct association between the things people consume and their general position in society, data on trends in the consumption of particular items such as consumer durables, actually tell us relatively little about the characteristics of particular households or household members. Although there are variations between households in the kinds of consumer durables they have, it is almost impossible to discover whether this is to do with some objective factor such as level of available income (or access to credit), or whether it is to do with the subjective preferences of household members. (The distinction between objective and subjective factors is important here as objective ones can provide a basis for comparing one household with another in some fairly concrete generally quantitative sense, whereas it is much more problematic trying to compare them according to subjective factors). Other than demonstrating that sufficient funds are available (or sufficient credit can be obtained) to do some spending, on its own, knowledge of the things which are consumed tells us very little else about that household and its members.

Findings from the *General Household Survey*, which, amongst other things, asks respondents if they have access to items on a list of 16 commonplace consumer durables, will help illustrate this point.[6] The survey reported in 2001 that households with older people are generally less likely to have washing machines, microwave ovens and mobile phones; that single-person households are less likely to have electrical domestic appliances; and that younger households were more likely than older ones to have entertainment items (*Living in Britain*, 2001: Tables 4.22, 4.23 and 4.24).

Although these findings add to our knowledge of the kinds of things that different households consume, they do not offer much beyond what common sense would tell us anyway. Older people may not see the need for consumer appliances which they have always done without; single-person households either have sufficient time to do household chores manually and/or can afford to pay for a cleaning, cooking or laundry service; and younger people simply have more time and income to spend on entertainment. As the authors of the report conclude 'there is very little difference between socio-economic groups in the ownership of most consumer durables' (*Living in Britain*, 2001: 29), which is to say that ownership or otherwise of a microwave oven does not provide much of a clue as to the kind of household it is, other than that its members eat food cooked in a microwave oven.

At the level of individual households then, and on its own, information about who is consuming what may not be very revealing. Adopting a slightly more subtle approach to this information however, and moving much more towards the idea that theories of domestic consumption should be about consumption in general rather than about any particular act of consumption (and in fact about its subjective rather than objective aspects), survey information can provide useful insights into the general nature of the new consumption which characterises modern society.

The new consumption

First, it shows how universally the current range of typical consumer goods is enjoyed throughout the households of contemporary Britain. Even when household consumption is cross-referenced with variables such as gross weekly household income, socio-economic group, or household type, only minor differences in patterns of access are revealed and often for reasons other than lack of income. Adopting the view that households with the lowest incomes might have *least* access to these items it is perhaps surprising that with the exception of access to the internet, dishwasher, fixed telephone (which has been superseded by the mobile phone) and car or van, lone-parent households in the sample (which are typically at the lower end of the income scale and definitely so if the parent has no earned income) were actually *more likely* than other households to have satellite television, video recorder, CD player, microwave oven, fridge-freezer, washing machine, tumble dryer and mobile phone (*Living in Britain*, 2001: Tables 4.20-4.24). If affluence is defined in terms of ability to consume a typical range of consumer durables (rather than in terms of income or some other measure), then almost all of the households represented by recent survey data could reasonably be categorised as affluent. Under conditions of the new consumption, affluent households are those in which household members are able to purchase any or all of the items which are typically available to households at a particular time. Members of these households are affluent in the sense that they are not restricted in the choice of consumer goods they are able to purchase (although they may have to make choices about which versions of a particular item they can afford). To repeat, in modern consumption-based society, affluence is defined in terms of a *general capacity* to consume rather than in terms of the consumption of any *particular item*.

Second, the relatively slow take-up of some items over time and across different types of household might suggest that they infringe some other and presumably more important need or expectation. The clearest examples of this are tumble dryers and dishwashers which even in 2000 were only 'consumed' by 54 per cent and 26 per cent of all British households respectively. (The same percentages were reported for more affluent households with incomes over £500 per week.) In contrast, over 93 per cent of households had access to a washing machine and 83 per cent to the relatively-recently introduced microwave oven. In the absence of detailed qualitative information from consumers about these choices (surveys do not ask *why* people consume things), one might infer the residual influence of a certain puritanism – tumble dryers are extravagant and dishwashers connote idleness. Washing machines on the other hand, connote cleanliness (which as we know is next to godliness) and, like microwave ovens, increase the efficiency of domestic time use (leaving more time for paid work or play).

Third, survey data indicate some of the ways in which the package of consumer durables which is considered to be 'normal' changes over time. The fact for example, that British households in 2000 with adults aged over 60 years are less likely to have a home computer or access to the internet (25 per cent and 17 per cent respectively) is most likely because older people are unfamiliar with the uses and benefits of these items. They therefore fall outside their range of expectations. The relatively rapid take up of some recently-introduced items such satellite television, internet access and mobile phones might be explained by the fact that increases in income combined with static (or in relative terms falling) retail prices make them cheap to buy. Within the next five-to-ten years it is very likely that almost all households responding to this kind of government survey will tick the 'yes' box for all these items. Ownership of cars and vans, on the other hand, which entail significant ongoing financial commitments in terms of maintenance and running costs has risen less dramatically from 52 per cent of households in 1976 to 73 per cent in 2000 (*Living in Britain*, 2001: Table 4.20). Data from this survey show that car ownership does vary by household type and especially income. (Other data show that average weekly household expenditure on motoring increased from £34.20 in 1980 to £57.70 in 2001/02. *Social Trends*, 2003:

Table 12.6). The close relationship between income and affluence is very evident here since it would seem that cost is the major factor determining car ownership. The consumption or otherwise of relatively expensive single or one-off items will continue to provide a fair indication of the level of affluence in society.

We can add that one of the key characteristics of the new consumption is that the stock of consumer durables which householders expect to have access to not only changes but at an accelerating rate. New items are added to the stock (reflected in the inclusion of internet access in the *General Household Survey from the year* 2000), or because of the substitution of new items for older versions (mobile phones for fixed line, digital audio tape for compact disc). Beyond what is included in the survey listings we can also note two other types of expansion. Commodities are continuously being upgraded so that consumers are encouraged effectively to purchase again items which are very similar to those they already own (the practical utility or 'added value' of making these purchases might be quite limited. Novelty would seem to be the main attraction). Second, there is a continuous increase in the variety of even the most routinely purchased commodities. Bread is no longer bread but is wholemeal, granary, malted, crusty, organic and so on. The reason why it is viable for producers to offer such a wide range of essentially the same product is that choice is always regarded as a good thing. People do not generally question or challenge the fact that the amount of choice continuously increases; they are much more interested in exercising it.

The new balance of consumption

Although knowledge of access to a particular range of consumer durables provides one way of understanding what the new consumption consists of, we need to widen our perspective and look at changes in the general pattern of expenditure between different types of consumption. To substantiate the claim that we are now living in a fully-fledged or mature consumption-based society, we need to show that people really are diverting their time and resources away from simple and towards complex types of consumption activity. These data are available from various surveys most notably the *Expenditure and Food Survey* (EFS), and in the *Classification of Individual Consumption by Purpose* (COICOP was introduced as a European standard in 2001–2) which record how households divide their expenditure between major expenditure categories. To the extent that increasing expenditure in categories such as 'leisure goods' and 'leisure services' indicates increasing participation in complex consumption, these data provide a useful means of assessing the move towards a consumption-based society.

14 FES items	12 COICOP items
Housing	Housing, fuel and power
Fuel, power	
Food and non-alcoholic drink	Food and non-alcoholic drink
Alcoholic drink	Alcoholic drinks, tobacco
Tobacco	and narcotics
Clothing and footwear	Clothing and footwear
Household goods	Household goods and services
Household services	
Personal goods and services	Miscellaneous goods and services
Motoring	Transport
Fares and other travel costs	
Leisure goods	Recreation and leisure
Leisure services	Restaurants and hotels
Miscellaneous	Other expenditure items
	Health
	Education

Figure 5.3   Household expenditure categories

Ideally, we would like to map the expenditure categories in Figure 5.3 onto the different types of simple and complex consumption we have described above (see Figure 5.1).[7] Unfortunately however, there is no entirely satisfactory way of doing this since items such as food, clothing and footwear are to be found in all types of consumption; food is obviously a basic necessity but can also be a highly indulgent luxury. The least unsatisfactory solution may be to match items of expenditure to types of consumption in the lowest category where they are most likely to be found, and to leave to one side varieties or instances which would generally be interpreted as falling into a higher or more elaborate type of consumption. For example, we could categorise housing, fuel and power as forms of simple consumption, but accept that the wood-burning stove or lavishly decorated house are indulgent, conspicuous and possibly even symbolic forms of consumption. Similarly we would categorise the luxury second holiday as conspicuous and even symbolic consumption, but accept

Basic type of consumption	Typology of consumption	Family expenditure survey headings
Simple	Necessary	Housing, fuel and power Household goods and services Food and non-alcoholic drinks Clothing and footwear Essential travel costs
	Elaborated	Food and non-alcoholic drinks Clothing and footwear Non-basic household items Basic recreational items
	Indulgent	Alcoholic drinks and tobacco Non-essential household goods Extended recreation
Complex	Affluent	Other travel expenses Alcoholic drinks and tobacco Luxury household goods and services
	Conspicuous	Leisure/recreational goods and services Conspicuous housing, clothing, motoring and travel costs
	Symbolic	Maximal exploitation of expenditure items for symbolic utility

Figure 5.4   Types and categories of consumption

that exceptionally, for some, it might provide a necessary break from work. This procedure generates a breakdown such as that shown in Figure 5.4.

An alternative way of approaching the information is to make a virtue of the fact that all items of expenditure can express different levels or types of consumption (which is itself a feature of the new consumption) and to assess different instances of each expenditure type as lying along a continuum of utility. At one end utility is understood in terms of basic, practical and unelaborated consumption, and at the other, utility is sought much more in terms of symbolic pleasures and satisfactions. Conceptually speaking, this allows us to address the consumption of a particular item, let us say a motorcycle, in all of its potential consumption types from basic getting-to-work utility to symbol of machismo.

To reiterate our main point, it is not the item or activity of consumption which matters in-and-of-itself, but the type and level of utility it yields to the person doing the consuming. Items and activities of consumption offer the potential for such satisfactions but are themselves inert until the act of consumption takes place. As we found to be the case with consumer durables, patterns of expenditure matter to our analysis because they show which types of consumption are available to different households and individuals. From the perspective that type of expenditure indicates the level of consumption which has been reached in society, if an increasing proportion of household expenditure is accounted for by non-essential household goods, then it is reasonable to conclude that levels of affluent, conspicuous and ultimately symbolic consumption are also increasing. If households habitually consume items which have a low capacity for these types of utility, the people who consume them and the society in which they live, is not going to be characterised by particularly high levels of complex consumption. The consumption of commodities matters not because any particular item is useful in itself but because of the potential for satisfaction it releases in the consumer; the more elaborate the item being consumed, the higher the potential satisfaction (utility) to the person doing the consuming. Habitual consumers of elaborate items are likely to have higher expectations of their consumption activities than are habitual consumers of the mundane.

Trends towards the new balance of consumption

So what trends in patterns of consumption do recent expenditure data suggest? Using *Expenditure and Food Survey* (EFS) categories, and measured in terms of total household expenditure between 1976 and 2001 (at 2001–2 prices), data from the 2001–2 survey reproduced in Table 5.1, clearly show that there has been a very noticeable increase in expenditure on items having high potential for complex consumption.

Expenditure on items offering only simple utility has increased by a much smaller amount or has decreased. Looking at fuel and power, and food and non-alcoholic drink for example – all of which can be regarded as basic necessities, it can be seen that the amounts spent in these categories have fallen by 23 per cent and 5.6 per cent respectively during the 25-year period covered by these data. Expenditure on clothing and footwear, also a basic necessity has increased but only by 4.7 per cent. In what we could call the mid-range where consumption becomes more elaborate, sometimes indulgent and occasionally affluent, expenditure on items such as housing (which covers rents, maintenance and repairs but not mortgage capital repayments) and household goods (fixtures, furnishings, domestic appliances and equipment), have increased a little more noticeably by 69 per cent and 75 per cent respectively. Expenditure on personal goods and services (toiletries, cosmetics, hairdressing) and leisure goods (recreational and entertainment goods and services) have also increased by 74.1 per cent and 79.3 per cent respectively.

The really dramatic increases however, have been very much in the range of commodities and services with high potential for affluent/conspicuous/

Table 5.1 Average weekly household expenditure, GB, 1976–2001/02

14 EFS items	1976£	2001–2£	% change
Housing	39.50	66.70	+68.9
Fuel, power	15.20	11.70	−23.0
Food and non-alcoholic drink	65.90	62.20	−5.6
Alcoholic drink	13.10	14.60	+11.5
Tobacco	9.80	5.60	−42.9
Clothing and footwear	21.40	22.40	+4.7
Household goods	18.90	33.10	+75.1
Household services	8.80	23.70	+169.3
Personal goods and services	8.50	14.80	+74.1
Motoring	27.50	58.30	+112.0
Fares and other travel costs	7.50	9.50	+26.70
Leisure goods	11.10	19.90	+79.3
Leisure services	15.90	52.30	+228.9
Miscellaneous	1.20	1.90	+58.0
All expenditure groups	264.70	396.80	+49.9
Average weekly expenditure per person (£) all expenditure groups	98.10	167.10	+70.3

Source: Calculated from *Family Spending: A Report on the 2001–2002 Expenditure and Food Survey*, London: HMSO 2003, Table 6.1.

symbolic consumption. Even allowing for increases in necessary private transportation to work, school and shops, expenditure on motoring has increased by 112 per cent (in 2001–2, of the £57.70 average weekly household spent on transport, 44.5 per cent went on purchasing private vehicles, 41 per cent on operating them and 14.6 per cent on public transport (*Family Spending*, 2003: Table 1.3). Expenditure on household services (i.e. services and facilities which are bought into the household such as cleaning, catering, general maintenance, some licences and fees) increased by 170 per cent. Leisure services, which include the cost of home entertainment, satellite, home computer and internet access, together with admission to sporting, cultural and entertainment activities outside the home increased by a whopping 230 per cent. From many points of view, this is very much the category of luxury or non-essential consumption activity where the emphasis is on pleasure, enjoyment, indulgence, escape and relaxation.

Having noted substantial increases in actual cash expenditure on items falling into our categories which facilitate complex consumption, it would also be interesting to know whether there have been significant changes in the way that households distribute their expenditure *between* different kinds of activities. Just because households are spending more on a particular type of activity does not mean that they are spending less on something else because the total amount they have to spend might also

Table 5.2   Household expenditure as % of total
expenditure, GB, 1976–2001/02

14 EFS items	1976	2001–2
Housing	15	17
Fuel, power	6	3
Food and non-alcoholic drink	25	16
Alcoholic drink	5	4
Tobacco	4	1
Clothing and footwear	8	6
Household goods	7	8
Household services	3	6
Personal goods and services	3	4
Motoring	10	15
Fares and other travel costs	3	2
Leisure goods	4	5
Leisure services	6	13
Miscellaneous	1	0
All expenditure groups	100	100

Source: Calculated from *Family Spending: A Report on the
2001–2002 Expenditure and Food Survey*, London: HMSO
2003, Table 6.2.

have increased. Table 5.2 expresses household expenditure between one
category and another as a proportion of total expenditure between 1976
and 2001–2.

It can be seen that there has been a noticeable shifting of expenditure
into our 'top five' categories of affluent/conspicuous/symbolic consumption. The proportion of expenditure on housing, household goods, motoring leisure goods and leisure services, have all increased, in the case of
household services and leisure services by over 100 per cent. Over the
same period, expenditure on items in the simple utility category (fuel and
power, food and non-alcoholic drink, clothing and footwear) has decreased
sometimes quite substantially.

On the face of it then, these data do point towards a significant shifting
of consumption activity in the average British household away from simple utility and towards things where expectations for pleasure and satisfaction are more complex and sometimes abstract. As we noted in respect
of incomes in Chapter 3 however, our arguments about the role played
by affluence as a primary mechanism for the emergence of consumption-
based society require us to show that even families with the lowest incomes
are shifting their activities in the direction of complex consumption. If
the least well-off households are gaining access to these kinds of activities then we could reasonably conclude that the new consumption really
has taken hold. Table 5.3 helps us make this comparison by showing

Table 5.3 Weekly household expenditure 2001–2, by income group

	None working	Bottom 10%	Bottom 30%	Top 30%	All
Food and non-alcohol	17.3	18.4	17.5	10.7	12.7
Alcohol and tobacco	3.9	5.0	2.4	2.9	3.5
Clothing and footwear	6.0	6.4	6.2	7.3	6.9
Housing/fuel, etc.	14.4	17.0	17.0	8.8	10.9
Household goods and services	10.2	10.0	9.8	8.9	9.3
Transport	12.7	9.7	12.0	19.6	17.6
Communication	3.3	4.3	3.9	2.9	3.2
Recreation and culture	15.4	13.4	13.7	17.4	16.9
Restaurants and hotels	7.7	7.4	7.5	11.4	10.2
Miscellaneous goods/services	9.2	8.4	8.0	10.1	9.3
All the above	100	100	100	100	100
Base for %: total spent in these categories, £/wk	122.20	150.90	464.10	1,609	328.00

Source: Calculated from *Family Spending*, 2003, Tables 1.4, and 3.4.

Note: Expressed as a percentage of total spent in the categories listed each week. Miscellaneous goods and services includes personal care and effects, social protection, insurance and some other fees and professional services. These data do not include expenditure on 'other expenditure items' such as mortgage interest payments, council tax, etc. Data presented in *Family Spending* do not use 'equivalisation' to take account of differences in the composition of different households in the same category. Some data are therefore not strictly comparable with data on incomes discussed in Chapter 3.

how households in the bottom 30 per cent and top 30 per cent by gross disposable income (i.e. income before deductions for income tax, national insurance contributions, etc.,) divided up their household expenditure (not including mortgage interest payments) between the main COICOP categories (excluding expenditure on health and education) in 2001–2.

Looking first at items at what we have called the 'simple utility' end of the scale, it can be seen that households with lower gross incomes (with 'none working', 'bottom 10 per cent' and 'bottom 30 per cent' by gross income) spend a proportionately larger amount of their income on basic items such as food and non-alcoholic drink, housing and fuel (typically around 17 per cent compared with 9 per cent or 10 per cent for those with higher incomes). Spending on intermediate utility items such as clothing and footwear, household goods and services and communication (postage, telephones) accounts for very similar proportions of weekly expenditure across all the income groups listed here.

In respect of the proportions being spent by different households on items at the 'complex utility' end of the scale, items which we have been arguing are characteristic of the new consumption, it is clear that a greater proportion of expenditure in households with higher incomes (which in this table means an average gross income in the range of at least £648 to £1,085 per week) is allocated to transport (nearly 20 per cent compared with around 12 per cent for lower incomes), to recreation and culture (17.4 per cent compared with 13.7 per cent) and restaurants (which includes bar meals, cafés, take-away and canteen meals) and hotels (11.4 per cent compared with 7.5 per cent). Having said this however, it is also evident that even in households with lower gross weekly incomes (meaning at least £175 per week), the proportion being allocated to items which offer the potential for complex types of consumption is not that much smaller. To the extent that the nearly 7,000 households responding to this survey are representative of all households in Britain in 2001–2, we can say that lower- and middle-income households do have access to nearly the full range of consumption activities currently available. As household incomes rise, the proportion of income allocated to items of complex consumption will rise also.

Summary

So where does this leave us in our attempts to distinguish a work-based from a consumption-based type of society? Well the first thing to acknowledge is that there are conceptual and practical limits to making such a distinction. Most importantly and as we have already emphasised, it is not very realistic to present the generally growing preoccupation with consumption within society as if it affects each and every aspect of that society. Consumption appears to dominate production, and particular kinds of consumption dominate within the realm of consumption itself, but that does not mean that complex consumption has become the dominating characteristic of late modern or postmodern society.

We also have to accept however, that during the course of the twentieth century, as people have come to expect an ever greater range and variety of means of satisfying ever-increasing types of needs, wants and desires the relationships between production and consumption on the one hand, and between these two and the business of satisfying needs on the other, have become increasingly complex. People's perceptions of the range of their needs and of the means of satisfying them have moved beyond what simple production and immediate consumption can offer. The search for alternative means of satisfying sometimes old but increasingly novel expectations of satisfaction and pleasure has stimulated a considerable expansion of activities in the realm of complex consumption. This has resulted in the development of new kinds of production and generated new combinations of production/consumption sequences and strands of action.

Simplistically, we still produce in order to consume in order to satisfy our needs, but in the late modern period the needs we experience, the priority we assign to their satisfaction, and the means we deploy for achieving these ends have expanded massively beyond the expectations of earlier generations. A key difference then between work-based and consumption-based social types, is that in the former, people's expectations are concentrated at the simple utility end of the scale. They are satisfied within and limited by participation in the realm of production, and through the provision of relatively simple commodities. The apparent limits of production set limits to people's expectations of satisfaction and pleasure. In consumption-based society in contrast, people have raised the levels of their expectations not only in terms of what is produced and their activities in producing it, but also and most importantly, in terms of the kind of satisfactions and pleasures they seek. Basic housing, simple food and sensible shoes are no longer enough. Since the demands of the new and complex consumer-as-consumer are much more variegated and irresistible than are the demands of old and simple consumer-as-worker, the realm of production must busy itself in meeting these new demands. Inevitably, it would seem, the new consumption becomes an important driving force in late modern society.

Applying these observations to society as a whole, we can suggest that societies which are heavily work-oriented are characterised by relatively few opportunities for intrinsically satisfying action, devote much time and resources to intermediate, abstract kinds of actions, and thus tend to be somewhat limited in the range and depth of pleasures and satisfactions which they enable people to experience. Consumption-based societies on the other hand, have altogether more sophisticated and elaborated expectations of the kinds of satisfactions which can readily be achieved and offer higher concentrations of autonomous, concrete, intrinsically satisfying, terminal kinds of activity. People come to expect that acts of consumption are more satisfying than acts of production both as activities-in-themselves, and in terms of the products or outcomes of those activities.

A THEORY OF THE NEW CONSUMPTION

As a first attempt at developing a theory of the new consumption we can begin with the following. First, and looking at production and consumption in terms of the ends which people hope to be able to fulfil through them, the fact that the realm of consumption expanded so continuously from the mid-eighteenth to the early twenty-first century (and looks set to continue to do so) strongly suggests that a similar expansion must have taken place in the kinds of satisfactions and pleasures people expect to be able to fulfil. Even if we allow that through advances in marketing and advertising producers have been able to push forward a bow wave of supply, there is no question that as consumers, the populations of the West have fairly willingly embraced the burden of demand. It is not a question that work- and production-side activities are no longer necessary, since clearly production continues to provide us with the commodities we want, and work continues to provide the mechanism through which we can obtain access to them (i.e. earned income), but that the type and variety of satisfactions have not remained static. If they had, the productive capacity required to satisfy them would have been reached long ago. Consumption has not displaced production; rather it has created a demand for ever-expanding production.

Second, and looking at production and consumption in terms of the intrinsic satisfactions they offer people while they are doing them (Weber's wertrationality), whilst it could be argued that the experience of producing relatively simple commodities for immediate final consumption is intrinsically satisfying – that it offers a sense of pleasure and satisfaction which is sufficient in and of itself – the necessary complexity of industrialised production inevitably pushes such instances to the periphery. Meeting immediate wants through simple production is fine as far as it goes; the trouble is that in modern societies it simply does not go far enough. In this sense, consumption is a category of activity which extends beyond production. To borrow a well-known advertising slogan, 'consumption refreshes the parts that production cannot reach'. Work thus remains a dominant realm of activity (we are still talking about a kind of work-based society), but it does not dominate all other realms in quite the same way as it once did because the satisfactions of consumption far exceed the satisfactions of simple production both as activities-in-themselves, and in terms of the desirables they produce.

Third, and picking up briefly on the fact that there are likely to be important differences *between individual consumers* in terms of how they construct and address their various needs, one might suggest that the degree and extent of this difference has, generally speaking, become much more marked as the choice of consumption-type activities has expanded. And the same can be said for levels of intrinsic satisfaction in that the routines and patterning of the actions of working life are much more regimented and predictable, much more similar from one person to another than are the kinds of actions which take place in the realm of consumption. Having said this however, and in terms of developing sociological knowledge of the factors which govern the way that people are divided or stratified within society, it would seem that patterns of consumption do not provide a very robust indicator at all. Objectively, knowing where someone is located in the division of production (occupation, employment status, level of income) still tells us much more about them than knowledge of their location in the division of consumption. A consideration of patterns of consumption and of consumption behaviour does have an important role to play but as a way of getting at the *subjective* experiences and expectations of consuming things. This interpretive, qualitative approach aimed at investigating the subjective side of consumption, means that we become less interested in what people consume (which as we have just seen is not always that interesting) than in *why* they consume it. And, following the typology developed at the start of this chapter, the 'why' assumes much more than basic utility but also includes more subtle and complex types of expectation and satisfaction. We can say then, that theories of consumption are likely to be much more useful if they concentrate on the subjectivities of consumption rather than on its objectivities.

Although we are not arguing that work-based societies are synonymous only with the work-based activities which go on there, or that consumption-based societies are synonymous only with the activities of consumption, what we can say is that societies are characterised by the types of activity which tend to predominate. The activities which people spend most of their time doing are bound to set a benchmark against which other activities are measured or assessed. In a subsistence-type society where people are mostly preoccupied with cycles of direct production and immediate final consumption, any form of light relief is bound to stand out and attract attention and discussion. The relative infrequency of non-survival type actions confirms the character of that society as survival- or work-based. Similarly, a preponderance of consumption-type activities is bound to affect the character of that society since 'consumption' becomes the benchmark against which other activities are measured. A consumption-based society is one in which the activities of consumption tend to predominate *in the sense that* other activities tend to be contrasted with them. Once the basic threshold of consumption has been reached, further or subsequent degrees of 'consumption-intensity' and 'consumption-centredness' could be assessed using the typology of consumption outlined above. The most intensely consumption-based societies are ones where it is not only consumption in general which predominates, but the higher or more complex varieties of it.

NOTES

[1]Showing off has always been a characteristic of modernity. The Great Exhibitions of the mid-nineteenth century, most notably at the Crystal Palace in London in 1851, New York 1853 and Paris in 1855, were a vigorous demonstration to the rest of

the world of the productive capacity and ingenuity of the then leading industrial nations. Few things have been more conspicuous than the Eiffel Tower (1889), (Greenhalgh, 1988).

[2]We could add to this list the new style of academic writing called 'post-modern cultural criticism' which has developed a mode of analysis and discourse peculiar to itself. See for example the essays in Featherstone (ed.), 1988 and Rojek and Turner (eds), 1993.

[3]The established point of departure for this perspective is taken to be Jameson, 1991. See also Harvey, 1989.

[4]For further discussion see: Kellner, 1989; Gane, 1991a and 1991b, and Gottdiener, 1994.

[5]Elsewhere, and very much following de Saussure's (1966) distinction between the abstract underlying deep structure (langue) of language and the concrete and accessible daily manifestations of it at the surface (parole) (see also Lévi-Strauss, 1972 and Barthes, 1973), Baudrillard distinguishes between the underlying, unconscious and structural aspect of the sign-system of consumption, and its lived, conscious and ethical aspect.

[6]The *General Household Survey* generates data from about 9,000 British households (a response rate of 76 per cent from 11,850 sampled households). Other data on 'household characteristics and ownership of consumer durables' are available from the *Family Resources Survey* which has 22,850 responses (response rate 66 per cent from 34,650) and the *Family Expenditure Survey*, from 2003 the *Expenditure and Food Survey*, which has results from around 7,000 households (response rate 60 per cent from sample of 11,450) (*Social Trends*, 2002: 230). Latest data from these surveys are reported in *Family Spending*, HMSO, 2003. The trends reported in *Family Spending* are similar to those discussed here. A useful commentary on the technicalities of the EFS can be found in Banks and Johnson (eds), 1998.

[7]In each classification the major categories are further divided to accommodate a large number of specific items. As can be seen from Figure 5.3 however, the 12 main categories in the COICOP do not match directly with the 14 EFS items which makes comparisons over time problematic. The time series referred to here are taken from *Family Spending: The Expenditure and Food Survey 2001–2002*, in which 'figures for 2001–2 are based on COICOP broadly mapped to the FES 14 main items' (p. 106). The 2001–2 survey results are based on responses from 6,809 households.

6 *Work, consumption and social identity*

As we noted in our opening chapter, our general aim in this book is to understand if and in what ways some transition from a work-based to a consumption-based social type might result in, or be associated with, changes in the meanings and purposes of people's social action. So far we have established reasonably strong grounds for suggesting that although work remains important, the realm of consumption has assumed a more dominant role in people's lives. We now need to consider in more detail what impact this development is having on the way people act in society. What does it mean to say that action is increasingly oriented towards consumption rather than towards production? Clearly there is insufficient room within one short volume to describe all of the different ways in which social action might be changing within and between these realms. In this and the following chapter we therefore concentrate on the more discrete issue of how a person's sense of who they are, of where they fit into society and how they should behave might change as the balance shifts away from work and towards consumption.

By choosing this topic we are following the current trend in sociology which is to see all things social as being reflected through the prism of identity: '"Identity" has become one of the unifying frameworks of intellectual debate in the 1990s … the sheer *volume* of discourse about identity has reached new magnitudes …' (Jenkins, 1996: 7–9). In order to deploy our material as clearly as possible we will see identity as multi-faceted in that a person's sense of themselves as a unique self has mutual or collective dimensions to it as well as individual and personal ones. People express identity both as objects in other people's perceptions and as the leading subject of their own lives. Similarly, some aspects of identity are unique to a particular person (a property which helps us make sense of the whole idea of identity) and some are shared in the sense that others in the same partnership, family, household, class, nation, etc., have the same identity-elements. In this chapter we will focus on the collective and in the next on the individual dimensions of identity.[1]

SOCIAL IDENTITY IN WORK-BASED SOCIETY

Defining identity

The basic argument we are relying on here, is that if a person's sense of themselves as a unique being in the world develops out of and is expressed through the various activities they habitually engage in, a change in those activities and/or a change in the balance between them is bound to affect their sense of who they are and how they should be acting (Goffman, 1969; Bourdieu, 1990). The social context of these behaviours (in our case the realm of work and the realm of consumption) has consequences for identity because the various social locales we occupy furnish us with useful indicators of what we should be doing, of how we should behave, of what expectations a person should reasonably have, when occupying that particular locale (Jenkins, 1996). Moreover, since the behaviours and expectations developed in one realm are never wholly contained within that originating realm, but spill over and affect our behaviour in other realms, we must recognise that some realms are more likely than others to influence identity and thus to affect the whole behaviour of the individual rather than one discrete part of it.

One of the presumptions we have been making about work-based society is that it is a kind of society in which the realm of production does dominate other realms of action. If I experience myself through my actions, and if taken as a whole, my actions are developed primarily to be effective in one particular context, then I might well end up behaving in all contexts as if I were always acting within this particular and primary domain. For Weber, the 'affinity' between the 'spirit' of capitalism and the Protestant 'ethic' is precisely this. It is a way of acting and behaving in the realm of business which is also effective in the realms beyond work. Vice versa, the ethic of ascetic Protestantism is effective in the spiritual realm (assuming one accepts this belief system as substantively rational) and is also, at the very least, supportive of the kinds of behaviours and protocols required within modern rational capitalism: 'When the limitation of consumption is combined with the release of acquisitive activity, the inevitable practical result is obvious: accumulation of capital through ascetic compulsion to save' (Weber, 1976: 172). Identity and action are intimately linked since the former cannot be expressed without the latter.

The question of the proportions different realms of activity contribute to the overall identity of the individual is obviously highly complex and lies beyond the scope of the current discussion (for guidance see Craib, 1998). It does seem probable however that some realms are more dominant than others in this respect. For example, developing or acquiring a sense of gender, or of being a parent, or of being an outstanding musician or sportsperson, might be the kinds of foundations which influence the whole of a person's identity. To the extent that identity is all about acting or behaving in one way rather than another (and of being conscious that one is doing this and enjoys doing so), one might expect to observe elements of femaleness in all aspects of the behaviour of a woman, or elements of parenthood right across the behaviour of people who have children, or of self-discipline and precision throughout the actions of a Tiger Woods or Yehudi Menuhin.

By concentrating on the social contexts within which people form and express their sense of identity we are consciously emphasising two things: first that the stuff of which identity is made is at least as much determined by environmental factors as it is by features of personality and psychology (for a summary of sociological treatments see Bocock, 1993: Chapter 4 and Jenkins, 1996: Chapters 5, 6. For a social-psychological perspective see Glover, 1989; Belk, 1998; Craib, 1998). To this extent at least, identity (both social/collective and personal/individual) is a social bequest and is subject to patterns and structures which are common both to the occupants of similar locales, and/or to occupants of the same locale at different points in time. These patterns and structures are also, one might add, outside or beyond the control of any particular individual.

One might object to this rather structuralist-sounding approach on the grounds that the various locales that people fill in society provide a means of expressing preferences, choices, desires and so on, which are developed prior to and thus outside or beyond the confines of these categories. 'I did not become an extrovert and rebel after I joined the circus, rather I joined the circus because these characteristics were already part of my personality'. The position adopted in the following account is that although it is certainly the case that each individual experiences the world uniquely, and that each person seeks out contexts for expressing their identity which yield the highest levels of pleasure and satisfaction, *the means of expressing identity* are not unique to any particular individual because almost all of these contexts are 'social' either in the sense that they have been socially constructed or because they are public rather than private.

Secondly, although the term identity is sometimes used to refer to a largely hidden or secretive self-impression, some unique narrative or biography of the self which resides entirely within the interior consciousness of the individual and to which only she or he has access, the concept of identity we are using here is one where identity and action are seen to be very closely linked together.[2] A person (the embodiment of an identity) can have no practical impact upon the world nor actually influence the behaviour of other people unless or until she or he acts. To misquote Marx, a yet-to-be-enacted identity is a non-identity.

Adopting a heavily action-based definition of identity obviously increases the significance of the contexts through which action (and thus identity) are performed. One cannot, for example, express a sense of gender identity, or ethnic identity unless there is some socially agreed means of expressing these aspects of selfhood and their various sub-categories. One might borrow Baudrillard's analysis of the sign-system here and suggest that in the same way that the meanings of acts of consumption are rendered intelligible because other consumers understand the relative position of these acts in the overall system or hierarchy of symbolic or sign values, people can only 'communicate' gendered ethnicised identities because onlookers understand the categories of difference which give such labels meaning. It is very difficult to conceive the gender or ethnicity of humans outside the systems of categorisation used to describe them (Hall and DuGay (eds), 1996).

This way of looking at things has a long and distinguished tradition especially within French, mostly structuralist, anthropology (for example Durkheim and Mauss, 1903; Lévi-Strauss, 1972; de Saussure, 1966; and Barth, 1969). Indeed, one of the major challenges posed by postmodernist conceptions of identity, is that identity is entirely constituted by the various discourses in which it is embedded (for example Foucault, 1972). As Hall puts it: 'the subject is produced "as an effect" through and within discourse, within specific discursive formations, and has no existence, and certainly no transcendental continuity or identity from one subject position to another' ('introduction' in Hall and DuGay (eds), 1996: 10). A similarly embedded and socially contingent notion of identity can also be found in social-constructionist accounts which presume, as Collin expresses it, that human beings 'create and transform their environment, they make of the natural realm in which they evolve as a species a new order, one brought into being and sustained by themselves' (Collin, 1997: 1). Clearly the selves envisaged here are very much a product of practical collective action.

The assumption here then, is that however private and intimate some of the dimensions of identity might be, the successful expression of identity presumes active recognition or approval, some confirmation of the correctness of our behaviour by others in our (ascribed or chosen) group. The sense of satisfaction we take from expressing our identity is at least partly dependent on the positive and supportive feedback of those we interact with. If a person persistently fails to achieve recognition or acknowledgement within the group, then they will have to find some other group to belong to (grouplessness is not much of an option). The sometimes difficult experiences of people changing class positions (Jackson and Marsden, 1966) or sexual orientation (Butler, 1990; Garber, 1992; Dunne, 1997), or cultural location (Lash and Featherstone (eds),

2002) are clear examples of how the collectivity bears down upon identity.

In speaking of identity then, we are referring to a combination of attributes which have become an integral part of who that particular individual is and therefore of how they act (or at least of how we expect them to act and thus behave towards them): the markers of action and intent which we most readily identify and associate with that person. In terms of how this core of a person makes itself manifest, we can define identity as that which a person retains and expresses in all their behaviour, across all their actions. However varied and complex the previous actions and experiences of an individual might have been, identity refers to the much more limited residue, those somehow essential nuggets which a person has retained and which continue to affect their future actions. In terms of engaging in any truly meaningful way with the social world, of actually making a practical difference to the behaviour of other people (and indeed for it to have any use as a sociological concept), identity needs to be regarded as a largely public, action-based and predominantly context-dependent kind of a thing.

Social identity and class

Looking at the social inputs and outputs of identity in a work-based society, one of the first things which comes to mind is the presumption of a very close relationship between 'identity' and 'working life'. If a person's life is dominated by work, if they live work-intensive, work-saturated and work-centred lives, then the relationships of work and the mechanisms of employment will necessarily provide key inputs to their sense of who they are (Bauman, 1998). Given the socialised, action-based conception of identity we have adopted in this discussion, this must be so because if sense of self is not sufficiently attuned to the requirements of work then clearly that individual is not going to function very satisfactorily 'at work' in a 'work-based' society. Until the late 1980s references to 'identity' in its now current sociological usage were relatively sparse not because sociologists were not interested in how people saw themselves, how they developed and expressed a unique sense of self and so on (although many would have regarded these matters as falling more properly within the territory of social psychology), but because, sociologically, these phenomena were conceptualised and analysed as being part of that bundle of factors and experiences which was a person's *class position*.

It is actually part of the sociological makeup of work-based society in the modern period, that it is the kind of society which operated with a pretty simplistic definition of social identity. Identity is determined by social class and social class is determined by occupation. In order to interact effectively with others in a society dominated by work, all you really needed to know was their occupation (which would enable you to read off their class and thus wider social and political circumstances and aspirations) or their class (which would allow you to read off their occupational type). Class-as-occupation is an extremely quick and easy way of sorting out some of the complexities of the modern social world. If you know nothing at all about how a person spends their time, then it is a fair bet that they have some kind of occupation, paid or otherwise, and that their motivations, aspirations and lifestyle will be quite closely associated with it. When meeting people for the first time it can take quite a deliberate effort not to ask directly 'and what do you do?' Even the simplest reply enables us easily to conjure up an edifice of expectations about many other aspects of that person's life and identity.

The range of encounters with people outside work, or with people having a different class location, might be relatively infrequent for many people, and when they took place, were most likely to be experienced as a somewhat ritualistic reinforcement of class/occupational group stereotypes. Although political, ideological even cultural gains and losses might be made during such encounters, very little of a person's identity is at stake because these encounters tend to confirm rather than challenge identity. And all this fitted quite well with the sociological characterisation of work-based society as one populated by work-saturated experiences and expectations (Goldthorpe et al., 1987; Goldthorpe and Marshall, 1992; Goldthorpe, 1996 and 1998). Bank managers were bankmanagerly in all their actions; the postman was always polite and deferential; the nurse and teacher certainly cared for people all the time.

This way of conceptualising the position of the individual vis-à-vis the work that they do and of how they are embedded within the economic structure more generally is one where the individual is taken to be somehow secondary or vulnerable to these structures. Since clearly there cannot be a distinct economic structure for each individual, it follows that this structure provides an organising principle for all the individuals acting within it. The most significant thing I have in common with others sharing the same occupation as myself is not so much the skills and responsibilities of the tasks we perform as the fact that we all occupy more or less the same identifiable position within the same economic structure. Employment provides a slot in the structure of society which I am able to occupy, and, equally important to my social functioning, a means of understanding how I stand in relation to occupants of the other slots. From an academic point of view, analysing the trivia of a person's daily actions at work and comparing these with how some other individual or group is occupied is pretty unexciting when these wider issues of social structuring and so on are at stake.[3]

This relating of everything to class/occupational group has until relatively recently been one of the core assumptions of the British sociological tradition (Savage, 2000). If work is structurally determined then so too is the person doing that work. It is easy to see why such a conceptual position has survived since there is something comforting and straightforward about explanations of social action which presume the presence of clear and determinate social structures. All one has to do is identify the structures and everything else will fall into place. The fewer the classes so much the better. Since the mechanisms of employment provide some of the clearest and most accessible instances of such structuring, and have undoubtedly shaped people's lives and identities in ways which are obvious and persistent, it is perhaps inevitable that one might become overly dependent upon these conceptual tools and the kinds of explanations of social action they provide. Ample confirmation of the dominance of this approach is reflected in the empirical research carried out by leading sociologists in Britain during the 1960s and 1970s. The *Affluent Worker Study* (Goldthorpe, Lockwood et al., 1968a, 1968b and 1969) for example, and Goldthorpe's later work on social mobility (Goldthope et al., 1987) are clearly and explicitly grounded in presumptions about the direct and causal connection between occupation and social position. As Savage puts it: 'It is difficult to find any sustained interpretation of social change in Britain from 1950 to 1990 that was not expressed [in terms of] arguments about how social classes are changing' (Savage, 2000: 6).

During the late 1980s however, research into occupations on the one hand (especially its labour process theory variant) and into class on the other, lost the hold they had previously enjoyed over the British sociological imagination. Within industrial sociology, analyses of occupation became narrowly focused on debates over the emergence or otherwise of post-Fordism. With the possible exception of those adopting a regulationist approach (e.g. Aglietta, 1979) who continued to point to a dynamic connection between occupation and other aspects of social and political 'identity', the remainder only seemed interested in the managerial and organisational efficiency of 'flexible specialisation', and various reorganisations of the workforce into 'core and periphery'. They had little to say about possible changes in the work-identity axis (for commentary see Pollert (ed.), 1991; Gilbert et al., 1992; Amin (ed.), 1994; and Kumar, 1995). The other main research topic, occupational segregation, also failed to do much more than re-state established knowledge of how labour market opportunity is unevenly distributed between men and women (for commentary see Fine, 1992 and Bradley, 1999). The exception to this general rule is the work of Catherine Hakim who challenges some of the presumptions of the feminisation of work, and points to important differences in employment opportunities *between women*, a position which theories of patriarchy (Walby, 1986; 1990 and 1997) and social reproduction (Charles, 1993 and 2000) are not well equipped to deal with (see Hakim, 1995, 1996 and 2000; Bradley et al., 2000).

Serious doubts were also being expressed at this time about class analysis itself. Given the dramatic expansion of interest within sociology in things 'cultural' and under considerable pressure from postmodernist social theorists to develop entirely new categories and discourses of analysis, people were bound eventually to ask how informative it was to continue to characterise people's expectations and behaviour solely in terms of occupation (the followers of Marx) and/or market position (the followers of Weber). And debates have subsequently raged over the very existence of 'class analysis' as a serious occupation for academic sociologists (Pahl, 1989; Goldthorpe and Marshall, 1992; Clarke et al., 1993), or even whether 'classes', as traditionally conceived, are 'out there' to be studied at all (Saunders, 1990; Pakulski and Waters, 1996).[4]

Social identity in transition

So where do these developments leave us and our current concern with the formation of identity in work- and consumption-based societies? Well the first point to note is that within sociology itself, 'identity' has been re-cast to mean much more than class/occupational position (for example Giddens, 1990; Beck, 1992). It is still sensible to identify class as one of the inputs to identity but without seeing identity as entirely filled-up with class issues and experiences. We should, as Bradley and her colleagues put it, 'adopt a more flexible, multidimensional form of analysis which is sensitive to the interaction of class with other dynamics of social differentiation, such as gender and ethnicity' (Bradley et al., 2000: 148).[5]

Although these authors conclude in their review of recent empirical evidence, that: 'production relations remain highly significant as a source of identity' and that 'class relations ... continue to have crucial effects on our lives' (Bradley et al., 2000: 132), people also draw on other fields of experience as well. Adopting the dictum 'no smoke without fire', the fact that this shift has taken place within sociology suggests quite strongly that something of the same sort is actually happening 'out there' in society. To the extent that work-based society is seen as being co-terminus with class-based society (which is the basic assumption of modernist sociology), the emergence of an expanded and much more widely sourced type of identity which is set adrift from class and occupation (an important tenet of postmodernist sociology) logically implies, at the very least, a pretty significant change in the nature of society as a whole. As entities in themselves, work-based societies lose much of their identity once occupation/class becomes a subsidiary contributor on the formative side of people's identity. To put this a little more strongly, work-based society cannot persist *unless* identity is primarily defined as class/occupational position.[6]

Looking a little more closely at this putative new reality, it is certainly the case that important and suggestive changes have taken place away from the one-time certainties of class-based social identities in work-based society.[7] First, and in terms of defining class as occupation, the relatively stable patterns of employment and occupations which formed the backbone of dualistic class categories in modern industrial society (manual versus non-manual, white-collar versus blue-collar, works versus staff) have been superseded as 'traditional' industrial working has been replaced by service-sector employment and occupations (Savage, 2000). If one does want to persist with a concept of class as occupation, the fact that the occupational structure is much more variegated and stratified than it was during the middle years of the twentieth century, clearly means that the number of classes which a person might belong to has increased, or, to put the matter the other way around, it becomes increasingly difficult to decide which class a person belongs to. Quite apart from the methodological difficulties this causes for sociologists of class (Marshall, 1997; Crompton, 1998), it signifies that *even if* class is taken to be strongly indicative of identity, the range of possible identity types is certainly greater than 'us' and 'them'. Even a relatively simple sub-division of 'the two great classes' into two or three sub-categories (lower-working class versus 'the aristocracy of labour', lower-middle class versus upper-middle class and so on) undermines the efficacy of the identity/class diagnosis of social encounter. Occupation still provides a key marker of social location, but in the late-modern period, there are many more occupations and thus many more markers than previously. Class-as-occupation loses its utility once the number of occupations expands beyond a few easily recognised and groupable types. Changes in the nature of work demand that significant changes are also required in the classificatory systems which are based upon them.[8]

The second important area of change affects our definitions of class in terms of the inputs they might have on the ideological, political and cultural identities of their members. Although *circa* 1850 the dualisms of capital and labour, proletarian and bourgeois, owner and non-owner of the means of production had a recognisable political consonance, these assumptions have become far less meaningful. By *c.* 1950, the expansion of the public sector and a proliferation of layers of managers and other intermediates who occupy senior positions whilst remaining employees themselves (the vast majority of those holding senior positions do not own the businesses or organisations they work for any more than the rest of the workforce do), makes it far more difficult to 'read-off' both the political priorities and characteristics associated with different classes, and to be certain whether each member of that class does actually hold to those beliefs.[9] Politically, we have rights and responsibilities as employees (and as consumers), but more and more we have political identity as citizens. The grounds on which we might express common cause with others and seek political representation and redress, might well be affected by our location in the means of production, but it is no longer adequate to assume that all our grievances are located here.[10]

Taking these two kinds of change together, in the late-modern period, the range and type of identity-forming encounters which people have are more and more likely to be ones where class/occupational group stereotyping provides a pretty inadequate guide as to how the interaction should be conducted. We can still draw effectively on our general knowledge of how people from particular classes and occupational groups might behave (what their motivations, interests and lifestyles are likely to be), but only to the extent of the class-based aspect of their identities. Class stereotypes as a guide to social conduct will eventually only be used for cultural and ideological purposes and not for industrial or political ones. Encountering others in terms of our own and their experiences of gender, ethnicity, cultural origin and so on, requires a much more subtle range of knowledge. We have, as it were, to speak the language of identity in many tongues, not just the soliloquy of class stereotypes.

SOCIAL IDENTITY IN CONSUMPTION-BASED SOCIETY

Turning our attention towards the formation of social identity in consumption-based society, the first thing we have to accept is that even in the most sophisticated manifestations of consumption people still have to spend a considerable portion of their time working. How else are they going to acquire the resources which are necessary for this level of spending? To this extent, the identity-inputs of work and of consumption reinforce each other because a person's self-perception as a consumer depends on a pretty effective sense-of-self as worker. As we have argued previously, the utility people seek requires activity on both the production and consumption side, and so, naturally, the identity of the individual is also cast under the influence of both.

Having said this though, we also have to accept that as the capacity to consume develops, we will have to abandon some of our assumptions about how work and identity are linked, and review some of the limitations which heavily work-based concepts of identity might impose upon our analysis. We mean 'limitations' in two senses. First, that in terms of the sociologist's craft, work-based concepts of identity, often drawn directly from Marx, are, as we have just seen, quite limiting in the kind of analysis that can be produced from them. Second, we are also interested in whether the kinds of inputs which work might have on a person's sense of identity are also quite limited when compared with the inputs they receive from consumption-side activities. What are the criteria of class membership in consumption-based societies? Are they best described as a nominal set of categories into which people can be sorted and enumerated by sociologists, politicians, marketers, etc., or are they actually-existing social entities which are lived and breathed by their members? In what ways is 'class membership', 'class consciousness', 'class action' ascribed to people (by political leaders, organic intellectuals, sociologists, etc.) in late modern, consumption-based society, and to what extent is 'class' something which people can choose for themselves?

From Marx to Weber

Representing a position which has been taken by many sociologists as a starting point for an alternative, and some would say, more modern conception of social ordering and identity formation, Max Weber offers a subtle and multi-layered characterisation of economic and social positioning. He introduces the term 'market position' to capture the idea that as capitalism has developed, the once direct linkage between a person's occupational prospects and the level and type of capital they control has been supplemented and in some degree superseded by possession of other less fixed forms of capital which are also crucial in determining a person's economic prospects and thus life chances. The greater the level of our credentials, our expertise and our experience, the more attractive we become to prospective employers and thus, given the competitive nature of employment relationships within capitalism, the more robust is our social and economic position with respect both to co-workers and to employers. The sense we have of where we stand in society is still formed on the basis of occupational and employment relationships, but contrary to what Marx implies, we are more able to affect the terms upon which we enter these relationships. To the extent that we are able to improve our market position through our own endeavours for example, by investing heavily in education and training, acquiring sought-after skills, developing employment networks, etc., we have some degree of autonomy when locating ourselves in the social structure.

Weber also suggests that people supplement their understanding of where they fit into society and of how they should behave by referencing other kinds of communal identification which may have nothing at all to do with occupation. He introduces the idea of 'status groups' to emphasise how people form associations with others sometimes in order to pursue political and economic goals, but also for largely social or recreational purposes. These associations offer just as important a sense of belonging and even solidarity as do the shared experiences at work but without being bound or constrained by the structures of occupation and employment. Once society has reached the point where these kinds of associations are generally available to people (associations which very often become possible because of increasing affluence) opportunities arise to develop a somehow multiple sense of identity, which is grounded partly in the shared experiences of work and partly in the shared experiences of consumption. A builder for example, who for Marx would plainly be a member of the working class and would presumably work amongst other working-class people and thus lead a working-class lifestyle, could be a member of a conservative political party, read a right-wing newspaper, join the local golf club and thus begin constructing their identity according to precepts more usually associated with the middle class.

Weberian concepts of status-group membership, differentiation by taste and other cultural skills have been taken up by Savage et al. (1992) (see also Butler and Savage (eds), 1995). They recommend adopting an 'assets approach' to emphasise that resources beyond simple occupation provide people with decisive means of marking out their social identity/location, and not just between one class or social stratum and another, but within particular groups. For example, '... variations in taste within the service class are less easily attributable to employment and work situations than to aspects of the possession of cultural capital deriving from education, social networks, openness to government propaganda, awareness of women's issues and so forth ...' (Savage et al., 1992: 254). Along with 'property assets' and 'organisational assets' they identify 'cultural assets', and suggest that the 'the old cultural distinctiveness associated with the public sector middle class [based on] traditional forms of "high culture", such as classical music, art, literature, and so forth', can be distinguished from 'the new conspicuous extravagance of the private sector professionals, who indulge in new types of sport and fitness regimes along with exotic holidays and luxury consumption' (ibid.: 212–3).[11]

The common experience of consumption

One of the key differences then, between work-based and consumption-based society is that in the former people somehow experience themselves as the product of processes and structures which were in place before they arrived, and over which they have relatively little control. Their expectations for the future moreover, are also very much determined by their origins. In consumption-based society on the other hand, people experience themselves much more as the instigators of their own actions. This is certainly what one would expect to find given that the activities of production are largely prescribed whilst those of consumption are much more open to choice and self-selection. Autonomy, choice and independence are, for the majority, characteristics of consumption not of work.

As sociologists, and in contrast to the relatively closed concept of social identity associated with class membership in work-based society, a concept which presupposes that economically, culturally and emotionally one is forever bound by one's class and occupation, the concept of social identity in consumption-based society is one which suggests that the formation of the self is a reflexive process as people constantly monitor their past actions and modify their future behaviour in light of ongoing experiences. In consumption-based society the range and depth of these experiences is greater than it was in work-based society and thus the process of reflection and modification is freer and more dynamic. As Craib has expressed it: 'the central feature of the self in modern society is its reflexivity, a constant questioning and reconstruction of the self in a lifetime project. We are constantly constructing and revising our personal stories and so reconstructing ourselves (Craib, 1998: 2).[12]

Consumption as a basis for social activity

In what ways then, does participation in the realm of consumption enable people to express the social aspects of identity? The first set of reasons are all to do with the central fact that like work, consumption is a profoundly social activity which relies upon some kind of cooperation with others. Although the content of the activities involved are obviously different, consumption is as much a socially embedded process as is participation in the world of work. It also provides excellent opportunities for satisfying our need for social contact. Most obvious are acts of consumption which involve groups of people consuming collectively at some form of public venue. Being a spectator at a sports event or part of the audience at some kind of artistic performance are clear illustrations of this. The element of participation is itself an important part of this kind of consumption (the experience of watching a film at a cinema is quite different from watching the same film on television at home).

Similarly communal are many of the preparations for consumption like going shopping or travelling to and from some leisure event. Although we are expressing a degree of individuality through such actions (the specific combination of items we buy, the actual car in which we drive to the leisure centre), many of the rhythms and patterns of our consumption are pretty much the same as those around us. Being part of a global television audience for the opening ceremony of an Olympic Games or the football World Cup for example, demonstrates that however unique this act of consumption feels to us we are simply behaving as many millions of others are. In fact, being aware of all these other people doing more-or-less the same thing becomes part of the experience we are having.

Further still, because much of the meaning of consumption, and especially of complex forms of consumption, is constituted by the feedback we receive from others, many acts of consumption (including many which we might regard as being intimate and private) require the active participation of others. Social bonding through consumption is not an incidental bi-product of the act of consumption, but is part of the utility of consumption. In terms of their socially-constructed sign-values, my new haircut, shirt or car mean nothing unless there is someone there to notice, to bear witness, to interpret the meaning of what I have done. Consumption is like a tug of war with consumers endlessly trying to drag recognition and acknowledgement from one another. For the duration of the struggle the two are almost physically attached. Each individual instance of such a connection is a thread in a much more extensive mesh of connections which also spreads backwards and forwards in time. The reinforcing experiences of successful consumption in the past are thus interwoven with expectations for even bigger and better consumption still to come.[13]

Consumption also produces effects of social bonding because in any particular time or place, it is one of the ways in which we express our underlying set of beliefs and expectations. At the level of substantive rationality, agreements about the desirability of particular outcomes have to be pretty much uncontested, while at the level of formal rationality, the day-to-day actions of consumption have to be seen as a valid means of achieving these ends. The precise outcome that a particular individual seeks, and the personal way in which they go about achieving it might be entirely unique to that person, but these aims and efforts will only be achievable if they harmonise with the efforts of the people around them. Those adopting ridiculous means to achieve impossible ends may celebrate the virtues of individuality, but will inevitably find themselves cast out by the rational majority. Madness and insanity are isolating rather than collectivising classifications.

Consumption and the meaning of social identity

The second set of reasons why consumption provides important inputs to identity is because it supplies us with new opportunities to experiment with and consume the meaning of identity. Recalling our discussion of complex consumption in earlier chapters, the objects and activities of consumption are heavily loaded with sign-value (Baudrillard, 2001). To the extent that work tends to be weighted more towards use-values and exchange values, than it is towards sign values, one can say that it is in terms of these kinds of inputs that consumption offers us much more in the way of identity-ingredients than does work.

As affluence increases and complex consumption thus becomes more readily accessible to people, the calibration of social identity becomes more and more subtle, and, some might say, more intangible. As we have already noted in our discussion of symbolic consumption, this most abstract realm is characterised by an apparently shifting set of relations between signifier and signified, between the thing in itself and the meaning which is attached to it. What we encounter here is the somewhat daunting prospect that the meanings or significances which are attached to the particular bits and pieces out of which our identities are made (gender, occupation, ethnicity, cultural group and so on) are somewhat 'up for grabs'. For example, although in an earlier period 'bank manager' connoted authority, conservatism, discretion, the 'bank manager' in the twenty-first century might connote something quite different (young, IT-skilled, entrepreneurial innovator). When added to the fact that 'bank-managernous' is now only one source, rather than all of, the identity of a person who has that occupational role, the permutations multiply very considerably. The disabled, ethnic-minority, urbanite bank manager occupies a very different position in the sign system of social identity than does that mature-age, white, male heterosexual treasurer of Backwoods, Virginia. Giddens' definition of self-identity being formed through 'coherent yet continuously revised biographical narratives ... filtered through abstract systems', and all of this 'against a backdrop of new forms of mediated expereince' (Giddens, 1991: 5), points very clearly towards an uncoupling of identity from its established markers and meanings.

Once the proportion of the population who are preoccupied with these more abstract and symbolic aspects of identity reaches a minimum level (something which is obviously closely linked with levels of affluent consumption), this creates a demand amongst consumers for ever more detailed and expert guidance as to how to deal with them. Conveniently, and entirely compliant with the productivist ethic, there is a corresponding proliferation of websites, magazines and television programmes which guide us through the minefield of the new age of identity formation (Hermes, 1995; Jackson et al., 1999; Benwell (ed.), 2003). These products service our need for information about what and where identity is these days. The capacity to massage the way that we interpret our identity and manipulate how it is interpreted by those around us, extends far beyond anything of this sort that can be achieved in the realm of work. Problems of identity are no longer defined as psycho-social conditions to be dealt with by trained professionals in the hospital or clinic, but as cultural problems to be dealt with by lifestyle-planning and lifestyle-choice consultants listed in *Yellow Pages*.

Divisions of consumption

The third set of reasons why consumption enables people to express the social aspects of identity is because, like work, it satisfies our need for *social orientation*. Just because class-as-occupation no longer provides comprehensive guidance, this does not mean that we have all been cast adrift in social time and space with no means at all of orienting ourselves in respect of other people. The alleged 'death of class' does not mean 'the death of any and all means of stratification in society'. Recalling Durkheim's highly influential conclusion that the division of labour is a primary mechanism of social solidarity in modern industrial societies, we can speculate that for late modern societies, something of the same sort is provided by the *division of consumption*.[14]

The division of consumption is based on assessments of how a person spends their money rather than of how they earn it. We can attempt to arrive at our own social orientation by considering not only what kind of job a person does, but also which group of consumers they belong to or have chosen to join. Like the division of labour, the division of consumption is hierarchic in that the higher up the scale a person is placed, measured in terms of levels of disposable income and thus spending power (rather than earning power), the greater will be the level of social prestige they enjoy. At its simplest, this initial allocation is meaningful in that it provides a basis upon which to make further assumptions about the probable habits, lifestyle and expectations of people who have particular levels of spending power. Capacity to consume transposes into likely patterns of consumption, and patterns of consumption are taken as a reliable basis for deciding questions of status- or consumer-group membership. In very much the same way that occupation provides a reliable guide to class membership, knowledge of how and what one consumes provides an increasingly important guide to status- or consumer-group membership. Knowing that a person has a particular level of disposable income, lives in a certain neighbourhood and reads this daily newspaper rather than that one provides at least as powerful a means of understanding social identity as does knowledge of the job they do. When both these sign-systems of interpretation and value-attribution are combined, the communicant will be able to build up a pretty clear impression of that person and their likely behaviour.

So what are the classes, strata, groupings, which we might expect to come across in consumption-based society in the late-modern period? Clearly a full analysis of the divisions of consumption in contemporary society requires a volume all of its own. What we can do here is indicate some of the main features which such a classification might bring forward, and how these affect social identity and social orientation.

Conspicuous consumption and expressions of social identity

Referring back to our typology of consumption developed in the previous chapter (Figure 5.1), expressions of social identity become increasingly involved as one progresses from simple and towards complex forms of consumption. Throughout the twentieth century in the Western economies, and especially with the coming of widespread affluence during the 1950s and 1960s, people were very happy to identify themselves simply as a member of consumer society. Being one of the masses in the age of mass consumption was a supportive and socially rewarding experience.[15] There may also have been some psychological benefits in that consumption provided a new pretext for togetherness but this time through enjoyment rather than through wartime struggles. Consumer mentality at this time was certainly characterised by a general consolidation of the thought (actively stimulated by the new sciences of advertising and marketing; see Packard, 1957; Tomlinson, 1990; Butler and Savage (eds), 1995) that it was quite normal to expect to have more and more of the goods and gadgets which were now available even if their manual and more labour-intensive forebears were still perfectly serviceable (Baudrillard, 1998: 112). The increasingly widespread use of hire purchase agreements, through which people could have the commodities immediately whilst spreading the burden of paying for them into the future, softened the feelings of guilt previously associated with being in debt. Owing a little on the fridge, or the car no longer meant social stigma and personal shame but was accepted as part of the process through which people acquired the means of expressing a modern identity. As we have already observed, the ethic of modern consumption celebrates the thrill of acquisition and rejects the sobriety of deferred gratification.

After a while however, the novelty of sameness wore off and people started to seek out ways of presenting themselves as 'different'. Having a washing machine and television was fine, but these former exceptions had now become the standard expectation. The emergence of various kinds of counter-culture during the 1960s and 1970s clearly illustrates the need people felt to resist what had become the conformities of mass consumerism (Hebdidge, 1979 and 1987; Willis, 1990; Heelas and Morris (eds), 1992; Plant, 1992; Thornton, 1995; Firth, 1996).[16] An essential part of this new game was to use consumption as a means of constructing and articulating a sense of identity which was all one's own. People still wanted to see themselves as part of society and take advantage of the support and protection this provides, but without becoming entirely assimilated into it. One trivial but instructive example of this was the craze for customising motor vehicles during the 1960s and 1970s. Although there are often impressive technical changes involved, what really mattered was that by changing one or two highly visible aspects of the appearance of the car or motorcycle or truck, the owner was somehow reconquering the vehicle's apparent ability to dominate through blandness – 'I need my car to get to work everyday, but I'm damned if I am going to let people think that this mass-produced commodity means that my social identity is also mass produced'.[17]

To the extent that the new age of consumer nonconformity developed at very much the same pace as did increases in the variety of ways of consuming, it is reasonable to conclude that the modern practice of liberated identity could not have emerged until society had reached the stage of affluent consumption. In order to be different (or, which very often amounts to the same thing, to express difference) people have to have access to the means of difference and consumption provides this in abundance. For example, the whole realm of mass-mediated popular culture offers itself as a fertile and easily accessible medium through which people can constantly invent and reinvent social identity. The culture-status of an Elvis Presley, John Lennon or Bob Dylan is partly to do with the impact they had on the genre of popular music, but is also, and perhaps much more significantly to do with inventing the idea first that popular music could be used as a direct marker of social identity, and secondly that there is nothing wrong with wanting to be an individual. As we shall be discussing more fully in the final chapter, one of the defining characteristics of postmodernism is the enthusiasm with which people shift signifiers between categories of interpretation or simply demolish the boundaries of the categories altogether. Clarity and continuity are rapidly displaced by ambiguity and novelty.

The capacity for complex consumption thus exacerbates one of the dilemmas which lies at the heart of the identity/consumption relationship which is that through consumption we are expressing a need to align ourselves with others, and yet we also consume in order to distinguish ourselves from them. The paradox of same-but-different stimulates our desire to consume but increasingly high levels of consumption dexterity are required to maintain a productive balance between being recognised and fitting in, and being ignored and left out.

In their analysis of the association between the cultural patterns of consumption on the one hand and class identification on the other, Pakulski and Waters suggest that it is no longer realistic to map 'cultural products and tastes' against 'organised classes' because of 'the recent shift from organised and standardised cultural production and consumption to diversified niche marketing' (Pakulski and Waters, 1996: 122). In the late modern period, 'a differentiation of consumption into individualised tastes' means that 'not only the community but the family ceases to be the significant consumption unit': 'Stylised consumption is radically detaching from family, community and class and is becoming self-referential ... When styles congeal into lifestyles, and when such lifestyles form identities, the process of cultural decoupling reaches its apex' (Ibid.: 125).

Following Rojek (2000), in the late-modern period, membership of 'taste cultures' (Thornton, 1995) offers one way out of this dilemma because they offer identity-inputs which are much more individuated than the collectivising inputs of the sub-cultural groupings of an earlier period. Being a member of a taste sub-cultural group no longer means substituting a group identity for a mass identity because group identity is itself defined in terms of the quest for an entirely distinctive and individual persona. Taste cultures emphasise 'a high degree of reflexive maintenance by actors ... the fantasies of identity generated and supported in taste cultures are a central source of pleasure ... [and they recognise] high levels of "drift" between identities and the reflexive switching of identities' (Rojek, 2000: 100).

Leisure consumption and class

We noted in the previous chapter that leisure consumption provides one of the most useful means of comparing one social group with another and of managing the complex business of social orientation. If we bundle together affluent, conspicuous and symbolic types of consumption, one of the most obvious ways of comparing one class or group with another is in terms of the kinds of leisure-consumption they enjoy. Consumption, that is, which is deliberately pleasure-seeking rather than aimed at satisfying basic needs. A useful example here, is Veblen's 'theory of the leisure class' which uses the capacity to enjoy particular kinds of 'leisure' as the defining characteristic of social position. In his analysis, 'the characteristic feature of leisure-class life is a conspicuous exemption from all useful employment' (Veblen, 1994: 40).[18] The dominant characteristic of the leisure class is that for themselves, they shun all activities which could be seen as carrying economic utility: 'the upper classes are exempt from industrial employments and this exemption is the economic expression of their superior rank' (Veblen, 1994: 1). To the extent that they are involved in 'honourable employments' at all, they are to be found in 'government, warfare, religious observances, and sports' (ibid.: 2).

As Veblen observes however, and as we have noted in our earlier discussion of work time, the preference for conspicuously non-productive leisure is not taken up by other social groups lower down the social scale. Although both conspicuous consumption and conspicuous leisure have in common 'the wasting of time and effort and the wasting of goods', it is evident that by the end of the nineteenth century, the trend 'is in the direction of heightening the utility of conspicuous consumption as compared with leisure' (Veblen, 1994: 85–6, 88). As consumption-as-leisure declines whilst leisure defined as conspicuous consumption-of-goods increases, there is a clear shifting in the criteria by which the divisions of consumption are arrived at: 'the conspicuous consumption of goods should gradually gain in importance, both absolutely and relatively, until it had absorbed all the available product …' (Veblen, 1994: 91).

This is useful in our current discussion because it shows that the productivist ethic, which by definition plays no part at all in the psychology of Veblen's leisure-class who actively shun for themselves all economic utility, does play a central role in the social identity of the emerging bourgeois or middle classes in modern industrial society. If, as Veblen suggests, the household can gain 'social esteem' 'only within the realm of productive efficiency and thrift' their struggle for 'pecuniary reputability' 'will work out in an increase in diligence and parsimony' (Veblen, 1994: 36). In the twentieth century, one of the clearest markers of social position is the capacity for conspicuous consumption of goods. And, as we have previously argued, this means an increased, rather than reducing desire for income through paid employment.[19] As leisure-as-waste recedes as a marker of social standing 'property now becomes the most easily recognised evidence of a reputable degree of success as distinguished from heroic or signal achievement. It therefore becomes the conventional basis of esteem … the possession of wealth presently assumes the character of an independent and definitive basis of esteem … a conventional basis of reputability … .' Social position depends to a very large extent on being able to meet 'the demands of pecuniary emulation', to live up to 'the normal pecuniary standard of the community' (Veblen, 1994: 29–30).

An alternative way of expressing these developments is to say that the practice of defining 'leisure' as a non-productive wasteful activity falls into disuse, whilst the practice of defining leisure in terms of commodity possessions and consumption takes over. Rojek argues for example, that at the start of the twenty-first century, the leisure pursuits of the very wealthy show none of the Veblen characteristics of leisure-as-waste. These hyper-wealthy individuals he finds, are much more interested in 'going to the movies for escape' while 'risk and competition feature prominently in their leisure' (Rojek, 2000: 80). Also interesting is the observation that many 'subscribe to the view that work should be fun' and that they 'hold a weak distinction between work and leisure' (ibid.: see also Pahl, 1995). As the range of activities which can be referred to under the heading of leisure becomes more and more open, it becomes less and less sensible to define social groups in terms of their leisure habits. In some respects at least, the distinction between work and leisure and their respective associations with particular classes might also come to be regarded as similarly unreliable (Rojek, 1995 and 2000). Both of these tendencies are especially evident under circumstances where the activities of consumption-as-leisure are directed primarily towards identity formation since their objective is, by definition, distinction and differentiation. To the extent that modernist approaches to class analysis had no problem recognising differences and distinctions *between* members of one class and another, they should have no difficulty in recognizing the possibility of differences and distinctions between individuals *within* the same group or class. It is sometimes useful to see class cultures, as Savage puts it, 'as contingently embodying forms of individualised identities which operate relationally' (Savage, 2000: 150).

Recalling our analysis of conspicuous consumption in Chapter 5, the point we want to emphasise in the context of social identity, is that in the late modern period, consumption is increasingly oriented towards commodities and activities whose primary purpose is to attract attention to the possessor or doer. Increased ownership of goods, measured perhaps by some inventory of possessions, attracts the attention of those around and is therefore 'conspicuous', but conspicuousness is more deliberately sought through goods which are entirely attention seeking. Veblen's notion that social orientation can be attained through possession of goods, becomes, in the late modern period, a quest for goods which have this property as their primary purpose. Their utility lies very much towards the end of the scale where conspicuousness is deliberately sought and valued.

SOCIAL IDENTITY AND SOCIAL ACTIVISM

In the final section of this chapter we need to address one other very important aspect of social identity (and one which was given great prominence in Marxist programmes of class analysis), which is the extent to which people act together in order deliberately to protect or further the interests of the particular group or class to which they belong. How that is, people act as social activists and not simply as social actors. Are there identifiable differences between work- and consumption-based societies in this respect?

The established notion of social activism in work-based society is that from time to time one is likely to act in support of the interest of one's class and its members. Classes are not just categories or groups of people developed by sociologists for the purposes of classification (Weber's nominalist position), but are entities through which, and in the name of which people express common cause. For followers of Marx, it is the shared experience of alienation at work which is expected eventually to develop through various stages of resistance into full-blown social revolution which is in the interests of every member of the working class. Class membership not only helps people to distinguish themselves from others, but emphasises what it is they have in common with members of their own class. The slight chill of difference helps one appreciate the warmth of sameness.

In addition to refreshing one's memory as to the causes one is fighting for, traditional class membership also provides helpful guidance about how and where one might go about expressing one's social activism. In work-based society, and given that the main focus of grievance and exploitation is the realm of production, the focus of collective action will be within the economic sphere. Not surprisingly, and especially in a society like Britain where the lines of class division have been most palpably drawn, many of the most noteworthy pubic disputes of the twentieth century were labour or industrial disputes centring on issues of working conditions and wages. As one would expect in a society dominated by work, these disputes took place predominantly at or around the place of work.

Beyond this important but none the less often rather narrow field of social activism however, it is far less certain whether even in Britain which is seen as the archetypal class society, class membership ever has played a leading role as a springboard for social activism outside work. Looking specifically at empirical research into class identity and class consciousness, Savage quotes from Marshall et al's., influential study that : 'there is no evidence … which can be said "to reflect a mature or developed class consciousness comprising class identity, class opposition, class totality and the conception of an alternative society"' (Savage, 2000: 38 quoting Marshall et al., 1988: 190). His overall conclusion is that: 'Britain is not a deeply class conscious society where class is seen [as] embodying membership of collective groups. Although people can identify themselves as members of classes, this identification seems contextual and of limited significance, rather than being a major source of their identity and group belonging' (Savage, 2000: 40). Although conclusions such as these depend on how exactly key terms such as 'class consciousness' are being operationalised for research purposes (Eder, 1993), only a true political romantic would argue that members of the industrial proletariat today have as their core belief the idea that revolutionary working-class activism will result in the overthrow of capitalism (Pakulski and Waters, 1996).

Social activism in consumption-based society

This does not mean of course that there is no such thing as collective social activism, but that in modern, and especially in late-modern society, it can no longer be categorised or analysed within the frameworks of traditional class analysis (Crow, 2002). In trying to understand these processes sociologically, there are two main routes to follow. The first draws directly from the modernist tradition of Max Weber for whom, as we have already noted, it is perfectly rational to expect people to find and express common cause with others. It is just that 'common cause' means different things to different people. In distinguishing between economic classes, status groups and political parties or pressure groups, Weber suggests that individuals are just as, if not more likely, to engage in collective action if they feel that their social status or 'estimation of social honour' is threatened, or if a single pressing issue grabs their attention, as they would be if their jobs are threatened. Moreover, it is not just the industrial proletariat which has feelings and interests to protect, but a much more formidable assemblage of groups and associations collectively labelled by sociologists as 'the middle classes'. Social activism in other words, is not confined to the realms of property ownership and economic well-being, but includes a much wider range of issues and social groupings which might spur people into action.

The second approach takes us into the realm of the 'new social movements'. Although there are a number of variants to choose from (Tilly, 1988; Melucci, 1989; Eder, 1993; Zald and McCarthy, 1987; and Tarrow, 1994; for a discussion see Charles, 2000), what they broadly have in common is the suggestion that social activism today is no longer centred in the economic and political realm, nor is it primarily concerned with economic issues. As Charles puts it: 'Their structural location means that [new social movements] are primarily cultural rather than political, bringing about social change through the transformation of cultural codes and collective identities' (Charles, 2000: 31). The various phases of the women's movement beginning with the suffragettes in the 1900s, the Campaign for Nuclear Disarmament in Britain during the 1950s, and the Civil Rights, Peace and anti-Vietnam Movements in the United States during the 1960s and 1970s, might be classified as 'new' rather than 'old' social movements for at least three kinds of reasons. First they are not an embodiment of 'old' class groupings but originate from across the social spectrum. Second, they and the claims they make are located outside the economic structure. Third, the demand for change expressed by their members focuses upon broad-based claims for universal rights. A female member of the middle classes has as much right to employment, political and cultural equality as does the black proletarian, and everyone has a right not to be vaporised in a nuclear Armageddon.

These ideas offer some useful pointers as to how the interface between social identity and social activism may have altered in late modern society. Following the analyses put forward by Jenkins (1996, following Beck, Giddens and others) and Savage (2000), a first point we can make is that increasingly, people tend to follow a more 'individualised' path in composing their social identity. They are not, and do not really see themselves as part of a clearly defined economic/political class (other perhaps than when they superficially locate themselves as such in response to the social surveyor), and therefore do not act as if they were. Even if the needs and expectations which people have are shared by most of the population – a nicer house, a faster car, a more adventurous holiday – it might not always be easy to decide whether it is better to act collectively or separately in order to achieve them. When sufficient consumers do act in a synchronised way (by for example boycotting a particular product or production technique) the kind of 'class' they are acting within is one which is based on individual interests rather than collective ones. Even though they may be acting together in seemingly common cause, they are actually acting as individual consumers in pursuit of their own individual aims. Any appearance of 'class-like' properties in their actions are little more than a coincidence.

Second, and notwithstanding the fact that people may develop quite a strong sense of allegiance to the various new social groupings and become life-long supporters, membership is not structurally determined like class membership is, but is based on choice. People may be born into the middle class (or even the Catholic Church), but nobody is born into the Campaign for Nuclear Disarmament or the Green movement. This difference in the basis of group membership obviously makes a major difference to the composition of the group as it can draw its members from across the whole of society.

With the coming of affluent consumption therefore, and along with it the general satisfaction of most common needs and simple expectations, people inevitably develop more individual perceptions of what they want and are prepared to try to achieve. To the extent that our social identities are grounded more in the realm of consumption than in the world of work, it seems sensible to recognise that people will be at least as interested in defending and protecting their rights as consumers as they are in defending and protecting their rights as producers. Although the integrity of the idea of the 'sovereign consumer' as the new focus of social and political action in modern society has been challenged by those who emphasise that in reality, modern-day consumers are actually the new victims of consumer capitalism,[20] the legal footing of consumer rights continues to strengthen. Our rights as consumers are now almost as formalised as our 'rights' as employees.

Third, the issues people take to heart are neither class-based in the sense that they are the grievances of a particular class, nor are they issues which can be resolved through the agency of class action. One might say that 'classes' in the economic/political sense were invented to deal with obvious and shared problems in a collectivised and collectivising way, and so by design, they, and the strategies and tactics which developed within them, are not a very appropriate way of dealing with other, more individualised kinds of complaints and grievances. One could take this idea a little further and argue that once the process of defining what constitutes a pressing economic, social or political issue has been uncoupled from the idea of 'class', the issues which might come to be defined as 'problematic' or 'pressing' might be quite different. For example, the issue of whether or not to purchase food commodities such as meat or vegetables if they have not been humanely and organically produced, is not a class issue (although level of income does have a bearing) but a moral and ethical one which bears directly on the conscience of the individual consumer.

Fourth, and with the notable exception of the 'anti-capitalist movement' (Callinicos, 2003), in late modern society, the main focus of social activism is not based on a wholehearted critique of productivism – the aim is not the overthrow of capitalism and all that. Contemporary activists target specific issues in the practice of consumption, for example the putative impact of genetically-modified products in the food-chain, but without directly challenging the fundamentals of the entire consumerist ethic. Concentrating on the ethical rather than economic and political aspects of an issue, various ad hoc single-issue groupings resist the seductions of consumption and draw attention to what they see as the excesses of consumer society, but without offering any alternative. Their approach is to attempt to cast doubt on the probity of day-to-day transactions of consumption rather than to undermine perceptions of the substantial rationality of consumerism itself. Typically, such campaigns highlight issues of animal exploitation (factory-farming, live animal exports), unfair trading practices (use of sweated labour in developing countries), and harmful environmental consequences (loss of natural resources, pollution and climate change).

The anti-consumerist movement

It must be said however, that these campaigns and the tacit counter-hegemony they hope to build based on the logic of limited production, renewability and sustainable development, have not ignited the imagination of those who adopt a more ethically relaxed attitude towards their consumption-side activities. Occasional spats from global even local campaigners sometimes make the headlines, but none has had much of an impact on the pro-consumption consensus. When looked at a little more closely, the 'countryside alliance' which emerged in Britain in the early years of the current century for example, was at least as interested in lifestyle matters as it was in genuine support for the agricultural economy. The banner of 'freedom' being held aloft was as much to do with cultural and leisure pursuits as it was with the viability of rural amenities (Stratford and Christie, 2000).

Adopting Gramscian terminology for a moment (Ransome, 1992), although there was a growth in support during the 1980s and early 1990s for Green politics in Europe (Dalton, 1994; Wallace and Wallace (eds), 1996; Bomberg, 1998, and Worpole, 2000), an alternative hegemony based on alliances from outside the productivist/consumptivist mainstream, has not emerged. Dalton and Rohrschneider report for example: 'While the British undoubtedly do more than they have in the past, a majority does not possess those characteristics which in other nations lead to the assertive movements challenging established policy-makers' (Dalton and Rohrschneider, 1998: 119). The tendency for expressions of environmental concern to be well ahead of preparedness to create the conditions for actual policy changes, remains a key characteristic especially of British environmentalism. In the early 1990s Witherspoon concluded for example: '... many environmental beliefs are rather superficial. Environmental concern is far more widespread than either support for environmental policies or environmental activism. The more specific and costly any proposal to improve the environment seems to be, the more rapidly support dissipates' (Witherspoon, 1994: 57). Taylor reached much the same conclusion some years later: 'When we examine attitudes towards policies aimed at environmental protection, we find generally lower levels of support than people's expressions of concern might lead us to expect' (Taylor, 1997: 13).

Similarly unconvincing are suggestions that some form of postmaterialist counter-culture is about to emerge as more and more people attempt to transcend the productivist ethic. Inglehart (1990, 1997) has argued for example, that Western societies are moving into a 'postmaterialist' phase associated with the progressive attitudes of people who enjoyed affluence during their formative years (particularly 1960s) (see also van Deth and Scarborough (eds), 1995). Ideologically, the new attitude involves a rejection of materialism and is demonstrated, amongst other things, by support for environmental politics. However, using data from the *International Social Survey Programme 1992–1996*, Bryson and Cutrice found little evidence of postmaterialist attitudes at least in Britain in the 1990s: 'the postmodernisation thesis did not pass this acid test …. Postmaterialists are relatively scarce, environmental concern is low, national pride is relatively high, and its social mores tend toward the illiberal' (Bryson and Cutrice, 1998: 141–2). Worse still for supporters of the postmodernisation thesis, such attitudes seemed to be more prevalent amongst the least rather than most affluent: '… the belief in the virtues of nature over science is more common among the less well-educated, the less well-off and older people … and is also unrelated to the measure of postmaterialism …' (Ibid.:).

A little less ambitiously, Etzioni expresses a neo-Gorzian perspective by developing the idea of 'voluntary simplicity' to describe people who wish to make alternative 'lifestyle choices'. He suggest that increasing numbers of people are 'down-shifting' away from their stressful and dramatic lifestyles: '… voluntary simplicity may appeal to people after their basic needs are satisfied: once they feel secure that their needs will be attended to in the future, they may then objectively feel ready to turn more attention to their higher needs …. Although their consumeristic addiction may prevent them from noting that they may shift upwards, so to speak' (Etzioni, 1998 in Millar, 2001a, Vol. I: 632). Again there is some irony here since 'voluntary simplicity' is a lifestyle choice for those who have already reached the top of the consumer hierarchy: 'my affluence frees me from the pursuit of affluence'. There is a very great difference between loin-cloth living as a lifestyle choice made by a handful of very wealthy people, and as a way of living amongst those genuinely grasping for survival along the margins of subsistence. As part of his 'theory of consumption' Baudrillard categorises such instances of the ostentatious rejection of conspicuous consumption as a renewed quest for differentiation – of emphasising how one is not the same as other people: 'Differentiation may take the form of the rejection of objects, the rejection of "consumption", and yet this still remains the very ultimate in consumption' (Baudrillard, 1998 [1970]: 90).

As if to prove its virility, the ethic of modern consumption repeatedly rises to these challenges, accepts a degree of moral approbation from the still peripheral 'green' and 'ethical' tendency (see Beck, 1992; Lee, 1993; Lodziak, 1995; Slater, 1997b), and then turns the concept of 'environmental friendliness' into a marketing ploy. Selling Mother Nature in all of her 'natural' and 'essential' forms extends rather than reduces the range of 'goods' which are available to the discerning ethically-sensitive consumer. Other examples of 'consuming with a conscience' might include the blending of environmentalism with gardening (natural planting, organic techniques), salvage and recycling with DIY (refurbishment and renewal), and ecotourism (Duffy, 2002).

Disciples of the ethic of modern consumption, characterised by the principles of pleasure, leisure and enjoyment, are not going to respond very positively to renewed pleas for restraint and self-discipline since these are the very principles which they have so recently cast aside. Without denying that many social activists do feel genuinely and passionately about the causes they are involved with, it can be suggested in the age of complex consumption, membership of some campaigning group or another has itself become a form of consumption. To be a good member of society it has long since ceased to be enough to be a good worker, or even a good consumer, now one has to have a cause to fight for. One has to be 'for' something or 'against' something. We need to consume with a conscience, hence the proliferation of entertainments with a charity twist: Live Aid, Children In Need, Sport Aid, Comic Relief and so the list goes on.

SUMMARY

In this chapter we have argued that concepts of social identity have altered to accommodate the greater variety of inputs and experiences which go towards the formation of identity in the late modern period. If a person lives at a time and in a place where work is dominant (measured both in terms of length of time at work and/or degree of economic necessity as previously discussed), then one would be justified in claiming that that person's life is heavily work-oriented and that their overall social position is mostly determined by their occupation. There is simply not enough of them left over to be significantly influenced by anything else. By the same token however, if a person lives at a time and place where consumption has become a major preoccupation, then both for the purposes of sociological analysis, and in our own lives as practitioners of identity, the importance of the consumption-side has to be properly acknowledged. It is because it impacts upon ideas about class, social position and identity, that the shift towards consumption poses major challenges to earlier presumptions about the constitution of society. If it had no significant impact in these domains then sociologists and others would not spend so much time discussing it!

Although the criteria which are used in defining the divisions of consumption have changed over time, there has been a general movement throughout the twentieth century towards using assessments of the level and type of possessions a person or household has as a key marker of social position. Given that the capacity to spend reflects the capacity to earn the logic of such a means of classification sits quite comfortably with earlier modes of classification based on occupation. Social identity still derives to some extent from occupational position, but we are much more likely nowadays to see our own identity, and for it to be judged by others, in terms of how conspicuously we consume rather than how conspicuously we earn. 'Conspicuousness' derives from the quantity of commodities and leisure activities a person can enjoy, but also from consuming things which are specifically intended to attract attention to the self. In late modern society, social identity tends to be formed more on the output side where consumption facilitates the (autonomous) expression of identity, rather than on the input side where identity tends to be limited by (heteronymous) occupational roles.

The assumption that the position a person held in the means of production was likely also to determine their position in terms of economic and social class, has itself been displaced by a new way of conceiving of social position and social orientation. There are two moves here. First (and not withstanding greater differentiation within the occupational structure itself), occupation is no longer taken to be the most important constituent of a person's class position. Following Weber and others, it is how one lives one's life as a whole which determines class not just occupation. The living of one's life is as much if not more to do with consumption as it is to do with production. Second, sociological analyses of individuals and what makes them tick have become very much based on the idea of identity rather than class. Class is seen as one important constituent of identity but by no means the whole of it. As a result of both these moves, the level of attention given to, and the significance attributed to that category of activities we call work has diminished, and that of consumption-type activities has increased.

In consumption-based society, social identity, social orientation and social activism are no longer determined by occupational role, occupational community and class, but converge upon the more individualised notion of citizenship. Perceptions of collectivism, of the desire to participate with others in some form of common purpose are carried forward but in a manner which also values individuality and choice. People choose the activisms they wish to belong to rather than inheriting them like ideological family heirlooms. The limits of traditional forms of class-based social activism have been reached because the sources of social identity upon which they depended and which they express, have been superseded by other experiences and concerns.

The new forms of social activism which have emerged to challenge aspects of the consumptivist ethic (principally the Green movement, various environmentalist campaigns, and the anti- or post-materialist tendency) differ significantly from those which emerged to challenge the productivist ethic in work-based society. The objections raised by these groups give very little clue as to other aspects of the lives of those who are raising them. Contemporary forms of social activism are not born of social class. They are not class issues, and cannot therefore be constitutive of class-based notions of social identity. What they indicate much more strongly, is that in consumption-based society social activism is made manifest as a further expression of choice. I *choose* not to buy certain commodities. I *choose* to recycle my domestic waste. I *choose* to campaign for animal welfare. To the extent that the individual is able to live their own life in accordance with these preferences, then the desired outcome has been achieved without any need to challenge the entire edifice of contemporary consumerism. It is not consumption that people are objecting to but what and how to consume.

NOTES

[1]For an introduction to the various labels given to the 'inner' and 'outer', the 'interior' and 'exterior', the 'I' and the 'me' of identity see Jenkins, 1996. This author deploys the concept of 'the internal-external dialectic of identification' to capture the way in which 'individual and collective social identities [emerge from] the dialectical interplay of processes of internal and external definition' (Jenkins, 1996: 20–5). A little more recently, Craib suggests that rather than having to choose between notions of the self as an 'assemblage of parts' on the one hand, or as 'more or less unitary' on the other, it should be possible to see the self as 'both at the same time', as a 'combination or dialectic of unity *and* diversity' (Craib, 1998: 5, emphasis added).

[2]The 'interactionist' concept of identity owes much to the work of the distinguished American social psychologists Mead (1934) and Cooley (1962 and 1964). This concept of identity as a reflexive undertaking has been carried forward by Giddens, 1991.

[3]One of the conceptual difficulties which arises here is whether 'the structure' or 'hierarchy' of occupations and of social strata more generally, has much of an existence outside the research programmes of sociologists. One of the responsibilities of class analysis is always to challenge the presumption that classes really do exist in the way that class theorists would like them to (Goldthorpe and Marshall, 1992; Savage, 2000).

[4]For commentary see: Marshall et al., 1988; Hamnett et al. (eds), 1989; Burrows and Marsh (eds), 1992; Marshall, 1997; Crompton, 1998; and Savage, 2000.

[5]This new approach is already having some impact within the albeit narrowing field of class analysis. Reformists such as Crompton (1998) and Savage (2000) are adopting a much more pluralist and culturalist perspective as they set about rehabilitating class analysis within British sociology.

[6]The modernist conception that the occupational structure becomes a defining characteristic of what modern society *is*, is most clearly represented in the work of Émile Durkheim [1893]. For Durkheim, modern industrial societies are inherently work-based because of the structuring and organising properties of the division of labour. To the benefit of members of these societies, participation in the division of labour preserves us from the dangers both of excessive egoism and of excessive altruism (Durkheim, 1933 and 1968).

[7]Proclaiming 'the death of class' Pakulski and Waters assemble a formidable inventory of recent social change: 'A wide redistribution of property; the proliferation of indirect and small ownership; the credentialisation of skills and the professionalisation of occupations; the multiple segmentation and globalisation of markets; and an increasing role for consumption as a status and lifestyle generator' (Pakulski and Waters, 1996: 4). In similar vein, Savage has re-emphasised the need 'to focus on the significance of the contemporary restructuring of organizations' which has very important consequences for the structuring of classes as 'new career technologies have radically reworked traditional class boundaries and have created new ideas about the relationship between the individual, hierarchy and organisation' (Savage, 2000: 121–2).

[8]The issue of how many classes there actually are has been a long-standing issue for sociologists. See for example Parkin, 1979; Abercrombie and Urry, 1983; Pakulski and Waters, 1996; Wright, 1989 and 1996; Savage, 2000.

[9]Savage notes for example that a 'major axis in the remaking of contemporary class relations ... has been the cultural and political defeat of the male, manual working class as a central reference point in British culture' (Savage, 2000: xiii). This author is also quite sceptical about whether there ever has been any significant class consciousness in British culture: 'There is precious little evidence which indicates the existence of strong collective and articulated class cultures in contemporary Britain' (ibid.: 34) See also Marshall et al., 1988 who reach an equally cautious conclusion.

[10]As Isin and Wood have recently commented; 'Cultural citizenship is not only about rights to produce and consume symbolic goods and services but also an intervention in this identity work .... Individuals and groups are excluded from the cultural sphere on account of their lack of access not only to economic capital but also to cultural capital, which means much more than education but also includes competence, social and symbolic skills, and credentials' (Isin and Wood, 1999: 152). See also Delanty, 2000; Millar, 2000; Stevenson, 2003.

[11]We can note in passing that Veblen also makes this kind of distinction between early and late formations of the leisure-class: 'This latter-day uneasy reaching-out for some form of purposeful activity that shall at the same time not be indecorously productive of either individual or collective gain marks a difference of attitude between the modern leisure class and that of the quasi-peaceable [early-modern] stage' (Veblen, 1994: 94).

[12]The established point of departure for the 'reflexive-project-of-the-self' definition of identity is Giddens; identity has become 'a reflexively organised endeavour' '... the pluralisation of contexts of action and the diversity of "authorities", lifestyle choice is increasingly important in the constitution of self-identity and daily activity. Reflexively organised life-planning ... becomes a central feature of the structuring of self-identity' (Giddens, 1991: 5).

[13]In the same way that the division of labour is formalised in law through legal statutes at local, state and international levels, the rules and regulation of work and employment, so also is the division of consumption. It is not just as workers that we have rights, but as consumers also. With the laying down of minimum quality standards for consumer goods and leisure services, and the consumer

associations standing ready to act against those found wanting, consumers in late-modern society can always expect a fair day's play for a fair day's spending. [14]Although space precludes a full discussion we can note that if the division of labour is being displaced by the division of consumption, then interesting possibilities emerge as to whether the organic solidarity Durkheim associated with the former is also being displaced. Perhaps the kind of solidarity which the division of consumption produces is also organic, 'super-organic' or even 'organic-plus'.

[15]For an informative, if sometimes rather abstract discussion, of the various manifestations of 'mass' in contemporary usage see Lee and Munro (eds) (2001).

[16]Something similar might be said of the Pop Artists of the mid-twentieth century who sought to challenge the apparent banality of mass-produced images by explicitly incorporating them into their art; for illustration see Russell and Gablik, 1969; Compton, 1970.

[17]Rojek (1995) has drawn a similar distinction between the generally conformist attitudes and expectations towards work and leisure associated with 'Modernity I' (1760–1960), and the much more non-conformist and fragmentary nature of leisure expectations in 'Modernity II' (post-1960).

[18]'The term "leisure" as used here, does not connote indolence or quiescence … [it connotes] non-productive consumption of time. Time is consumed non-productively (1) from a sense of the unworthiness of productive work, and (2) as an evidence of pecuniary ability to afford a life of idleness' (Veblen, 1994: 43).

[19]Following Gershuny (1993), Hakim makes the point that as far as sheer levels of market and non-market activity are concerned in the latter part of the twentieth century, it is the middle classes and not the working classes who are doing most of the work: 'As the leisured class has become the overworked class and the working class now does far less work of any kind, the working class has more leisure than the middle class' (Hakim, 1996: 50).

[20]Consumption does not offer relief from alienation but is actually the post-production form of it. See for example Fine and Leopold, 1993; Keat et al., 1994; Ritzer, 1996; Mort, 1996; Slater, 1997b; and Bauman, 1998).

7

Identity crisis – workers versus consumers

PAID OCCUPATIONAL ROLES, UNPAID OCCUPATIONAL ROLES AND IDENTITY

In the previous chapter we looked at how identity is affected by the different kinds of activities which take place in the realms of work and of consumption, and at how these realms promote different kinds of class-or status-group-based expectations and activities. These experiences provide an important context within which people develop the mutual or collective dimensions of their identity. The issue we are considering in this chapter is that if people are becoming less dependent upon occupational role, and more reliant upon consumption-type behaviour, as a means of understanding and expressing who they are, how they should behave and where they fit into society, then what impact is this change likely to have on their sense of personal identity?

Occupation: the bedrock of personal identity in work-based society

First, and as the discussion in previous chapters has shown, the importance of occupational role in defining identity is one of the essential characteristics of work-based society. Occupational role is like other roles such as sibling, partner, parent in that it provides us with a means of developing and expressing ourselves as individuals through the medium of convenient and orderly pieces of social practice. Whilst personal identity is clearly affected by factors such as culture, ethnicity or gender, it is inevitable that if one is living in a form of society in which people are largely preoccupied with work, personal identity will be closely associated with the various occupational roles people take on.

In work-based society, the occupational hierarchy provides an indispensable guide as to where one stands in relation to others. Data on the distribution of people according to occupation provide sociologists with a representation of those relationships (we noted in the previous chapter for example, that sociological analyses of class and social mobility often set out from data on occupations). Moreover, since this mapping applies across the whole of the society in which a person lives (and in fact across all other economies of a similar type) a person can work out where they stand, not only in relation to people they actually come into contact with, but many whom they will never meet. I can as easily and accurately work out where I stand in relation to an airline pilot in Canada, as I can to a postman in Carmarthen, and quite irrespective of whether I have met either of them. Following Durkheim's observations about the role of the division of labour in maintaining social solidarity (Durkheim, 1933 [1893]), a knowledge of the positioning properties of the occupational hierarchy is not only helpful but entirely necessary if we wish to remain socially integrated. I might have some choice over which bit of the hierarchy I occupy, but the relation between this particular slot and all the other slots is entirely beyond my control.

Occupations for all

Second, and stemming directly from this, in a work-based society everyone has an occupation. The occupation/identity relationship thus affects everyone in that society irrespective of whether they are currently engaged in their occupation or not, and/or irrespective of whether that occupation is one for which they get paid. Although, conventionally, 'occupation' is taken to mean 'formal paid employment',[1] the term serves just as well to describe what occupies a person during the many hours of their non-resting and non-leisure time, and quite irrespective of whether it provides them with earned income or not. In a society saturated with work, there is no such thing as an unoccupied person. Everyone is classifiable by occupation. The occupational hierarchy has slots for those in occupations for which they get paid (the *Standard Occupation Classification* provides a comprehensive list), and if a person is temporarily not active in their usual occupation they are classified as 'unemployed', 'resting' or 'sick'. The non-paying occupational roles have labels such as 'child', 'student', 'housewife'/'househusband', 'retired' and so on.

When asked to state 'occupation' on an official document, it would be idiotic to put 'none' or 'not applicable' since plainly, everybody is doing something identifiable with their non-leisure time. All occupational roles are located somewhere within the occupational hierarchy and so they, and the people who fill them, can be compared quite directly with all other paid and unpaid occupational roles and their occupants. The capacity of the occupational hierarchy to provide an essential element of social stability is not at all affected by the fact that in other respects, unpaid occupational roles might not be regarded as particularly comparable with paid ones. In practice, in work-based society, all occupational roles are treated as if they are comparable.[2]

Looking a little more closely at non-paid occupational roles, particular attention has to be paid to the large number of people who are preoccupied with childcare responsibilities, domestic and family life. Trying to develop a sense of personal identity through these roles can pose difficulties for those concerned because, as we saw in Chapter 2, the economic rationality of work-based society dictates that paid occupational roles, and presumably the people doing them, are superior to those which do not yield income (Ransome, 1996). For as long as the prospects of economic and social advancement depend upon increasing the financial resources of the household, then it is rational to give priority to activities which produce income (Becker, 1981 and 1985). To do otherwise would mean challenging the whole idea that some occupations are better paid than others (no pay is after all just another kind of low pay). Even though people who are preoccupied with unpaid tasks and responsibilities in and around the home might in many ways be regarded as having a higher social standing than those in paid work, the comparison immediately breaks down when notions of status based on income are invoked. Not being on the pay roll dramatically reduces one's economic and social status however necessary, worthy, or fulfilling one's activity might be in other respects.

Without belabouring this point, it is not just housewives or househusbands who sometimes lack income-oriented forms of social status, but also those having other non-paying occupations such as students, those supported by welfare payments, even elderly and retired people. The more elevated a position people acquire by having a secure income, the more depressed are those who have none. As Glucksmann (2000), Hakim (2000) and others have continued to point out, as individuals or as members of households people need to find some kind of balance between paid and unpaid occupational roles since the outcomes of both kinds of activity are necessary for securing the survival and prosperity of the household. There is nothing irrational about doing unpaid domestic chores – since clearly households could not survive unless these tasks are done – but it would seem irrational to replace income-based notions of social status with some other notion reflecting the qualities and virtues of unpaid occupational roles within the household as this would simply alienate all those people who do associate income with status. It is important not to confuse the productivist (economic) rationality of income-getting with the (reproductivist) rationality (based on the desire to raise offspring in a clean safe and healthy environment) of doing things around the home which need to be done. The only way out of this dilemma it would seem, would be if an alternative means of provisioning the household became available thus weakening the link between paid occupational roles and social status. Conflicts over attributions of social status are complicated by the fact that people generally take on more than one occupational role. As we shall see when we look at the breadwinner role later in this chapter, one of the changes which has been taking place in work-based society is a weakening of the presumption that the paid occupational role a person has is always and everywhere the dominant feature in forming their personal identity.

As one would expect then, the occupational hierarchy is a flexible, even organic structure since obviously there is a constant displacement of out-dated roles (the diminishing status of clerical work during the twentieth century, or the demise of domestic service) and an influx of new ones (computer programmers in the 1980s or call-centre workers in the 1990s), and an ongoing interchange between paid and unpaid occupational roles (Gershuny, 2000; Hakim, 2000).[3] The stability of the hierarchy as a structuring feature of modern industrial societies is not particularly affected by changes in the precise contents of the various strata of which it is made. One of the key characteristics of work-based society – an essential part of its basic structure – is the presence of an occupational hierarchy with the capacity always to revert to a state of equilibrium. Even very considerable changes in the contents of the occupational hierarchy caused by paradigmatic shifts such as those brought about during the first (1760–1850) and second (1975–2005) industrial revolutions have been accommodated without any real threat being posed to the hierarchy itself.[4]

Occupation, identity and status

Third, and equally inevitable in work-based society, is the fact that the status-identity of an individual will be evaluated in terms of the rewards that are known to accompany particular occupational roles. Of first importance is whether the occupation offers an income, and at what level. In the market economy, income determines how elevated a position that role will have within the occupational hierarchy. The status of the person having that occupational role is also directly determined by the level of income which comes with the occupational role they fill. The greater a person's level of income the more easily they can satisfy their survival needs. Prosperity (or happiness as Mr Micawber would put it) is simply a measure of how much distance there is between income and necessary expenditure. As we have described it in earlier chapters, 'affluent' is the name we commonly give to people and households which are routinely able to exceed their basic expectations and to consume for pleasure and enjoyment. Occupational roles which provide income are more highly valued than those which do not. Those which pay more are more highly valued than those paying less because higher pay suggests that they will provide household members with better opportunities for survival, prosperity and complex consumption.[5]

Occupation, identity and lifestyle

Fourth, the status differential which holds between one occupational role and another (or of one class or group of occupational roles and another group or class) is also constructed in terms of differences in the lifestyles of different occupational/income groups. Income obviously affects the degree of choice and control the household has over the kind of lifestyle it can afford to adopt. Although it seems probable that there will be broad similarities between households having comparable levels of disposable income – that there will be an evident similarity between all low-income households, or all middle-income households in their manner of living, we can further speculate that the degree of variation between households in the same income bracket becomes greater as the level of income rises. The lifestyles of low-income households are likely to be more similar one to the other than the lifestyles of high-level income households. To the extent that these categorisations depend mostly on income, and that income mostly comes from earnings, we can see another important sense in which occupation determines lifestyle. If we replace the term 'lifestyle' with the term 'class' one might say that the impact of occupational role on class position is more direct and predictable for people filling low-income, low-grade and thus low-status occupational roles than it is of people holding mid- or high-status occupational roles. And it would not be surprising to find that class analysts have become increasingly pre-occupied with 'the middle classes' amongst whom, clearly, there is a much greater variation in occupational groupings (Marshall, 1997; Crompton, 1998; Savage, 2000).

Work-lifestyle choice

In addition to its impact on income, status and style of life, the occupational hierarchy also affects a characteristic which we can call work-lifestyle choice. A knowledge of the broad distinctions which persist between different types of economic activity and different types of identity are revealed in the different terms such as 'occupation', 'trade' and 'job' which people use in referring to them. Hierarchically speaking, 'occupation' connotes some degree of professional status and expertise in the work that a person does, whilst 'job' connotes a more casual and lower category of paid activity. Professionals describe the bits of work they have as 'cases' and 'projects'; non-professionals just do 'the job'. Arguably, 'occupation' plays a more significant or dominant role in the identity of a solicitor than 'the job' does for someone employed as an unskilled labourer. The building-site worker obviously sees the income-getting side of themselves in these terms – labourerness is part of their occupational identity – but the flavour of their working activity carries over less into other aspects of who they are. For others on the building site, such as the plumber and the electrician, and even more so for the architect and surveyor, their trade or profession is much more integral to who they are. Having invested heavily in their occupational status, they naturally expect to get something pretty significant back from it. Somewhere between the apex of professionalism and the broad base of unskilled labouring are the various strata of the experienced unskilled, the semi-skilled, the skilled, those with recognised trades, craftspeople, and white-collar workers through the range from routine to complex tasks.

The association of level of skill and expertise with position in the hierarchy draws attention to another important aspect of work-lifestyle choice which is that the greater the level of skill and refinement required, the more easily a person can disassociate themselves from the particular task in hand. The occupational identity of those doing the least skilled tasks is more transient or insecure and needs to be made over again and again as each task is performed. Working identity in this stratum barely survives the task being performed. The occupational identity of the most highly skilled craftsman or professional on the other hand, remains much more separate from any particular instance of their work. The durability and purchase of occupational identity therefore, does not remain constant throughout the hierarchy but varies in form and intensity according to the level of skill or expertise required in that occupation. In this sense, and much like the benefits of having elaborated rather than restricted codes of speech, that portion of overall identity which is made up by the occupational role is more transferable for some people than it is for others. Being more transferable, its traits and characteristics are more likely to be expressed in all the activity of that person and not just whilst they are 'at work' (DuGay, 1996)

Another view of this situation can be had by looking at a list of occupations such as the *Standard Occupational Classification* used by statisticians in the United Kingdom, the number of sub-divisions increases as you move up the hierarchy. 'Unskilled labourer' has very few sub-divisions – it is a lumpen category, whilst 'professional-managerial' has many more and is an individualised or 'individuated' (Jenkins, 1996) category. The opportunity which work-tasks offer people to build and express their identity varies through the hierarchy. Deprived of opportunities to express their identity through work, people in the lower tiers of the occupational hierarchy necessarily have to look progressively outside work in order to do so. Their identities are thus less distinctly work-based.

To the extent that a work-based society is the kind of place where work- or occupation-based sources of identity are particularly highly valued, the 'outside-work' sources might be regarded as comparatively trivial or insignificant. The labourer who is the leading goal scorer for the local football team, will still be largely located within the occupational hierarchy as 'labourer' rather than within a leisure hierarchy as 'striker'. In work-based society, the occupational hierarchy outranks all other social hierarchies. The celebrity status of the highest-paid sportsmen and sportswomen in no way guarantees that they will be taken particularly seriously by other more conventionally employed professionals.

The benefits and risks of occupational roles

If work-based society presumes a close association between identity and occupational role, to be without a clear occupation, and moreover one in which one is actively engaged and from which one earns an income, means that a person is going to be regarded as something of a lightweight in the identity stakes or that the identity they are developing will not be entirely suited to the requirements of a paid occupational role. This does not mean that people who develop their personal identities in ways other than through paid occupations are bad people or social failures, but that in doing less well in the world of employment (where more deliberately work-oriented kinds of personal identity are likely to be more successful) they will end up occupying lower status positions in the mainstream social hierarchy. They may occupy a superior position in an alternative or minority hierarchy – perhaps of the itinerant craftsman or entertainer, or 'the ever-popular tortured artist' – but not in the mainstream, conventional work-oriented social hierarchy which the majority recognises and approves.

Neither does the presence of a dominant social hierarchy mean that people are forever trapped in one kind of social hierarchy or another. At different times and for different purposes we may switch between one role and another and between one code and another. In his analysis of the 'romantic ethic' for example, Campbell suggests that: '… the romantic and rational-utilitarian values are serially institutionalised in the life-cycle of bourgeois man …' (Campbell, 1987: 224) meaning that over time, individuals move from one ethic to another depending on their immediate needs. The bohemian youth turns into the conservative adult. (An argument we shall be examining shortly is that one of the most important identity-related features of consumption is that it opens up a wide range of artistic/aesthetic social hierarchies for people to participate in.)

Losing work, losing identity

The importance particularly of paid occupational roles is most vividly demonstrated by those who are unable to find or retain paid employment (Ransome, 1995; Gallie et al., 1998). To be actively employed in one's occupational role brings social status, honour and prestige; to be unemployed deprives a person of these crucially important social markers. The unemployed or insecurely employed person runs the risk of losing these ingredients of their sense-of-self. There is no honour or positive social status in being unemployed; it connotes failure and anti-identity. Being unemployed without wishing to be renders one socially invisible. Research has repeatedly uncovered a direct association between loss of work and a powerful sense of loss of identity: 'Discussions of human consequences of unemployment are full of references to how it lowers self-esteem, saps self-confidence, undermines self-reliance, induces self-disgust, heightens self-consciousness, and so on – all of which cumulatively implies a profound change in the individual's self-concept' (Kalvin and Jarrett, 1985: 44); 'several studies of people anticipating and experiencing unemployment have found that these people suffer loss of self-esteem, loss of personal identity, worry and uncertainty about the future, loss of a sense of purpose, and depression' (Keefe, 1984: 265). Other well-documented consequences of loss of identity through loss of work include increases in stress leading to physical and psychological illness, while for some a total collapse of a sense of identity can lead to the ultimate abandonment of self through suicide (Fineman (ed.), 1987; Gallie et al. (eds), 1993; Hayes and Nutman, 1981; Nicholas, 1986; Portwood, 1985; Ransome, 1995; R. Smith, 1987; Westergaard et al., 1989).

The persistence of the impact of occupational role on identity can also be seen in considering the situation of a retired person for whom occupational identity is in abeyance (Lyon, 1987; Bond and Coleman (eds), 1990). Clearly, retired people continue to rely upon their previous occupational role (whether paid or not) as a basis for their personal identity but with less immediacy than formerly. To the extent that a person is able to enjoy a comfortable retirement because their working life has been active and prosperous, then they are continuing to enjoy both the material and the psychological benefits of their previous occupational role. They can also set themselves free from full dependence on their former occupational role because they have both the time and financial resources to do other things and thus to alter the basis of their identity. In stark contrast is the situation of the person whose working life has not been sufficiently successful for them to liberate themselves from their basic material needs. Rather than using their former occupational roles as a springboard for something new, they are obliged to continue to see themselves through the lens of their former occupation simply because they have done little else. Assuming that the work they used to do was done mainly to provide the bare necessities, then they are doubly trapped as they must continue to see themselves as someone who has yet to meet these needs. Although they are now without an active occupational role, they are still occupied with meeting their needs.

Although then, the link between occupational and personal identity can be a positive thing, it does entail certain risks. There are winners and losers in the occupational hierarchy. One only has to consider how doubly damaging loss of work has been to the identities of those formerly employed in industries such as mining, ship building or steel manufacture, where people have lost not only their own particular jobs but any opportunity of expressing their chosen occupational identity. Being an unemployed miner in a district where mining no longer takes place presents the severest test not only of loss of occupational identity but of identity as a whole (Fricke (ed.), 1973; Newby, 1979; Beynon (ed.), 1985; Harris, 1987; Morris, 1995). Similarly, and given what we have just been saying about work-lifestyle identity, there is some evidence to suggest that being an unemployed professional is more harmful to identity than is being an out-of-work unskilled worker.[6] If one expects one's employment to be mainly short-term, intermittent and unreliable, then one might invest less heavily in the identity/ occupation axis. Of necessity, the range of jobs one might take on is likely to be quite broad and alternative sources of income might be sought by engaging with the black economy. Whatever the financial impacts of unemployment might be for different individuals and households, identity is certainly affected, and especially so for those who have invested most heavily in their occupational identities (Pahl, 1995).

Summary

Different types of occupational role then, offer different kinds of opportunities for the expression of personal identity, differences which result partly from the characteristics of the tasks involved, partly from the expectations and motivations of the person doing those tasks which that occupation requires, and partly from the styles of life and work-lifestyle which are typically associated with people who occupy the various occupational strata. People are aware of these differences and, given the closeness of the occupational role/identity relationship, the process of making occupational choices already tells us something about a person's identity. If a person desires or requires an occupational role which will bring reasonable rewards, and invests heavily through education and training in order to achieve this, they are much more likely to end up in superior position in the hierarchy (more pay, greater autonomy and variety at work and in lifestyle, higher status) than a person who does not seek a well-paid, or just a paid occupational role at all. The superior social status associated with top occupational and especially professional-occupational roles is seen as a reward for the hard work that has gone into securing those positions. It also serves to legitimate the liberal-pluralist perception of society as an essentially meritocratic place where privilege and social standing are not inherited but are earned through hard work.

Relatedly, and also directly reflecting the proportion of time and energy which has gone into achieving this position (number of years in school, higher education, professional training, etc.), the personal identities of high achievers in well-paid occupational roles are likely to be more closely associated with their occupational identities than those who do not invest so much. The differentiation between higher and lower occupations, and the status differentiation it creates between their occupants is what renders occupational differentiation hierarchic. It is of course in the interests of those occupying higher positions and thus enjoying greater social status to maintain the differential between themselves and those below. They will actively seek to protect the considerable personal investment they made to gain an elite occupational role.

This is not to suggest that people who have occupational roles at the base of the hierarchy always positively desire them, or that it is equally easy for everyone to climb the ladder towards occupational success, paid or otherwise, since clearly some people end up in largely unrewarding positions for reasons which might be beyond their control. Many people are just not in a position to choose a paid occupation at all.[7] What we are saying here however, is that higher-grade, often professional occupational roles cannot be had *without* making considerable investments of time and effort. One can be grossly over-qualified for a low-grade or unpaid occupational role but it is much less common to find grossly under-qualified people in top professional positions. Being secure and well-paid in one's occupational role is no longer something which happens by accident of birth, treaty, plunder or conquest. The Protestant career- and work-ethics gain much of their legitimacy from the fact that real tangible and sometimes substantial rewards actually do come from achieving high-paying, high-status occupational roles.

GENDER IDENTITY AND OCCUPATIONAL ROLES

The homemaker and the getter of income

Having looked at the general features of the occupational hierarchy and the relationship between occupational roles and identity, we now need to look at particular instances of these processes. How do different kinds of occupational role actually and specifically affect personal identity? At the risk of jumping in at the deep end, we will illustrate our general case for the way occupation affects identity by looking at one particular instance of this relationship, that is the association of occupational role with gender identity.

Whatever else they may signify in terms of identity, occupational roles certainly provide valuable opportunities to express a sense of gender-identity, that is, to exhibit patterns of behaviour which are recognisably either typically male or typically female according to conventions currently in place (Crompton, 2001). In the following discussion 'gender' will be defined as a pattern of behaviour which is generally taken to be associated with biological sex. With the exception of the very specific activities which can only be performed by a person having one biological sex or the other, it is accepted that these associations are socially constructed.[8] To illustrate this part of the discussion we can usefully refer to research recently carried out in South Wales which interviewed people from three different organisations to investigate gender and job insecurity. The relevance of the data to this discussion is that it sheds light on perceptions of paid and unpaid occupational roles and how they relate to gender.[9]

We will begin by making a number of comments about the general association between occupational role and identity. This is a complex domain for analysis because the association between gender and occupational roles circulates around and between a series of uncomfortable and difficult to resolve loops of practice and signification. For example, to what extent do people acquire particular elements of their gender identity from their occupational role and to what extent do occupational roles reflect characteristics associated with the gender of the people who typically carry then out? If a person is inclined to align their sense of personal identity with an occupational role which is 'appropriate' for them in the sense that current social convention marks it up as a 'male' or 'female' role, then they will gravitate towards occupational roles which match their gender. If, on the other hand, they want to develop their personal identity by challenging the conventional associations of gender with occupation, they might well make occupational choices which run contrary to these conventions. If sufficient people do this, then this might result in a change in the gender-marking of that occupational role (for example the feminisation of clerical work which, in the nineteenth century, was regarded as a male profession, see Lockwood, 1989).

In terms of the social status of the occupied person, who is to say whether one occupation is regarded as more prestigious because of the gender of the people who typically fill this kind of (paid or unpaid) occupational role, or whether one gender is regarded as having a higher social status than the other because of the kind of work that people of that gender do? The fact that women spend more time than men caring for others does not mean that only women can take on these occupational roles, but it does reinforce the general expectation that carers are female. For as long as large numbers of women continue to carry out the activities of carer, it is convenient (even if ideological) to continue to assume that they are predisposed to act in this way. The pitfalls in this area of analysis are many and deep.[10]

Blood, sweat and toil

However these dilemmas might be resolved it is generally accepted that occupation provides a central constituent of a person's sense of gender. Activities within the realm of paid occupations provide men with an extremely powerful forum for establishing and expressing basic elements of what it is to be male. Conversely, activities within the domestic realm, and particularly those involving the care of children provide many women with an important means of expressing what it is to be female (Butler, 1990; Griffiths, 1995). Seidler has suggested for example, that '[Men] no longer have a sense of self which exists separately from our sense of male identity. We are so anxious as boys to prove that we are *not* girls ... that we come to identify our sense of self directly with our sense of male identity' (Seidler, 1989: 18).

One of the central ways of expressing a male self, of being a man is through having a paid occupational role. To the extent that agricultural production and early-industrial production in the West required that a high proportion of the workforce not only perform but begin to specialise in physically demanding tasks, a clear association was established between men and physically demanding occupational roles, and, with the coincidental spread of wage-labouring, of men with income-getting (Pahl, 1984; Tilly and Scott, 1987). Although the association of manliness with physical work and income-getting has become more tenuous, first as many fewer people have physically-demanding occupational roles and second because women make a more forthright contribution to household income, does not mean that the breadwinner stereotype has fallen from use; it has simply become more and more ideological (Ransome, 1999).[11]

If one's sense of personal identity as a male is constructed largely or entirely in terms of a successful performance of a paid occupational role, then one of the reasons why loss of occupation is so catastrophic for men is precisely because it deprives them of part of the foundations of their sense of who they are. Asked to describe what the consequences would be for her husband if he lost his job, one of the respondents to the South Wales study replied:

> I think it would knock his confidence, especially if he was made redundant. He's always worked since he left school and college. He's never been out of work. He's never been on the dole, and I don't think he ever wants to be really. Out of choice. I don't think so. I think he feels he's got self-respect when he's working full-time. He would lose that. I think he'd lose all his self-respect, he would. (42-year-old female part-time general assistant/checkout operator, 017B)

On your own two feet

A second important aspect of the breadwinner/male identity association picks up deeply-embedded ideas about the importance of self-reliance and individuality which developed following the Protestant Reformation in Europe particularly during the seventeenth and eighteenth centuries. In combination with Enlightenment notions of the superiority of reason over emotion, men not only identified themselves with an unending responsibility for providing for themselves and their households, but insisted that this productivist orientation towards life, was the only rational and reasoned way to proceed (Seidler, 1989. See also Winter and Robert, 1980; Giddens, 1991; Rojek, 1995; and Connell, 1995). Success in this effort, both inwardly as measured against one's conscience (saving one's soul), and outwardly as measured against one's social and material status (saving one's capital), became a signifier of other highly valued attributes such as psychological integrity perseverance, endurance and stamina (Seidler, 1989: 50–143). Within the Protestant psyche, the aspect of (male) personal identity aimed at pragmatic self-reliance is complemented by a spiritual aspect wherein the individual also takes responsibility for their own spiritual salvation (Weber, 1976; Marshall, 1982; Campbell, 1987).

This view was strongly expressed by other respondents in South Wales:

> Traditionally [the man] is the breadwinner … . he is the responsible one, the head of the family. And should be taking care of his wife and he's the provider in real terms. Traditionally I [am the breadwinner]

... since we've been married I've always had the senior, or the better paid job and more stable job. [its] my responsibility and psychologically I will always be a man ... . it's up to me to provide. (57-year old male part-time general assistant, 0028B)

In successfully performing the provider/breadwinner role then, men are confirming one of the key markers of what it means to be male. Particularly in work-based society, not being a successful provider, or not being a provider at all, signifies an immanent and possibly imminent failure of male identity. This is not to say that Western male personal identity is exclusively and always based on the performance of a demanding occupational role, but to acknowledge that this is the background from which it has developed in work-based society. If carried out successfully, the provider role also enabled a person (in principle of either gender but in practice usually a man) to develop a particularly robust and public sense of *individuality* based on their capacity for self-sufficiency and thus independence. Since the provider role necessarily requires active, visible and public engagement with a paid occupational role (very few can provide without earned income, and very few paid occupational roles are private), the notion of individuality developed through the breadwinner role inevitably demonstrates a high level of adaptation to the demands of living in a work-based society.

Given the wide range of other (paid and unpaid, public and non-public) occupational roles which are available to people however, other kinds of individuality have also developed. Most important is that associated with people (in principle of either gender but in practice usually women) who are primarily involved with provisioning roles in and around the household. In addition to the fact that the tasks performed as part of the domestic occupational role require many of the same skills and competences found in the public sphere of paid occupations, and that they might equally need to demonstrate spiritual cleanliness though good works, their individuality and the recognition and status which stems from it, is reflected in the status and social standing of the household taken as a whole rather than in terms of them as a distinct individual within that household. A mature-age female respondent to the South-Wales study is quite clear that: 'Home life ... is more satisfying than work .... you take pride in what you do, you know. It reflects you. Your home reflects what you are and who you are' (68-year old female, part-time general assistant, 0018B). (Interestingly, and in addition to this apparently home-centred sense of identity, this respondent also reported having a particularly rich and varied working life including running small businesses like shops and public houses.)

To the extent that men (and many women) have got into the habit of assuming that the public provisioning role, and the particular version of self-reliant individuality which goes with it, falls to men, the notion of the successful, independent provider has come to be seen as an attribute of persons of the male rather than of the female gender. The public/independent/self-sufficient ideal of individuality is associated more with men than with women because these are the attributes of paid occupational roles, and it is men who more often than not have taken on the most demanding and rewarding paid occupational roles. At the same time, an alternative version of individuality, one which also draws heavily on pragmatic self-reliance and independence but which is less dependent upon the public sphere for its expression and fulfilment, has been generally associated with persons of the female gender because, more often than not, it is women who have taken on the most demanding and rewarding unpaid occupational roles. In speaking of the different versions of individuality associated respectively with Protestantism and Romanticism, Campbell suggests that women might be the primary bearers of the romantic ethic and men of the puritan one. Within the household, the child aspires to live up to the expectations of the hard-working father, whilst being nurtured in the comfortable and comforting bosom of the mother who emphasises emotional expression, sensitivity, empathy and so on: '… modern individuals [especially those in the middle-classes] inhabit not just an "iron cage" of economic necessity, but a castle of romantic dreams, striving through their conduct to turn the one into the other' (Campbell, 1987: 227).

Over time however, and as more women take on a shared if not leading role as income-getter for the household, and as more men are attracted to the less public varieties of individuality and independence found in the domestic realm, stereotypical presumptions that male identity is inevitably linked with breadwinning and that female identity is inevitably linked with home-making will gradually weaken (Crompton, 1997). As Bradley et al., put it: 'Employment is becoming increasingly important in women's lives as they strive for independence and self-fulfilment' (Bradley et al., 2000: 91). A 42-year old general assistant working part-time clearly expresses the sense of independence which comes from having a paid occupation role:

> I've got my own wages, you know and a bit of independence. I don't like relying on my partner for everything, you know. I like the independence, I like being able to run my own car … I can go without going cap in hand to him. Ask him for money all the time … I enjoy working, you know, I feel better when I'm working … more self respect [and] pride then. (017B)

Women, occupation and identity

One of the impressions that comes across quite consistently from the South Wales study is that male identity is seen by women as being heavily dependent on having a job:

> He wants to be the main breadwinner. I think it would knock his confidence, especially if he was made redundant. He's always worked since he left school and college. He's never been out of work. He's never been on the dole, and I don't think he ever wants to be really. Out of choice. I think he feels he's got self-respect when he's working full-time. (42-year old female part-time general assistant, 0017B)

A similar view was expressed by a 53-year old female part-time customer assistant:

> It's a status thing innit? A man having a job? I think that my husband is proud of the fact that he's got the job albeit it's a menial job ... And I'm proud of the fact that he's working, know what I mean? There's a lot of blokes there that's not working that want a job and can't get one ... they're proud that they're doing their bit. (0015B)

Although this is exactly what one would expect since obviously the whole notion of the male breadwinner assumes that this is the case, what is more surprising, and a little depressing, is that a number of the female respondents portray their men folk as not really having anything else to base their identity on other than their paid occupational role:

> I feel quite sorry for my husband sometimes. He's home all the time because of his health and I'm working. Poor bugger. He'd like to be out and about if he could. It must be horrible to be stuck in there all the time and that's why I go home for my dinner because I only live by the hedge. I go home for my break – which is only half an hour – but I think I might as well go and keep him company for half an hour and I go home for dinner. He has my dinner ready for me and we sit down and have a cup of tea and a chat. (48-year old female full-time receptionist/trainer with disabled husband at home, 001B)

Men are portrayed in these responses as either having a job and thus an identity, or not having a job and thus no identity, and no prospect of developing one either. Although respondents were not asked to expand on the other kinds of interests and activities that their (male) partners might be involved with, there is very little spontaneous comment about these other kinds of activities apart from the occasional reference to voluntary work. In fact when instances of past redundancy were recalled, the emphasis was very much on all the effort which was put into finding an alternative paid occupational role and certainly not on exploring non-paying alternatives.

In contrast to this a number of female respondents (and largely irrespective of whether they are working full- or part-time, and of whether they are the leading income-getter) portray themselves, and often women in general, as having a much more multi-dimensional route into developing and expressing their identity. They might choose to work. They might have to work for financial reasons, but they consistently report that if they are not working, then they can fall back towards, and, depending on their position in the lifecycle, return to, unpaid occupational roles within the domestic realm in order to consolidate their sense of personal identity. A number of respondents are quite certain that women have more of a choice than men, that their identities are more stable than those of men (in general and particularly) because they have at least two realms of occupational role which they can take on:

> *Would you say that home life and working life are equally as important to you*? Yes, they are equally as important. Obviously, for it to go smoothly I've got be working to have money ... They are both dependent on each other really? Having the job allows you to do things at home and whatever. *Do you get the same sense of satisfaction from working and what you get out of your home life*? Oh yes, I enjoy it. Now, like I say, I'm in a different job and it's a challenge. Something new to me, and something that I am enjoying. (28-year old female in-store part-time laundry person, 022B)

One of the interesting aspects of this one-dimensional versus multi-dimensional strategy of identity formation, is that for many women it enables them to get along with a more realistic and thus less fragile perception of the importance of paid occupational role for personal identity. Female respondents often reported that even though they might be earning higher incomes than their male partners, and that their income is vital to household finances, they feel that it would be more important for the man to regain employment if lost than for the woman:

> I will say that I'd rather *he* was out working and me at home ... because a man is the person who thinks that *they* should be the one, the breadwinner. Because that was the killer to start. He thought he was letting us down. That was a year of hell ... he thought, 'Why the hell is *she* having to go out there to work when I've got to be here with the kids?' ... I think the man looks upon himself to be the breadwinner.

> But those days have got to go now anyway, I think. Because you've got a lot of househusbands today anyway, and you've got to pull together. Or its not going to work. You've got to pull together. (48-year old female full-time receptionist/trainer with disabled husband at home, 001B)

With further probing, respondents typically explain this apparently irrational view by saying that because men are so dependent on work for their sense of who they are, they are less able to cope with loss of employment than women. Women cope better because, unlike men, not all their identity-eggs are in the paid-occupational-role basket. (The rationality operating here is that both emotionally and financially, supporting and restoring an identity-light male partner would represent an even greater strain on the woman's and thus the household's resources than would loss of financial income alone.)

The consequences for personal identity of combining paid and unpaid occupational roles is not always straightforward. Referring back to the responses of the apparently work-centred female respondent quoted above (017B), later in the same interview she also displayed characteristics of home-centredness:

> Well my family comes first. You know, they've gotta come first. My home life comes first. That's why I wouldn't go for [promotion] … because of the stress in work, I don't want it really. I like a job where I can just come in, do my job, go home, and not have to worry, you know? I wouldn't like to be going home and worrying about my work. You know, in the evenings. I don't want it sort of, erm, I don't want it coming into my home life if you know what I mean. I want it to be separate. (42-year old general assistant working part-time, 017B)

These apparent contradictions appear quite often in the South Wales data and indicate that in reflecting on their sense of personal identity women and men might as it were, alter their angle of view depending on the issue being addressed (in the manner perhaps, that one rotates an object to look at it from different points-of-view). When asked about 'work' they present the work-centred aspect of their identity; when asked about 'home' they present its home-centred aspect. This combination might not always and for everyone be an easy compromise since, as Charles and James find in their analysis of the same data set: '… when women's paid work was part of their identity it was defined as separate from (and potentially in conflict with) their identity as wife or mother. Paid work was an assertion of themselves as individuals as opposed to being a mother, wife or housewife' (Charles and James, 2003: 250).

This does not mean of course that the work commitment of women who are in paid occupational roles is less than it is amongst men (Hakim, 2000; Crompton and Harris, 1998; Charles and James, 2003), but it might help explain why, for the many women who choose not to take on paid occupational roles (individuals who might fall into the 'home-centred' category in Hakim's typology), or are quite content to combine a full-time commitment to the domestic sphere with a part-time commitment to a paid occupational role (individuals who might fall into the 'adaptive' category), they do not suffer a crisis of gender-identity as a result. Similarly, and although they are still in a minority, the prospect of switching between an identity based on paid occupational role and an identity based on unpaid occupational roles does not seem to be a barrier for men who want to express their home-centredness.

Breadwinning, income-getting and homemaking revisited

As far as the relationship between occupational role and gender is concerned, although it is undoubtedly the case that most women and men 'do not have one central life interest' and that home- and work-centredness 'is expressed in gendered ways' (Charles and James, 2003: 255), these ways of expression (primarily for men going out to work and taking on the provider role, primarily for women continuing to take major responsibility for the household and the carer role) continue to manifest themselves through traditional associations of role with gender. As an interim measure however, whilst people are coming to terms with the potential confusions of identity caused by shifts in the nature and allocation of these roles and responsibilities, the idea of 'breadwinner' might be separated from the role of income-getter. Thus women in households who earn more than their husbands or male partners, might still refer to them as 'the breadwinner' in a social or psychological sense even though economically these men do not actually bring home all of the bacon. Breadwinners still 'provide' but not always and simply by delivering the highest incomes. They also bring essential psychological and physical benefits to the household through their practical and parenting skills, and through companionship and moral support. Conversely, homemakers still deliver the children, and help cook, wash and clean for them, but not always and simply by staying at home. They also trade their practical skills and competences for income in the public realm. The pattern of their engagement with paid occupational roles might not be the same as it has traditionally been for most men, but this in no way lessens its significance as part-and-parcel of making the home.

Whilst it is clearly ridiculous to suggest that the structures of paid and unpaid occupational roles, and the various income, status and lifestyle hierarchies associated with them are suddenly going to disappear (not least because people – men and women, have already invested very heavily in them and would not want to give them up until or unless alternative structures bearing equivalent statuses developed), there are indications that people are becoming more imaginative in their articulation of occupational role with personal identity and with gender.

Discussing the nature of masculine identity for example, Connell suggests that rather than treating perceptions of appropriate roles and behaviours as 'pre-existing norms which are passively internalised and enacted' i.e. that gender is just something which is 'already there', a more autonomous and proactive approach is that these stereotypical assumptions and the categories through which they operate are not inevitable: 'Masculinities are configurations of practice structured by gender relations. They are inherently historical; and their making and remaking is a political process affecting the balance of interests in society and the direction of social change' (Connell, 1995: 35–44).

By taking on paid occupational roles women might be 'feminising' the nature and content of the tasks which those roles require for example by changing styles of decision-making or on how particular tasks are carried out (although some observers are quite sceptical about whether 'feminisation' in any really meaningful sense is happening at all).[12] Much more importantly however, women are in some cases widening, and in other cases consolidating, the base upon which they develop their sense of personal identity. The point is not so much to change the marker of the paid occupational role from 'male' to 'female' as to enlarge the category 'female' to include the denotation 'person who becomes socially recognisable on account of the paid occupational role they take on'. Once everyone has access to paid occupational roles, occupancy of those roles would no longer signify 'gender'.[13]

These changes might also undermine the automatic association of self-sufficiency, determination and so on with the expression of a male rather than female gender, and of the apparent superiority of the public/independent/self-sufficient version of individuality which goes along with it. A new perception might emerge that all forms of individuality are equally worthwhile as vehicles for the expression of personal identity. Although it is certainly premature to suggest that the divide between paid and unpaid occupational roles is about to collapse just because a few people are 'breaking the rules' the fact that virtually the whole concept of 'gender' is socially constructed certainly nudges us towards accepting that the boundaries between one kind of social role and another can and do change over time.

In order to transgress the work-centred/home-centred dichotomy and its association with persons of one gender or the other, two things need to happen. First, and as Gershuny (2000) has suggested might already be happening, the propensity for persons of one gender always to perform one kind of occupational role needs to reduce (the duality becomes a dualism). Second, and as Hakim (2000) has suggested, additional categories need to be recognised giving space for expressions of personal identity but without the gender-baggage which accompanies existing roles (the choice is no longer limited to one or other kind of 'centredness' but includes various kinds of 'adaptation'). Crompton has recently suggested for example, that a key factor in the (largely socially constructed) 'gender order' or 'gender regime' in late-modern society comes from the gender relations of the division of labour, and that these relations can usefully be seen in terms of a continuum ranging from the 'traditional' male breadwinner/female carer model at one end, to the 'less traditional' dual earner/dual carer scenario at the other. She concludes that:

> [The] erosion of the male-breadwinner model might be followed by a number of possible alternatives – there is not going to be 'one best way' of organising the gender division of labour that meets every possible set of circumstances ... . The most stable solution overall might be some version of a dual-earner/dual-carer model, backed up by some kind of state or collective provision. (Crompton (ed.), 2001: 213)

IDENTITY IN CONSUMPTION-BASED SOCIETY

Given that the boundaries of paid and unpaid occupational roles are shifting in the ways just described, and that to some extent at least, the significance of these roles in the formation of identity and of gender might be reducing, one is bound to ask what other sources of identity are available to people? Does a decline in the importance of occupational roles mean that people in late-modern society have less identity, or does it mean that they are drawing it from other parts of their lives? For the remainder of this chapter we will consider whether the role of 'consumer' might be displacing the role of (paid or unpaid) 'worker' as the primary source of identity.

Less work, more play

In the age of affluence people have increasingly come to realise that although occupational role is an important marker of identity and of gender the latter are not reducible to the former. Personal identity is no longer slave or servant to the occupational role but reflects more evenly the range of activities and interests they are involved with, not least in the realm of consumption. Describing the emergence of this way of looking at things, Mort suggests that: 'Carrying the significance which once had been ascribed to work, it was argued that consumption had now come to occupy the 'cognitive focus of life' ... Self-reflexivity – the cultivation of the self, physically as well as psychologically – was understood to be enshrined in the current orchestration of consumption' (Mort, 1996: 6). There are a number of stages in this progression.

The first stage is the simple fact that under conditions of affluent consumption, people are able to spend an increasing proportion of their energy and resources doing things other than work. As we have already seen, a good deal of this additional time is now being spent on activities in the realm of complex consumption. Where activity leads so identity will surely follow and thus the balance of experiences out of which people develop their identities tilts away from the experience of producing things and towards the experience of consuming them. If one wishes to retain a rich notion of personal identity and yet also wants to claim that (especially paid) occupational role makes less of a contribution than it used to, then the ever-expanding realm of consumption is an obvious place to look for alternative sources of identity.[14]

Affluence and identity-rich consumption

Second, the major sites of increasing consumption are not (as they were during the 1950s and early 1960s) devoted to buying more and more of the basic necessities on which physical well-being depends (a capacity which has already been far exceeded in the West), but on purchasing new kinds of goods and leisure services the utility of which is measured in terms of satisfaction at the more elaborate or symbolic end of the scale: 'A "poor" society is one which must devote the bulk of its time to low-value-added activities ... Economic development [...] allows the society to shift its time progressively towards production and consumption activities relating to more sophisticated wants' (Gershuny, 2000: 19). Increasing choice allows greater discernment, not just for the wealthy minority who have always been able to underscore their elevated social position through consumption of expensive items, but for the majority. The shift towards complex consumption, added to a burgeoning desire to express identity through participation in pleasure-giving leisure-consumption gives further impetus to the volume and quality of consumption available to people:

> Rising overall affluence and changing production methods have provided both the desire and the means to move away from mass-produced products and hence mass consumption. In this environment less status accrues from the simple ability to buy goods and services, but more from what specifically is bought and how that is different from what others buy. This has resulted in the increasingly fragmentary nature of consumption. (Stewart, 1992: 217)

As we saw in Chapter 5, this transition from consuming things associated with simple necessities towards consuming things which satisfy new or acquired needs has been used within the Fordism/post-Fordism debate to help explain why the mass consumption of the 1950s and 1960s has been superseded by the individualised consumption of bespoke commodities during the 1980s and 1990s. It is no longer sufficient to be able to purchase the same goods and services as everyone else; it is the differences in the choices we make and the things we buy which make us different. Mass consumer goods are now only 'mass' in terms of how they are produced but not in terms of how they are consumed. Production in the late-modern period emphasises variety and difference but without abandoning economies of scale.

In these arguments we find a clear and direct association not only between the production and consumption of things but a change in the presumed direction of this relationship. Broadly speaking, and following our earlier line of argument, one would say that consumption remains the servant of production while commodities are consumed in order to satisfy basic needs because one cannot negotiate away one's basic needs. I need bread to eat and will thus consume bread in whatever form the producer wishes to sell it to me. However, once consumption takes place mainly for pleasure and enjoyment (once pleasure becomes the object of enjoyment), the direction is reversed as producers have to respond to changes in consumer demand for this kind, colour or shape of product rather than that one. Fordism is needs driven and producer led whilst post-Fordism is desire driven and consumer led. We can note then, that there is a very substantial difference between societies which mainly produce subsistence goods and societies which produce things which are mainly consumed for pleasure.

The central factor which triggers the transition from one form of producer-society to another form of producer-society is affluence. One could actually define 'affluence' as the condition which renders a subsistence-producing society into a society characterised by choice. Reiterating an earlier point, we can also note that these changes in the nature of consumption tend first to stimulate rather than inhibit production (they do not signal 'the end of work') and second, they indicate the emergence of an increasingly sophisticated kind of consumer: 'The high-value-added society must collectively develop new high-value-added occupational specialities and matching new high-value-added consumption habits … as the range of services increases, consumption patterns necessarily become more diverse, there is more scope for personal choice …' (Gershuny, 2000: 29).

Consumption as identity

Moving up the hierarchy of complex consumption from affluent consumption and towards conspicuous and symbolic consumption, the third stage in the putative ascendancy of consumption as a source of identity has been to use consumption as a clear and deliberate route towards the formation of personal identity; 'Consumption has ceased to be purely material or narrowly functional – the satisfaction of basic bodily needs. Today consumption is both symbolic and material. It expresses, in a real sense, a person's place in the world, his or her core identity' (Stewart, 1992: 204 drawing on Gardner and Sheppard, 1989: 3). Consumption can directly affect identity because of the kind of activity it is. As we saw in Chapter 5, acts of consumption provide the terminus for the strings of productive activities which preceded them. In consumer society, consumption is the pleasure dividend to which our previous efforts have been directed. These moments of satisfaction are highly significant for identity because part of what we experience at these moments is a strong sense of who we are: a momentary confirmation of the selves we want to be.

Unlike production, which as we have already argued is largely a means to an end, consumption actually is an end. And this contrast is just as valid whether one is discussing production/consumption in terms of the goods it produces, or whether one is discussing them in terms of how identity is formed. Although I am partly who I am because of the actions I perform in order to furnish myself with the things I desire, it is only by fulfilling these expectations, by actually making the purchase or eating the meal or reading the book or listening to the music or watching the film, that I am truly expressing my identity. For example, the particular variety of recognition I get from others when I dress in one way rather than another enhances my perception of how I want to be seen and thus how I see myself. Variations in the levels of pleasure associated with different forms of self-presentation reinforce and consolidate one's preference for consuming one mode of dress rather than another. Since I cannot avoid being seen in one way or another – only H.G. Wells' invisible man has this doubtful advantage – what I wear at any particular time is, even if only momentarily, constitutive of my identity. Over time, and through repetition and habit, patterns will emerge in my choices of what to wear. Eventually the number of chosen alternatives diminishes which means that I have become more certain (or at least less sensitive) about those aspects of my identity which are made manifest through my choice of clothing.

This point is well made by Belk (1988) who puts forward the notion of the 'extended self' to capture the idea that 'possessions are incorporated into self-concept':

> Having possessions can contribute to our capabilities for doing and being ... When an object becomes a possession, what were once self and non-self are synthesised, and having and being merge ... possessions are all-important to knowing who we are. People seek, express, confirm, and ascertain a sense of being through what they have. (Belk, 1988: 183–93)

In the same way that collective aspects of identity are expressed through conspicuous consumption, participation in various registers of 'taste', 'style', 'fashion' and so on, personal identity is also expressed by and through the commodities and services we consume: 'Just as clothing, accent, grooming, and jewellery can distinguish an individual from others and express an individual sense of being, they can also indicate group identity and express belonging to a group' (Belk, 1988: 208).[15] One convenient way of proving this simple truth is to consider how difficult it can be to relinquish some piece of clothing or habitual item which we have got used to seeing ourselves in possession of. One of the reasons why giving up smoking is difficult is because smokers see themselves as smokers and miss the paraphernalia of being a smoker. A retired professor of sociology of my acquaintance still carries his pipe in his pocket despite not having smoked it for five years!

Consumption also affects identity because the activities of consumption tend to be concrete rather than abstract. Either they provide satisfaction and thus positively reinforce the kind of identity we wish to express or they do not. This sense of satisfaction enters people's behaviour since it either motivates them to carry on acting/consuming in that way, or discourages them from so doing. Continuing with our clothing example, if I am repeatedly laughed at for wearing a particular item (and assuming that I am not trying to be deliberately contrary or working as a clown), then it will not be long before I stop wearing it. These expressions of choice are much more difficult to come by in the realm of production where one is much more likely to be required to do something like it or not. Similarly concrete is the fact that when itself considered as an act of production, the formation of identity is entirely contained within the personage of the actor; we do not produce the identities of others in the same way that we produce packed lunches for them.[16]

In summarising these developments, we can therefore say that as affluence increases, and along with it the various registers of complex consumption, the need to develop and express identity comes more and more into the foreground of our expectations. Consumption provides exciting new ways of developing one's identity within established parameters, but it also shifts these parameters so offering altogether different kinds of identity options. One of the ends to which the various acts of consumption are a means, is precisely the formation of identity. As this dual trend gathers pace it is almost inevitable that people will become ever more identity conscious. Identity thus emerges as a core fixation of consumer-based and consumer-oriented society. The alienation, 'estrangement' or 'anomie' which confronts people in consumption-based society is of the same order as the alienation found in work-based society, since both are caused by the feeling of loss of self. For Marx, 'the worker feels himself only when he is not working; when he is working he does not feel himself'. For people today, in consumption-based society, the individual does not feel 'when they are not consuming, and when they are not consuming, they are not feeling themselves either'.

CONSUMPTION AND THE IDENTITY REVOLUTION

New choices, new identities

As we noted earlier in this chapter, one of the basic associations of occupational identity is with the provider role, and in its turn, of this role with a particularly vigorous sense of provider individuality. If it is the case that work-based society is characterised by the person-as-provider/producer concept of individuality, then we need to consider whether consumption-based society might be associated with an alternative concept based around the idea of person-as-consumer. In the context of our discussion of occupational role and gender identity this is an important issue because, as we have just seen, male identity has been so closely associated with the provider/ producer role and the high-status public concept of individuality that goes with it. This is however a very complex area of analysis since for as long as provisioning remains essential to the well-being of the household, the provider role will continue to dominate. It is not therefore a matter of calculating the diminishing returns of the provider role, but of understanding whether and how this role is being uncoupled from assumptions about what constitutes male/female behaviour. Perceptions of individuality, even autonomy, are obviously closely involved in these processes.

A first point we can make, is that the traditional occupation/provider conception of identity and individuality tends to be quite static and conservative when compared with the much more dynamic conceptions of identity which are to be found in the realm of consumption. As we have already seen, one of the major attractions of the realm of consumption is precisely that it provides a much more exciting range of possibilities for developing one's identity and sense of individuality. It is not just a question of moving out of one field of identity formation and into another, but of recognising that in this respect at least, the realm of consumption is streets ahead. As Stewart puts it:

> Once an individual acquired certain real features, in terms of age, sex, and so on, then the expectation was that they would acquire a fairly narrow set of values which 'limited' their behaviour. Increasingly, as society has become more affluent and the old social mores, relating to age, class, and gender have broken down, it seems evident that we are free to 'appropriate' meanings into our lives from just about wherever we choose. (Stewart, 1992: 220)

A very similar diagnosis of the possible breaking down of these traditional markers of identity and individuality, and of the 'authority structure' which goes with them was famously put forward by the Henley Centre for Forecasting as early as 1986. Suggesting that 'deference to traditional authorities in Britain has now hit an all-time low', they proposed that the new source of 'authority' comes from *within* people rather than being *imposed* upon them by society:

> Whilst the authority of class, of the production side of life, has declined, that of the consumption side has risen ... we talk of a more discriminating form of materialism in which, in essence, the motive has changed from one of seeking to keep up with the Joneses to one where we are seeking to keep away from them (so to speak). The authority we tend to use for this is from within rather than external. (The Henley Centre for Forecasting, 1986: 117, quoted in Mort, 1996: 103)

At the centre of this new approach, and in many ways its driving force, is the desire to develop a new sense of individuality which is very much centred on the self: 'The demise of the ethos of production, together with a corresponding rise of a reformulated code of individualism, was generating a more internalised hierarchy of authority. It was the self, Henley claimed, which now functioned as the highest court of appeal' (Mort, 1996: 103–4). Rather than trying to develop a sense of personal identity which constantly had to reconcile itself with a very specific and dominating concept of individuality, there was a growing sense that in consumption-based society, the concept of individuality would have to be remodelled in order to accommodate an almost infinite number of different identities. Individuality is now plural rather than singular.

At a slightly more generalised level of analysis, and very much in line with those who have characterised late-modern capitalism as 'disorganised' (Offe, 1985; Lash and Urry, 1987, 1994), Rojek suggests that there are significant differences between the practice of consumption in the earlier and later stages of modernity, differences which are directly related to this burgeoning sense of liberated identity. In the period of 'Modernity 1' (say from around 1780 to 1980), which is characterised as being orderly and controlled, individuals were faced with relatively limited choices, choices which only offered a semblance of true individuality and freedom:

> Our consumption and leisure experience is composed of mass-produced items and standardised accessories which can be found anywhere. On this reading, leisure in mass culture is not about a search for authenticity or fulfilment; instead it consists of distraction activity. What one is distracting oneself from is the realisation that originality, uniqueness and spontaneity are dead. (Rojek, 1995: 85)

With the coming of 'Modernity 2' (from the 1980s onwards), which is characterised as being disorganised, fragmentary and thus tendentially out of control, people's experiences, both within and outside work have become much more transitory and diverse. With diversity of experience comes diversity of identity.

One of the reasons why a more liberated notion of identity and individuality emerges in consumption-based society is because ultimately, it is impossible to exhaust all the different versions of identity/individuality which are available. Consumption presumes that there must be at least as many versions of identity/individuality as there are people and even more if one allows that one person might experience more than one version of their personal identity. This contrasts with the situation in work-based society where the identity one develops by taking on the provider/homemaker roles is limited by the type and extent of the needs of household members. In terms of providing basic necessities such as food, drink, shelter and clothing for example, although these items are always required, and will always therefore keep the provider/homemaker busy, the degree of satisfaction which comes from making this provision might not be that great and especially not once basic, if not quite developed, kinds of satisfaction can be taken more-or-less for granted. How much satisfaction can there be in having a full refrigerator or a clean house? The needs which consumption is intended to fulfil have no such limitations and especially not when they become centred on the desire to satisfy identity needs. It is possible to have more and more identity, to be more and more of an individual.

Extending the logic of productivism, the limitlessness of consumption does not destroy the need for the provider/homemaker roles, it actually gives them new life by creating a demand for all kinds of new ways of having an identity and of being an individual. Whilst it might be supposed that this partial discarding of identity markers based on occupational roles would result in a kind of anomie of the self, a new kind of self-alienation, the business of seeing one's self as an object of consumption is actually a continuation rather than an abandonment of the logic of productivist individualism. Only this time, it is the self which becomes the object (or subject to be worked on) of consumption rather than being the (active) subject which does the consuming (Seidler, 1989: 25–6).

Gender, identity and the new individualism

Looking finally at the possible impact of these developments on the formation of gender identity, if the identity markers of acts of consumption are more often gender neutral when compared with the identity markers of paid and unpaid occupational roles, then a shift away from the latter and towards the former might serve to reduce the allocation of different activities and the kinds of identity/individuality associated with them as between one gender and the other. The difficulty with this line of argument, is that the markers of gender identity are already and just as fully-formed in the realm of consumption as they are in the realm of production. They may in fact have come from the realm of production in the first place.

When men do turn towards the realm of consumption it is likely that they do so in search of traditional images of masculinity and male identity and not out of a desire to explore alternatives. Rather than transcending the realm of production and the provider role in matters of identity, the realm of consumption might simply provide a mirror image of it. Male consumers might be craving alternative means of proving their maleness not of escaping from it. Gender markers are to be found across the full range of activities which men and women are involved in and not just in their occupational roles. It might be tempting to imagine that earlier stereotypes and assumptions about what constitutes male or female identity have been laid to rest in the consumer-oriented world of late-modernity, but there is clear evidence that advocates of the old gender-hegemony will not give up without a fight, and that new and reactionary counter movements will also emerge to fight this rearguard action (Connell, 1987; Bly, 1992; Abbott and Wallace, 1992; Pfeil, 1995; Benwell (ed.), 2003).

Where there might be more of an impact on gender identity however, is that in work-based society people tend to invest less heavily in realms of activity other than work. For men in particular, identity in work-based society tends to be a one-realm kind of identity. Whilst this is an entirely rational strategy to adopt in the kind of society where heavily work-based forms of identity really do enhance one's sense of being a good provider (real jobs provide the highest rewards and real jobs are for real men), it does somewhat limit the desire and opportunity to explore alternative sources of identity. Because they always have had to spend a considerable proportion of their time in more than one realm, women have a more fully-developed capacity to draw their identities and their sense of individuality from a broader range of experiences.

Escaping occupational identities

To the extent that paid occupational roles still dominate the lives of most men, the activities of consumption may provide a means of escape from work, a kind of anti-work, but they cannot provide an alternative to work. For men, the way that activities outside work are interpreted in terms of what they have to say about gender, are still tied in with the gender markers of the occupations they have. It is difficult to imagine that an individual experiences one sense of a gendered self in one realm of activity and a different sense of gendered self in another. Gender may be multi-faceted but there are only two genders. Expectations about gender are not abandoned when people turn from paid to unpaid occupational roles or from these to activities in the non-work realm. Rather these expectations travel with them across all their activities. In this respect gender is the same kind of concept as identity which we defined at the start of the previous chapter as an essential something which transgresses all the boundaries between one aspect of a person's activity and another and yet is partly grounded in each of them. However, unlike positions in the occupational hierarchy which have been consolidated over many years, the hierarchies of consumption are still fluid which might mean that the gendering of acts of consumption is still in a state of flux. A turn away from production and towards consumption might imply a more general process of reconstructing established assumptions and perceptions of gender. Sport as leisure might be one example of a non-producing category of activity which is not deemed to be the prerogative of one gender or the other.

New concepts of individuality

As far as concepts of individuality are concerned, commercial commentators and academics alike have certainly identified a correlation between forms and patterns of consumption directed explicitly at identity-building and the emergence of a new concept of individuality. Responding to the need 'to assemble a type of synthetic male personality out of the flotsam and jetsam of contemporary commodities', Mort (1996: 18), suggests that the agents of social-cultural engineering defined and described various species of the new man, rising phoenix-like from the carcass of traditional manhood with his new sense of liberated individualism, a new pride in his autonomy, and a flatteringly high level of regard for other members of the cast. Conveniently, and in direct contrast with the apparently static and unimaginative origins, the fixed menu of choices from which the old man had to make his choices, the resources now available for identity reconstruction, for the makeover of identity and selfhood are multiple, dynamic and cafeteria-like:

> These speculations were produced through multiple concepts, which varied according to the goods in question and their position in the marketplace. There was no one model of consumption which dominated, despite the evangelical claims of the creative innovators and the style *cognoscenti*. The dynamics of transformation were plural and diverse. (Mort,1996: 144)

We will be looking at some of these issues in more detail in the following chapter but for now we can conclude with the following. First, and in contrast to the somewhat ascetic psychology of Protestant notions of individualism, 'the new individualism' of late-modern consumption-based society has absorbed the idea that it is all right to feel good about one's sense of self; it is not necessary to feel embarrassed about exploring new ideas about identity, nor to feel that consumption is somehow self-indulgent as compared with the honest and more earthly business of providing and homemaking. Indeed, being positive in these efforts is an essential part of the new game plan.

Secondly, and as an extension of the idea that identity-markers have been set free from earlier constraints, the search for the paraphernalia of identity-formation has been represented as being as much an ideational, semiotic or symbolic process as it is a material one. Featherstone for example, applies the cultural studies schemata in describing what he calls 'the change from an industrial manufacturing order to post-industrial and informational order':

> [The] seemingly empty and universalist signs circulating in the world informational system can be recast into different configurations of meaning. That these transformed social semantics can – in the context of traditional and self-reflexive social practices – instead inform the (re)constitution and/or creation of individual and communal identities. (Featherstone et al. (eds), 1995: 2–3, 'introduction')

Thirdly, and picking up on themes developed earlier by Weber (1976), Simmel (1978), and Veblen (1994), both these new emphases have shifted the centre of gravity of academic debate away from the productivist stance of 'industrial sociology', and towards the wider cultural arena in which ideas about the meanings and purpose of work are debated. Within cultural theory for example, these changes have been reflected in a move away from 'the concept of cultural manipulation' as represented in the critical theory of the Frankfurt School during the 1940s and 1950s (e.g. Horkheimer and Adorno, 1972) and of 'rational choice theories of consumer sovereignty' (Mort, 1996: 6), both of which had tended to represent the consumer as the passive plaything of market forces, towards a much more reflective and active conception of the consumer. The explicitly culturally-oriented contributions of writers such as Featherstone, Baudrillard and particularly Bauman and Bourdieu, have since suggested that differential social position, and thus the identity markers which go with them, need to be assessed in terms of the consumption-oriented 'habitus' as constituted by the signs and expectations of taste and lifestyle, rather than in terms of the grit and toil of productivism.

Summary

Occupational roles are important in that they provide individuals with space and opportunity, a framework even, within which to express themselves. Identity remains virtual until it is expressed (the comatose hospital patient appears to have no identity) and so the contexts within which we express ourselves are an integral part of that sense of identity. Identity needs an environment which lies beyond or outside the confines of the mind and body of the individual to become real, and this is what the social universe provides. In societies where paid occupational roles remain the dominant form of activity and provide the most enduring basis for the economic and social hierarchies, it is inevitable that the activities and protocols, not just of work in general (i.e. simply having a paid occupation or not having one), but of particular kinds of occupation (manual or non-manual, casual or professional) become especially important as contexts for the expression of personal identity.

We appear to be dominated by the occupation-based dimensions of our identity, not just because they do actually preoccupy us, but because we regard them as a suitable venue through which to express our sense-of-self. The hegemony of the self we experience in work-based society is peculiar to that kind of society because of the hierarchic structures of paid and unpaid occupations which dominate it, and literally make it what it is. One of the paradoxes of the struggle for gender equality has been the need to participate in these structures whilst at the same time trying to alter their shape (Walby, 1997; Charles, 2002). These structures, and the ideas and expectations about gender which are associated with them, develop over time and thus provide the context for many of our most important activities. Whilst we might prefer to think that we are autonomous in living out our occupational roles, this sense of autonomy is an illusion which arises from the mistaken idea that just because we act in real or present time, our actions are not constrained by things which happened in the past.

The hegemony of the self which develops in consumption-based society operates in the same way (there are structures and hierarchies of consumption which exceed the capacity of any particular individual to change them), but it has a somewhat different impact on identity because these structures are still being formed. In consumption-based society and particularly those devoted to complex and symbolic forms of consumption, identity is no longer an unintended consequence of action, a by-product of producing and consuming things, but has become a central focus of many activities. Identity has fully come out and people are allowed home early from work so that they will have plenty of time left over for identity-work beyond the confines of the traditional workplace. Consumption therefore provides opportunities for identity to float free from the confines imposed upon it by activities within the realm of production. It is able to do this first because the nature of the two kinds of activity is different (terminal rather than intermediate, self-contained rather than abstracted), and second because the content of consumption-type activities is often explicitly geared towards the satisfaction of identity needs.

Since gender forms an essential part of identity – there is no such thing as a gender-free identity – important linkages are bound to develop between gender and the different realms of activity in which people are involved. In work-based societies gender has become closely associated with the kind of occupational role a person fulfils. Originally for fairly simple practical reasons and more recently as a matter of convention, the paid occupational role (which is what the breadwinner/provider role is in modern households) has traditionally been associated with persons of the male gender and unpaid occupational roles (a continuation of the nurturing/homemaking role) with persons of the female gender. One of the most important implications of a transition from a work-based to consumption-based social type is that these associations will be revised firstly as women invigorate their engagement with paid occupational roles and men warm to the attractions of the unpaid ones, and second because across society, identity has become a major preoccupation in the realm of consumption.

Although we do not have space to develop it properly here, one of the most interesting things about these changes in the associations of gender with particular kinds of activity, is that these changes suggest that it is differences in the kinds of activities which people perform which give them an opportunity to express those aspects of identity called gender. In answer to one of the dilemmas we raised at the start of this chapter, we can say that people have the genders that they have because of the kinds of activities they are mainly involved with. 'Gender' is not an innate capacity which predisposes a person to act in one way rather than another, to seek out this activity rather than that one. Rather we acquire a gender because of the actions we perform. If the balance of those activities begins to alter, then one can conceive, in theory at least, of a situation where ideas about what constitutes male gender or female gender might also be revised. There is however, no danger that the certainties we currently rely upon in relating to others as being of the same or the other gender to ourselves are suddenly going to collapse, because the activities of biological reproduction will always require that there are two genders. These most fundamental and irreducible biological functions will continue to provide the basic marker of gender identity:

> The social semiotics of gender, with its emphasis on the endless play of signification, the multiplicity of discourses and the diversity of subject positions, has been important in escaping the rigidities of biological determinism. But it should not give the impression that gender is an autumn leaf, wafted about by the light breezes. Body-reflexive practices form – and are formed by – structures which have historical weight and solidity. (Connell, 1995: 65)

NOTES

[1]This convention – that 'occupation' is synonymous with 'paid employment' illustrates again how the productivist ethic subordinates all activities to the category of paid work (Gorz, 1989; Ransome, 1996).
[2]Although Glucksmann is particularly interested in how market and non-market activities are distributed between different members of the household, the notion of occupational role I am using here as encompassing all the activities in society and not just those in the category 'formal paid employment' is broadly compatible with the idea of the 'Total Social Organisation of Labour' or TSOL she has recently put forward:

> [TSOL] [includes the recognition] that 'work' is not simply synonymous with paid employment, and does not take place only in a structurally distinct 'economy' … but may be undertaken within a variety of socio-economic

relations and take a variety of forms … . TSOL refers to the manner by which all the labour in a particular society is divided up between and allocated to different structures, institutions, activities and people. The TSOL is a kind of higher level of division of labour, referring not to the technical division of tasks within one institution or work process, but rather to the social division of all of the labour in a given society of whatever kind between institutional spheres. It is the organisation of activities from the standpoint of their economic constraints and tensions. (Glucksmann, 2000: 18–19)

[3]As noted in chapter four, Gershuny highlights 'convergences' between the activities of men and women in the proportions of domestic and non-domestic activity each performs, and between these and the balance of work and leisure activities within the household. Hakim has recently put forward 'preference theory' which directly examines how, as a result of the contraceptive and equal-opportunities revolutions of the mid-twentieth century, new kinds of choices have been made available to women 'between a life centred on private, family work, and a life centred on market work or other activities in the public sphere' (Hakim, 2000: 2).

[4]The idea of paradigmatic shifts in economic development, usually described as cycles of investment and technical innovation has been thoroughly researched by economists. Dunford (1989: 114, Note 1) offers the following definition: 'A new industrial paradigm is made up of a series of technically and economically inter-related radical innovations that have pervasive effects on the whole of economic life and involve major changes in the capital stock and skill profile of the population; the development of computers and communication technologies is a contemporary example.' For original contributions to 'long-wave theory', see Kondratiev, 1935; Schumpeter, 1989; Freeman et al., 1982; Perez, 1985. For a discussion see Ransome, 1999.

[5]We stress 'are perceived to provide' because as we saw in Chapter 3, household prosperity depends on composition and expenditure not just on income. A single high income might not stretch as far in a household which includes five depen dent children, as might the income of two pensioners in a household without children. We should also pause to consider here, that although some occupations are seen as being more socially worthy or valuable than others (as having high use-value) it does not follow that this positive evaluation will be reflected in the levels of pay they attract (their exchange value). This observation provides the point of departure for most if not all of the criticisms of capitalism as a system which promotes exchange values above everything else. Many of the most socially worthy occupations, such as looking after house and home, are not paying occupations at all and yet many people are engaged in them. It is possible to have a 'good' job in the nuclear industry and a 'bad' job in a hospital (Gorz, 1989; Beck, 1992). This raises a number of vexing questions about how, within a capitalist market economy, qualitative criteria of evaluation are generally displaced by quantitative criteria). Where an occupation does offer a reasonably high level of intrinsic satisfaction, this is taken to be reward enough. Correspondingly, high pay often becomes a compensation for work which lacks intrinsic satisfaction. For a discussion see Ransome, 1996.

[6]In his account of the effects of job insecurity on professional workers for example, Portwood found that: 'Under conditions of redundancy, many of these [FE] lecturers suffered severe mental anguish even to the point of temporary loss of identity and purpose. Their career commitment became a major handicap ... many considered that monetary compensation could not make up for the loss of style of life associated with their careers' (Portwood, 1985: 457–61).

[7]There is a truly vast literature which examines occupational segmentation, the 'glass ceiling', employment inequality and so on. Currently, there is much conflict within sociology between those who argue that most people are in a position to make 'rational choices' when choosing occupational roles (Hakim, 1995 and 2000), and others (Ginn et al., 1996) who argue that for many, the choice is between taking various kinds of 'poor work' or facing financial difficulties (Allen, 1997; Rowbotham, 1998). For reviews see Procter and Padfield, 1999 and Bradley et al., 2000.

[8]There is much complexity here since it would seem logically impossible to separate 'gender' from the ways in which it makes itself manifest in society. Can we understand human social interaction without a concept of gender? How might 'gender' express itself unless it is by means of particular social roles? If one removed all the stereotypical paraphernalia of what constitutes 'maleness' or 'femaleness' from a person, how might one relate to the de-gendered remainder? Would all such de-gendered beings be equal? For further discussions of these matters see: Devor, 1989; Butler, 1990; Garber, 1992; Dunne, 1997; MacInnes, 1998; Alsop et al., 2002.

[9]ESRC-funded research project 'The Gender Dimensions of Job Insecurity', Nickie Charles and Paul Ransome, L2122520120, part of the *Future of Work* Programme 1999–2002. Other interpretations of the data have been published as Charles and James, 2003 and Charles, James and Ransome (forthcoming 2004). The interpretation presented here in some respects concurs with earlier work and in other respects moves the analysis forward. This book is not written from a feminist perspective, and does not prioritise material/structural factors over ideational/volitional ones. The analysis is that of the author and has not been discussed with other members of the research team. For more details of the research protocol see Charles, James, and Ransome (forthcoming 2004).

[10]It is worth emphasising that in order to be effective, perceptions of what constitutes a typically male or typically female role at a particular time and place, have to be held both by the men and by the women living there. Stereotypical perceptions of gender roles are as much a part of how women see the world as they are of how men see it. For a detailed discussion of how this gender ideology of work is thought to operate and why it is so difficult to shift see Fine, 1992; Charles, 1993; Scott (ed.), 1994 and Ransome, 1999.

[11]The association of breadwinning with physical exertion does however survive. As one of the respondents to the South Wales study put it (see Note 9 above): 'I think his [job] is more important because – I don't know – the old school really, where the man is the breadwinner. His wages are more than mine, his job is far more physically demanding than my job is. Bending and stretching. And he gets more tired. Physically tired. Whereas mine is more mentally tired. But I always think of his job as more important than mine, definitely' (50-year old female full-time wages clerk, 004B).

[12]Bradley et al., conclude that whilst there has been a 'feminisation of the workforce' in the sense that a growing proportion of it is accounted for by women, 'feminisation of occupations has been limited ... while the cultures of work and organisations are deeply gendered in ways that persistently disadvantage women' (Bradley et al., 2000: 91).

[13]Which is not to say of course that everyone would be equal since as we have been at pains to point out, the occupational structure is hierarchic by virtue of the economic, political, social and cultural distinctions it gives rise to.

[14]At this point in the discussion we are looking equally at women and men although some of these developments affect men more than women in the sense that women already have an expanded range of activities from which they build their sense of identity. Men on the other hand, have really only just started their quest for alternative sources of identity as they have been relatively slow to recognise the limitations of occupational identity.

[15]Simmel suggests that fashion offers 'on the one hand, a sphere of general imitation, the individual floating in the broadest social current ... and on the other hand, we have a certain conspicuousness, an individual emphasis, an individual ornamentation of the personality' (Simmel [1904] in Frisby and Featherstone (eds), 1997: 196).

[16]One exception might be the dressing of babies and young children since they are largely unable to choose what to wear for themselves. Temporarily at least, parents construct an identity on behalf of their children – a procedure which has sometimes raised the objection that some parents treat their children as if they were some kind of prop or fashion accessory for their own (the parents') identity.

8

The cultures of work and consumption

Introductory discussion

The purpose of this final substantive chapter is to consider whether the work-based and consumption-based social types we have been discussing are associated respectively with a work-based culture and a consumption-based culture. If such a distinction could be made, this would certainly support the argument that a transition is taking place from one social type to another. We are defining culture as a realm of social activity and associated artefacts which provide people with a means of exploring the meanings of their action. These meanings, and the ideas that are habitually used to describe and discuss them, are closely bound up with the values people want to express through their actions.[1] In this context 'meaning' can be defined as the sense of satisfaction or pleasure which accompanies successful instances of value expression or value fulfilment through action.[2]

Our argument is that if living in a work-based society is different from living in a consumption-based society because (a) people are involved in different kinds of activities and (b) they have different understandings and expectations about their actions than formerly, then these differences are likely to show up in 'culture' since culture is the realm in which ideas about the meanings/values of action are collectively developed and expressed. A difference in shared meanings/values implies a difference in culture, and a difference in culture implies a difference in social type. As Slater puts it:

> The spread of consumption values to the general society occurs firstly because consumption itself becomes a central focus of social life (... other foci, e.g. work, religion, politics, become less important or meaningful); and secondly because the values of consumer society acquire a prestige which encourages their morphological extension to other domains ... (Slater, 1997b: 25)[3]

Although there is certainly more than one way of expressing ideas about what actions mean (there might be as many interpretations/modes of expression as there are individuals), in this discussion we are mostly interested in values/meanings and the ideas which are generally used to express them, which are collectively produced and can thus be presumed to be relatively stable and ordinarily understood by everyone living in the kind of society which has produced that type of culture. Because these shared values are collectively produced they also establish a sense of legitimacy and validity around actions which reflect those values.[4] We are particularly interested in ideas which are used to validate, justify and legitimise what we have previously referred to as the ethics of production and the ethics of consumption. Although we have argued that it is false to assert that a decline in the importance of the ethic of production necessarily or automatically heralds the demise of work-based society as a whole, there are important differences in the meanings/values of production and of consumption and these differences give rise to important cultural differences. Whether one regards these differences as sufficiently large and persistent as to justify claims about radical social transformation depends in large part on how much freedom is given to 'culture' in one's analytical framework.

We approach our analysis by deploying the idea of a clear contrast between the culture of work-based society on one hand and the culture of consumption-based culture on the other, cultures which prioritise respectively the values of production and the values of consumption. We can tentatively assemble the following list of possible associations which it might be useful to bear in mind as our discussion proceeds.

Work-based society	Consumption-based society
Modern society (from 1760)	Postmodern society (from 1985)
Modern capitalism	Late-modern capitalism
Modern culture	Postmodern culture
Production-side values	Consumption-side values
Ethic of production	Ethic of consumption
Modernist perspective in styles of discourse, aesthetics, etc.	Postmodernist perspective in styles of discourse, aesthetics, etc.
Modernist theories of culture	Postmodernist theories of culture

Figure 8.1   Associations

To get the ball rolling we will concentrate in the first instance on the ways that 'culture' has been constructed in social theoretical discourse, and try to understand whether alternative means of theorising culture are characteristic of societies dominated by work and by consumption respectively. We will use the term 'modern theory' to refer to modernist theories of culture which were developed to understand modern culture in modern society. To distinguish this established perspective from those more recently emerged, we will use the term 'postmodern theory' to refer to post-modernist theories of culture which emerged towards the end of the modern period or at the commencement of the late- or postmodern period to understand postmodern culture. One can of course adopt a modernist perspective and use a modernist style of cultural theory in looking at phenomena which are classified as 'post-modern', and conversely, use a postmodernist perspective and theory of culture in looking at phenomena classified as 'modern'. Care does need to be taken however, when looking at phenomena which occur outside the historical period from which they take their name. It might be argued for example, that those who persist in looking at postmodern phenomena with modernist eyes are not seeing the same thing as people who see them contemporaneously through the postmodernist gaze. Similarly postmodernist theory might be poorly equipped for looking back at things which are rooted in a period before its own conception. Commenting on important differences between 'postmodernism' as 'one style among others' and as 'the cultural dominant of the logic of late capitalism' for example, Jameson stresses that 'the two approaches in fact generate two very different ways of conceptualising the pheno-menon as a whole: on the one hand, moral judgements … and on the other, a genuinely dialectical attempt to think our present of time in History' (Jameson, 1999 [1991]: 342).

THEORETICAL APPROACHES TO CULTURAL TRANSITION

Locating 'culture' in the social structure

The most crucial area of disagreement between modernist and postmod-ernist accounts of cultural change is that they make quite different assumptions about how to understand the (structural) relationships between the cultural and other realms within which people act. Theories of modern society tended to regard 'culture' as something of a poor rela-tion when compared with other bits of the social universe such as the economic or political. According to the modernist view, culture was a super-structural phenomenon which was largely determined by the economic base. The relations between culture and economy were therefore quite straightforward: wherever the base would go, culture would surely follow. If modern culture is an inevitable accompaniment to modern (let us say twentieth-century) capitalism, postmodern culture is the inevitable accompaniment to end-of-twentieth-century capitalism. For Jameson (1991) for example, postmodernism is 'the superstructural form' of late capitalism. It is the reflection within the superstructure of the changed economic base of capitalist economic relations in its multinational or globalised stage of development.[5]

During the 1980s however, this characterisation of culture as a somewhat subordinate realm of activity was challenged by an increasing number of theorists who argued that culture warranted much greater attention than it had been receiving (Harvey, 1989; Connor, 1989; Featherstone (ed.), 1988; Featherstone, 1991). Now it was culture rather than economy that was seen as being able to act independently of other constituents of social structure, and even more dramatically, of having the capacity to determine activities within those other realms:

> Culture was too often regarded as readily circumscribed, something derivative which was there to be explained. It was rarely conceived of as opening up a set of problems which, once tackled, could question and overturn such hierarchically constituted oppositions and separations [including economy/culture, production/consumption, work/leisure ...] A set of problems which, when constituted in its most radical form, could challenge the viability of our existing modes of conceptualisation. (Featherstone (ed.), 1992: vii)

The logic here is that established theories of how the various bits of society fit together and of how these bits influence people's behaviour need to be looked at afresh. Even more alarmingly for those who anchored their social theory in a relatively simple (conceptual and empirical) relation between base and superstructure, given the relational nature of concepts as they are typically used in sociological theory this process of reassessment inevitably required that all the other concepts related to culture (and arguably ideas about what constitutes such a relationship), including ideas about the economic realm, would be subjected to renewed scrutiny (Kumar, 1995: 112ff; Swingewood, 2000: 218ff.). Theorists of the labour process and economy were thus relegated to the bench as fit young replacements, many of whom were familiar with beguiling European concepts and tactics, took to the field. Culture was being offered the leading role in a whole new conceptual drama; a veritable *whodunit?* of theoretical intrigue and debate and the outcome was a great outpouring of detailed accounts of some of the new kinds of activities people were now engaging in (many of which were directly associated with 'the new consumption') and proposed cultural explanations of such activities (for example, Rojek and Turner (eds), 1993; Keat et al., 1994; Gabriel and Lang, 1995. For a more panoramic view see the collections in the four volumes of Millar, 2001a–d).

Modernism versus postmodernism

We have then, a major difference of opinion between (progressive) post-modern social theorists who emphasise the importance of the study of the cultural realm and (reactionary) modern theorists who prefer to rely on the established view that things cultural only warrant limited attention since they are largely determined by things economic. Modernist academic discourse regarded cultural elements as having limited (structural) independence, whilst post-modern academic discourse conceived of the cultural realm as having considerable independence (Mouzellis, 1995). One useful way of resolving this apparent impasse is to recognise that changes within the cultural realm are not the same as changes in the relationships between the cultural realm and other realms of social activity. It is perfectly consistent to accept that something important is going on in culture whilst at the same time sticking with the modernist view that 'culture' operates within limits set by things economic. Significant cultural change is not necessarily accompanied by a change in the significance of 'culture'. One explanation of why this confusion tends to arise is because debates over the transition from (society-wide) modernity to (society-wide) post-modernity have been subsumed within debates over a transition from (the cultural form) modernism to (the cultural form) post-modernism:

> I take the stand that postmodernism does reflect important changes, not so much in the structure of industrial capitalism, but in the place and nature of culture …. The weakness of traditional sociology has been its inability adequately to analyse culture. Postmodernism as a style of analysis can be seen as an attempt to provide an analysis of culture in late capitalism. (Turner in Rojek and Turner (eds), 1993: 73–4)

To the extent that the transition from the historical period called modernity to the historical period called postmodernity has been treated as if it were a transition from modernism to post-modernism (i.e. from one kind of aesthetic and mode of theoretical investigation and philosophy to another mode), this transition has been defined as profoundly cultural. Once defined as cultural, the kinds of explanations which are sought are, by definition, going to be cultural ones.

The price one has to pay for this theoretical directness however, is the assertion that the cultural realm sets its own limits (rather than them being set by economy), and this argument requires an altogether much more robust level of justification. A weakening economic sphere and a strengthening cultural sphere is one thing, but the idea of an autonomous cultural sphere is much more challenging. Cultural-explanation-type accounts of the transition out of modernity and towards postmodernity have generated much novelty and interest but changes in the contents, artefacts and activities of culture do not automatically indicate that 'culture' has become a free agent in the social structure. Certainly some of the changes which have been going on in the postmodern cultural realm are quite revolutionary, but none of this signifies that anything very revolutionary has taken place regarding the relations between culture and everything else. Although the (modern) characterisation of culture as the by-product of economic processes might have resulted in an under-playing of the important changes which have been taking place in the cultural realm, it is just as likely that the (postmodern) characterisation of an independent cultural realm has resulted in an underplaying of the continuing importance of goings on in the economic realm. Conceptually, autonomous cultural explanations of social transition repeat rather than overcome the shortcomings of traditional modernist accounts.

Culture and the transition from work- to consumption-based social types

Where then, does this leave us and our more immediate concerns about whether a transition is taking place from a work-based to a consumption-based social type? Beginning with changes in the general size and shape of 'culture' we can apply the modernist view that the cultural realm expands and contracts within limits that are set by the economic structure. Change has occurred as a result of the fact that work-based society has produced increasing affluence and increasing affluence means that people find it much easier to satisfy their basic needs. No longer preoccupied with satisfying these basic needs people have increasing amounts of time and resources which they can devote to other activities according to their own choices and preferences. As we have already noted, many of these freely-chosen activities take place in the realm of consumption. Greater choice in matters of consumption, lifestyle, identity and so on stimulates the need for fresh guidance as to the meanings and purposes of these new kinds of activities, and, as the leading provider of these collective values, the cultural realm also expands. Conversely of course, loss of affluence would result in a foreshortening of choice, a contraction of activities in the realm of consumption and so the cultural realm would contract because the meanings of action would cease to be ambiguous.[6]

If we accept that in the late-modern period, 'culture' is increasingly associated with the expanding non-work realm and especially with leisure-consumption (it would be difficult to argue persuasively that the 'culture of work' is expanding even though it might be occupying more space in textbooks and seminars about 'managing organisations'), it follows that in a consumption-based society, 'culture' plays a more vigorous role in people's lives than it does in work-based society. This is not to say that work-based societies are somehow devoid of culture, since as social historians of culture have pointed out, the development of British workerliness was a profoundly cultural thing (Hoggart, 1956; Thompson, 1963; Hobsbawm, 1969; Steadman Jones, 1984 and Williams, 1985). Rather we need to acknowledge that in work-based society, the realm of culture was, as it were, 'used up by' ideas about work, family, church, community and class.

In consumption-based society however, a much greater range of experiences and concerns clamour for attention. One might say that production-side values are more transparent than are consumption-side values and so take less cultural work to explain and communicate them. Consumption-based society creates fresh appetites for the exploration of values through culture. Following Baudrillard, we could go so far as to suggest that one of the things we consume is the melting-pot of cultural debates, and discourses about consumption itself:

> Consumption is a myth. That is to say, it is *a statement of contemporary society about itself*, the way our society speaks itself. And, in a sense, the only objective reality of consumption is the *idea* of consumption; it is this reflexive, discursive configuration, endlessly repeated in everyday speech and intellectual discourse, which has acquired the force of *common sense*. Our society thinks itself and speaks itself as a consumer society. As much as it consumes anything, it consumes itself as a consumer society, as *idea*. (Baudrillard, 1998: 193, original emphasis)

Although the rate of production of cultural artefacts is particularly evident at times of crisis and upheaval,[7] one can suggest that it is also likely to increase as people have more time and resources at their disposal for reviewing the ideas and values they hold. As Veblen noted at the turn of the nineteenth century, a prerequisite for the acquisition of 'taste, discernment and culture' is the availability of plenty of comfortable leisure time in which to intellectualise: 'the criteria of a past performance of leisure therefore commonly take the form of "immaterial" goods [such as] quasi-scholarly or quasi-artistic accomplishments and a knowledge of processes and incidents ... which may in some sense be classed as branches of learning' (Veblen, 1994: 45). A similar point is made by Campbell as part of his explanation of how eighteenth-century 'sentimentalism' not only allowed people to take pleasure in a way that seventeenth-century asceticism had denied, but associated pleasure with culture and aesthetic appreciation:

> [T]rue to their religious heritage, [the middle classes] regarded 'taste' as a sign of moral and spiritual worth, with an ability to take pleasure in the beautiful and to respond with tears to the pitiable equally indicative of a man (or woman) of virtue ... an ethic which inevitably provided powerful legitimation for the pursuit of emotional pleasure. (Campbell, 1987: 205)

Whether one is describing the emerging 'middle class' of eighteenth century, 'the leisure class' of the late-nineteenth century, or the 'celebrity class' of the early twenty-first century (Rojek, 2000), it is clear that affluence is a key facilitator of increased cultural activity and a growing preoccupation with ideas, beliefs and values. Allowing a fairly inclusive definition of what constitutes 'culture' (i.e. that mass popular culture is not excluded on grounds of taste), one could say that affluent societies are always more cultural than non-affluent ones. Being cultured means being interested in meanings and values.

The importance of culture as the refinery of ideas about collective values raises the possibility that much of what constitutes the transition from work-based to consumption-based social types is in fact 'cultural'. One of the most obvious characteristics of the kinds of changes we have been discussing in previous chapters is that they are to do with how people come to understand, give meaning to, even justify their behaviours. It is not just that important changes are taking place in the balance of people's activities (away from work and towards consumption), activities which people need to apply meaning and value to, but that the 'old' meanings which are applied to established activities are also under review. And as we have defined it above, 'culture' is the realm where these shared meanings are collectively constructed and communicated.

New relations of culture and economy

A transition from work-based to consumption-based society does not mean however, that 'culture' has broken free from the constraints which are set for it by the production side, because the conditions which have given rise to its greater importance in people's lives are primarily economic conditions. Although affluence, which is the most important of these conditions (others are the restructuring of employment and occupations, changes in the techniques and practices of production, economic globalisation) has often been treated as a cultural phenomenon and has been readily incorporated into cultural-explanation-type accounts of social transition (Keat et al. (eds), 1994; Bocock, 1993), in crucial respects it remains a production-side phenomenon (capacity to consume depends on earned income and earned income depends on employment).

Moreover, the continuing influence of the production side over the consumption side (in theory terms of the economic over the cultural) is not historically accidental but plays an essential role in providing much of the evident continuity which binds work-based and consumption-based phases of social development together. In the same way that work persists in consumption, and that work-based sources of identity lie behind those expressed through consumption, so economy continues to set the limits within which culture operates. By the same token there must be elements which carry through from pre-modernity and modernity, and from modernity to post-modernity (from Fordism to post-Fordism, modernism to post- modernism and so on) or there could be no such thing as social development as this idea is commonly understood. Even if we switch into a postmodernist way of thinking and suggest that modernist concepts of development and of 'history' are 'part of the problem' (that the forward movement of social practice over historical time is not incrementally progressive and smoothly evolutionary, but is profoundly unstable, discontinuous and potentially disorganised: Lash and Urry, 1987; Giddens, 1990; Fukuyama, 1992) it is evident that practically and ideationally we live in a world of artefacts, practices, ideas and values which continue to manifest the modernist past as well as the late- or postmodernist present. To give one trivial example, it is usually quite unsatisfactory to draw a parallel between postmodernity and postindustrialism because although fewer people are occupied in heavy industry and many more are occupied in services, this does not mean that contemporary Western societies have ceased to be 'industrial'. The immediate form has altered but the substance remains pretty much the same.

Values

As we have already noted, when we talk about differences in the meaning and justification of action provided by work-based and consumption-based cultures, what we are really talking about are differences in the collective values people profess to.[8] To the extent that the activities of production and consumption are distinct one would certainly expect to find differences in the collective values each is trying to express. At the same time, to the extent that some of the same values are found in both fields (we have already seen that production and consumption are linked both motivationally and practically as production-consumption sequences), one would expect to find differences in the ways in which the cultures of production and of consumption express those values. For example, and referring again to Campbell's modernist narrative account of the 'romantic ethic', this author suggest that although following Weber's account, it appears as if the hedonism of an emergent consumerist ethic is incompatible with the Puritan ethic of abstemious production (which rather inconveniently means that the production and consumption revolutions 'have to be separated by more than a century' (p. 204), the two can be resolved when recast into a form of modernist romanticism: 'The romantic ethic can be seen to possess a basic congruence, or "elective affinity", with [the spirit of modern consumerism], and to have given rise to a character type and ethical conduct highly conducive to the adoption of such attitudes':

> Whilst the rationalistic puritan [Weber's Calvinism 'evolving into rationalism and utilitarianism'] and romantic [Weber's Pietism 'evolving into Sentimentalism and Romanticism'] traditions differ, and in some respects are even opposed, it is really a form of sibling rivalry which divides them, joined as they are through a kinship which can be discerned psychologically and sociologically as well as historically. (Campbell, 1987: 220)

What this account shows, is that apparent differences between the cultures of work and of consumption are often to do with how ideas, meanings and values are represented and expressed rather than from any substantial differences in value systems which lie beneath them. As we have seen in our earlier analysis of the basic similarity between the ethics of production and of consumption, although the cultural artefacts of work and of consumption are different, they take different forms and adopt different modes of expression, the core values which they transmit are actually very similar. One trivial illustration of this is that although they may be separated by as much as 50 years, the central themes of many popular television situation comedies and soap operas, have barely changed at all. The characters and contexts of the 2000s are not the same as those of the 1950s, but the relatively settled and moderately affluent depiction of ordinary working and family life which underpins them remains largely unaltered. A similar case could be made about continuity in the themes of popular music enjoyed by young people. Rebellion, rejection of authority and desire for change are as characteristic of jazz and rock 'n' roll as they are of rap and hip hop (Lhamon, 1998).

In recognising that continuity of meaning and value persist despite evident changes at the surface of culture, it becomes clear that in comparing the types of culture and cultural artefacts which are typical of work-based and consumption-based society respectively, we are much more likely to be comparing techniques of presentation rather than of substance. For example, one of the most important characteristics of postmodern or postmodernist artefacts is that they challenge the modernist tendency to assume that the relationship between the object or phenomenon we are trying to understand (the signified) and the word or idea we use in referring to it (the signifier) is relatively stable. It is very much a modernist way of doing things to try to understand the world in terms of clearly defined opposites or dualisms, to see things in black *or* white, this *or* that, etc. Since it is impossible to articulate and communicate our understandings of the values we express through action without using words and labels the signifier/signified relationship is fundamental to the whole process not only of understanding how 'meaning' is constructed, but also of how particular meanings come to be associated with particular activities (how signs and what they signify become related). A heightened sensitivity to how meanings are constructed, by whom, how durable they are and how they are transmitted is one of the main characteristics of postmodernist culture and cultural criticism.[9]

Not surprisingly, participants in this discourse define postmodern society as a society where the realm of culture has expanded in order to provide an enlarged context within which people can research the meanings of their actions and explore their values. And in this respect at least they are certainly correct because in consumption-based society people actually do have a much expanded range of activities to participate in. One of the things which marks the period of transition from modernity and towards postmodernity (say from 1950 to 2000) is that the rate of increase of new activities and expansion of the range of meanings which are associated with them has been particularly marked.

THE CULTURES OF WORK AND CONSUMPTION

The debates we have just been discussing provide us with a number of useful strategies for understanding how and why changes in the balance of people's activities away from work and towards consumption might be reflected in the realm of culture. We know that as a result of increasing affluence people have been able to divert more time and resources towards consumption. With increasing consumption comes more choice and a greater range of activities and this in turn increases uncertainty about the meaning and purpose of those activities. Levels of cultural activity increase in order to meet the demand for value-guidance; to make good the value-deficit caused by an excess of novelty made possible by new forms of consumption. Clearly then, the focus of our attention needs to be on the values which are used to justify different kinds of activities, and on differences in the modes of expression which are used to keep those values in cultural circulation. We must however be careful not to assume that differences in form automatically indicate differences in substance. We must also be wary not to confuse differences in the general function of culture as a realm where the meanings and values of action are debated, with differences in the contents of the value systems which provide much of the substance of those discussions.

What one would expect to find is that 'culture' fulfils largely the same function in work-based and consumption-based social types but that such variations as there are in the values which are articulated through culture will show up as cultural variation. The degree of cultural variation obviously depends (a) on how different the activities are which people typically and habitually perform in the society which that cultural type reflects, and (b) on the similarity or otherwise of the value systems which are used to justify those activities. The cultures of otherwise largely similar societies (societies which actually share the same basic value system) might appear to vary a good deal if the ways they express those values through culture are not the same. For example, differences between North American and Australian culture are largely attributable to differences in the ways that each expresses values through its particular style of cultural artefact, rather than to differences in the basic value system (an acknowledgement of the Christian belief system, respect for hard work and perseverance, acceptance of rights and obligations developed through democratic processes). A similar continuity at depth combined with variety at the surface helps us understand why key values in British culture have survived over long periods of time despite considerable changes in other aspects of society. It is the longevity of such core values which gives particular national cultures – the Anglo-Saxon in our case – their distinctiveness. Discussing 'the great traditions' of English society in mid-twentieth century for example, the writer J.B. Priestley listed the following:

> First, the liberty of the individual. So long as they do no harm to others, men must be allowed to develop their own way. Second, that which goes with liberty – toleration. Third, voluntary public service. Fourth, a very deep love, a poetic love, rooted deep down in the unconscious, of England and the English way of life, of the fields and the woods, flowers and birds, of pastimes, of the poets and storytellers. Fifth, which you will find everywhere among the common people, humour and irony and along with these a profound depth of sentiment. (J.B. Priestley, quoted in Richards, 1988: 55–6)

Making sense of it all

Beginning with the basic question of how people make sense of their various activities in the two kinds of society we are interested in here, we can say that the meanings/values which people draw from culture in work-based society are relatively stable and universally understood by everyone in that society, and much of this is attributable to the fact that over time these meanings/values have become heavily collectivised. Similarly, the ideas and expressions which are used to promulgate these meanings/values (the contents of culture) have had plenty of time to establish themselves and thus tend not to be very ambiguous. Such debate as does go on is relatively easy to follow since the meaning of the terms which are being used and the ideas they represent travel along well-worn and familiar paths. This is very much what one would expect to find in a society where the activities which people spend most of their time doing, i.e. working, tend to disallow much in the way of autonomy. If people are doing similar kinds of things in a similar kind of way and with similar ends in mind, then it is not too difficult to identify a set of meanings/values which most people identify with. 'Culture' is a shorthand way of referring to this set of agreed values. The meanings/values and thus the cultures which circulate in work-based society are relatively simple because the objectives of action are relatively transparent.

Another way of saying much the same thing, is to recognise that even if the intended meaning of action can seen ambiguous, reference to the context in which the action takes place usually resolves the matter. To the extent that the contexts of production-side activities are less varied than the contexts of consumption-side activities (one office or retail outlet is pretty much the same as another from the worker's point of view), the likelihood is that levels of meaning-ambiguity will also be pretty low.

The core values of work-based society

As one would expect then, the value systems of work-based societies are relatively simple not because people living in this kind of society have limited ambitions when it comes to understanding the meaning of their actions, but because the meaning of action in such societies is actually pretty straightforward (which is not the same as saying that these meanings are unimportant). The same simplicity is evident when these values are drawn upon to justify or legitimate the activities of production. Material survival is the prerequisite to all other kinds of action and so the physical actions and practical outcomes of work are entirely justifiable for as long as they produce these ends. Given that in this kind of society it is non-productive to develop too many alternative means of achieving the same end (an over supply of rational technique is irrational), there might not be much variety in the way that work is done (the labour processes of all industrialised economies really are very similar).

Beyond basic survival lies material prosperity and this also is an entirely legitimate and justifiable pursuit because prosperity signifies that one can take one's basic survival pretty much for granted: prosperity is survival writ large. If the utility of particular ends and their associated means survives constant practical testing and repetition over long periods of time (people actually do survive and prosper) then the usefulness of these means and ends might become translated into an abstracted notion of 'value' in the sense of some kind of general 'good' (meaning a goal or objective which has withstood all attempts to discredit it). Work is 'valued' firstly because the ends it aims to achieve (survival/prosperity) have high utility (are valuable), second because it has established itself as a most effective (valuable) means of achieving those ends, and third because both as action and as outcome, work enables people to express the values they hold about the importance of being productively active. In work-based society, and quite beyond its indisputable utility as a means of producing highly desired practical outcomes, 'work' signifies the expression of a more generalised or disembodied sense of 'value'.

These generalised values express the socially agreed meanings which characterise particular societies and provide culture with much of its subject matter. For example, one of the dominant cultural values of Western industrialised societies is the 'value' that it is right and proper always to try to achieve more. Belief in this general value has spawned other more colloquial sayings or expressions which reflect the same basic idea – 'there is no such thing as enough', 'more is always better', 'onwards and upwards'. Work-based society can be defined as a type of society where work is more highly valued than any other activity. It is by no means a coincidence that one of the reasons why this form of society has been so successful is because at the core of its value system is a belief in the 'value' that satisfaction can never really be achieved (the battle for survival goes on). It is for the same reason of course, that the decline and fall of many of the great societies of the past has been triggered by an abandonment of the values of 'blood sweat and toil' in favour of the values of pleasure and enjoyment. Affluence results in hedonism and hedonism is not known for its capacity to produce material goods (or values).

The core values of consumption-based society

Looking at how value is associated with activity in consumption-based society, we can say that the same basic rules apply (people seek out the meanings of their actions and often this has to do with the pursuit of values), but that although the value system which is used to legitimate and justify consumption-side activities is largely the same (not least because it shares the same roots as the ethic of production), the way it expresses these values is slightly different. People remain involved in production-type activities and so inevitably continue to refer to the 'values' of economic activity when trying to understand and legitimate this part of their lives. These values are also applicable to consumption, and especially if we are talking about simple consumption. It would be ridiculous to suggest that economic values cannot be used to legitimate any kind of consumption at all. To the extent that production and consumption serve the same ends, most forms of consumption can be straightforwardly legitimated by referring to the core values of productivism. However, the situation becomes more complicated with the emergence of complex forms of consumption ushered in by sustained affluence, and especially with activities which provide satisfaction in terms of symbolic meaning. Within culture, new ways have been found first to exploit the value-potential of novel satisfactions which lie at the novelty-rich end of the utility continuum, and secondly, to explore new ways of representing established values.

From around the late 1950s it must have been quite a shock for people in the industrialised West to discover that a whole new range of values had come into view, and one moreover, which sanctioned the kinds of indulgence and satisfaction which ascetic productivism had tried to repress (or had at least tried to defer until retirement). Although always sanctioned as a legitimate means to an end, consumption for pleasure was rapidly becoming an end in itself. The satisfactions of work remain, but they are overtaken by the kinds of satisfaction which come from activities which express self-indulgence and personal pleasure rather than necessity. To those who accept ascetic productivism as a reliable basis upon which to develop a sense of value and purpose about their activities – that is to value 'work', and this includes most of the population of the industrialised West who had been born before about 1930, it literally makes no sense to squander these hard-earned securities on personal satisfaction and enjoyment. Affluence challenges this apparent certainty by giving people an opportunity to separate the dull routine of work from the novelty of consumption not only in terms of the activities themselves, but much more importantly, in terms of the values which they can express through these activities.

For example, the cultural rift which occurred most explicitly in North America but also elsewhere during the 1950s and 1960s between young people and their parents is actually a rift between those-born-of-affluence and those-born of-austerity.[10] What was challenging about the newly affluent younger generation was not simply that they lived at a time when the grip of work over people's lives had loosened a little, but that they embarked on a vigorous campaign to develop new ideas about the meaning of their activities and especially how to justify their non-work activities. Leisure was no longer the bits-and-pieces of time left over after work but was becoming a significant realm in its own right and with its own practices, codes of conduct and thus values. One of the things which made this expanding realm an attractive and exciting place to be and especially so for younger people, was the fact that the means by which these new values were being explored and expressed were in the field of popular culture. To those with money in their pockets and increasing amounts of free time, the leisure-consumption realm of music, fashion and entertainment was very much 'the in scene to be seen in'.[11] The rewards and satisfactions of consumption were sought because the ends to which they are the most effective means, namely enjoyment and pleasure, were now deemed to be highly desirable ends in their own right. By the 1970s it was no longer ridiculous to talk about 'the values of consumption', or 'consumption-side values'. Indeed in a society where production and consumption are balanced against each other what could be more natural than to supplement the core value of 'work' with a new core value called 'consumption? Consumption had acquired the status of being universally 'valued':

> [W]hilst the media invite certain interpretations, young people have not only learnt the codes, but have learnt to play with interpreting the codes, to reshape forms, to interrelate the media through their own grounded aesthetics. They add to and develop new meanings from given ones. The young are the most sophisticated 'readers' of images and media of any group in society. The meanings they derive from these things inform all their activities. Most importantly the cultural media are used as a means to vitality, to provide and construct dimensions for what they are and might become. (Willis, 1990: 30)

Degrees of value satisfaction

Another useful way of differentiating between work-based and consumption-based societies and cultures, in terms of the contents of their respective value systems, is to consider whether consumption is more satisfying because it offers greater opportunities for value fulfilment than does work. This might be so in two senses. First, and in contrast with the activities of production which tend to be fairly task-specific and whose meanings and purposes can therefore be readily explained and justified by reference to a limited range of values, the activities of consumption are more complex and thus require more in the way of explanation and justification in terms of meanings/values. Simplistically, one has to put more effort into understanding the meaning/value of an act of complex consumption than one does into understanding a simple act of production. Greater satisfaction might come from solving more complex meaning puzzles, or, which amounts to the same thing, reaching higher levels of understanding. To the extent that an increasing need to devise ever-more complex explanations of the meaning and value of action requires more in the way of cultural activity, then consumption-based societies will be more 'cultural' in the sense that cultural artefacts are required to do more work, and that more cultural artefacts are available to do it.

Second and following on from this, the hierarchy of consumption we discussed in Chapter 5 might reflect a hierarchy of values in the sense that the more meaning-laden a particular activity is, the more vigorously it will be sought. Simple acts of production/consumption directed towards the satisfaction of basic necessities allow people to express what we might want to call first-order values, while complex acts of production/consumption directed towards the enjoyment of more symbolic outcomes allow people to express second- or third-order values. Instead of using values only as a means of understanding the meaning of an activity (the meaning of my actions is intelligible to me because it comes partly from the values I seek to express through my actions), the expression of values in-and-of-itself becomes the primary reason for performing a particular kind or range of activities (value-expression is my primary intention). It is an expression of meaning/value as an end in itself which is sought, not merely a general explanation of the meaning of an action which makes reference to the expression of values as part of the explanation of that action (that is, as a means to an end).

Although there is no such thing as an unimportant value (if an ideal or objective is not actively sought, it will not constitute a value) it is not unreasonable to think that people try especially hard to express some values more vigorously than others, and/or invest particularly high levels of value significance in some activities than they do in other activities. Arguably, if the value content of a particular activity is high, then that activity might be sought ahead of other activities which have a lower value content. If as terminal-type actions (rather than intermediate ones as discussed in Chapter 5) acts of consumption are closer to the moment when satisfaction is achieved and if value-fulfilment is the mode of satisfaction being sought, then consumption is bound to come across as a more value-ridden, or somehow more intensely 'valuable' kind of activity. Such questions would ultimately have to be settled by resolving how or in what ways one kind of satisfaction is more 'satisfying' than another kind. One would have to ask whether levels of value satisfaction depend (a) on how much raw pleasure one gets from an action which is highly 'valued' because if its association with that pleasure outcome (sex-n-drugs-n-rock-n-roll) or (b), whether it comes from the fact that one is pursuing a highly sought-after 'value' which is difficult to achieve ('it is better to have loved and lost than never to have loved at all'). Failure to achieve completely something with a very high end-value (b) might still be more satisfying than completely achieving something whose action-value is actually quite trivial (a). People marooned on a desert island for example, might yearn for the satisfaction of an ice-cold beer although actually a fish and rice soup would be much more genuinely satisfying. Activities which combine high levels of action-satisfaction with important end-values (for example sexual intercourse with a much loved partner) are obviously going to be located right at the top of the value/activity hierarchy.[12]

Themes and contents of culture in work-based society

Moving on from our brief comparison of the value systems of work-based society, we should say a little more about the themes and contents of the cultural artefacts typical of each type. Given the production-related pre-disposition of meanings/values in work-based society, one would not be surprised to find that many of the leading cultural artefacts of the modern age are centred around the themes of working life and the various changes it has undergone. One could easily construct a chronology of key works of English literature which matches the chronology of developments in the organisation of work. From the early emergence of organised home working described in *Silas Marner*, the collapsing idyll of rural life in *Adam Bede*, *The Mayor of Casterbridge* and *Far From the Madding Crowd*, the coming of modern industry and commerce in Dickens and Trollope, to the examination of industrial utopia and dystopia in the works of Wells, Huxley and Orwell. A bitter examination of the consequences of the coming of factory production and the spread of urban dwelling forms a constant backdrop to many of the events and characters in the turgid world written by D.H. Lawrence. In modernist fine art also, the mark of industrialism is indelibly stamped. From the dreamy but restless images of the power of steam and coal in Turner's *Rain, Steam and Speed* (1844) and Monet's *Gare Saint-Lazare* (1876), to the futurists' child-like obsession with the energising turmoil of revolutionary industrialism, the aesthetic of pre-war modernism in Europe is heavily preoccupied with the quest for the meaning of productivism and the productivist work ethic (Gombrich, 1972; Parker, 1998; Roberts (ed.), 1994). The heavy emphasis on practicality and utility, a basic characteristic of productivism, is also reflected in other fields most notably in architecture where early twentieth-century designers such as Le Corbusier and Lloyd Wright were much concerned with the balance between form and function (Pevsner, 1973).

The prevailing theme of cultural artefacts of this period are very much a reflection of the work-oriented style of life that the majority of the population were leading. Not surprisingly this concern with working life within the artistic intelligentsia is also found in the academy. In post-war British cultural theory for example, Edward Thompson focuses full-square on the emergence of the 'English working class' and its coming of age during the twentieth century. For Raymond Williams and Eric Hobsbawm, the culture of postwar Britain is one which has its roots in the experiences and expectations of the mass of ordinary working people. As we saw in our discussion of social identity and class in Chapter 6, a very similar set of themes dominates academic accounts of people and society put forward by British sociologists during the 1960s and 1970s. Whether we are looking at Newby's account of agricultural labour, Beynon's or Hebdidge's explorations of industrial community and heritage, or Pahl's fine-grained dissection of life in work, British sociology at this time was pretty much a sociology of working life only. Interest in other areas such as the family or social stratification and mobility are also firmly rooted in this same tradition.

Themes and contents of culture in consumption-based society

One of the most pressing reasons why ideas about the meaning/value of various kinds of activities seem to have moved on so dramatically in consumption-based society is that the means of expressing and discussing these ideas have changed. At the surface, it is not only the 'what' of culture that has changed but the 'how'. One could make a strong case for saying that movement from one social type to another (in our case from work-based to consumption-based social types) goes hand-in-hand with developments in the technical means of cultural transmission. One does have to be careful however, not to be entirely seduced by the apparent novelty and technical wizardry of the new digital media since, as we have already pointed out, there are actually quite strong continuities both in the means and the contents of cultural communication over time.

Again we need to maintain a distinction between changes in the means and changes in the message. Just because new means of cultural communication are available does not mean that the messages they contain will necessarily be new. For example, paper-based media such as books and magazines are used in both the social types we are concerned with here, as are captured visual images in photography and film, and various kinds of performance such as dance and theatre. Reading Shakespeare off a computer screen might not be quite the same experience as reading him off the paper page and certainly not the same as attending an actual performance, but the basic plot of the play remains constant. The difference in listening to the same piece of music in live performance, as recorded on digital or audio tape, on compact disc, on magnetic tape, or on a vinyl record, is largely one of audio clarity; it would be difficult to argue convincingly that the music itself is different in each of these manifestations. One of the reasons why cultural continuity over time and between one social type and another is possible is because established means persist alongside new developments in the range and variety of media through which cultural artefacts and their associated (if contested and arbitrary) meanings are articulated within the population.

It must be acknowledged however, that one of the most important developments in means of cultural transmission characteristic of consumption-based society is that they are themselves highly consumable. As we saw in our analysis of patterns of consumption in Chapter 5, in its latest manifestations, digital communication and all the paraphernalia that goes with it now features very prominently in categories of household goods and services and leisure goods and services which households typically spend their disposable income on. Consumers not only want to consume the message, they also want to consume the means by which it is transmitted and received.[13]

One thing then, which distinguishes what we might want to call the mode of culture in the two types of society is that over time, the ideas and messages about the meaning/value of action are increasingly consumed in themselves as tasty cultural morsels. We no longer need these artistic dramatisations or representations of what goes on in the world of work to help us understand what is going on at work. We already know enough about these things. What we do want to do however, is to show off just how knowledgeable we now are. Whereas comedy about work has always been an escape from work, an antidote to the Monday-morning feeling, in the cultural artefacts of consumption-based society a much more knowing even arrogant self-confidence has emerged. Cultural artefacts in consumption-based society represent a real sense of liberation from the ordinary, rather than simply a translation of the signs by which 'the ordinary' is represented.

Relationships

One of the most important functions of culture, and again one which is common to both the types of society we are interested in here, is that it provides dramatised re-enactments of how social participation and solidarity operate in that kind of society. Not surprisingly then, a dominant theme running right across the cultural artefacts we have just been referring to, is that they carry essential messages about the meanings and purposes of our interactions with other people. In the same way that we relate to people in terms of the material or practical outcomes of their actions, we also relate to them in terms of the values they appear to be pursuing.[14] The age of complex consumption opens the possibility that people are expressing more than one set of values in their actions and therefore that there is more than one value-level upon which we might want to interact with them. In modern work-based society the tendency is to relate to people in terms of their occupation and perhaps the social or economic class to which they belong. In consumption-based society people are much more likely to relate to others in terms of their gender, their ethnicity, their sexual orientation and so on. What this amounts to is a more forthright recognition that the range of values people hope to express through their actions, is no longer limited by economic values but also expresses other values including those associated with consumption. The linkages between value, activity and identity, linkages which certainly preoccupy the producers of cultural artefacts, become more complex as levels of affluence increase. One of the 'values' of affluent-consumer society is the value of being able to express different aspects of our needs and desires through different parts of our identity, in effect of being able to relate to others on more than one level.

Summary

Figure 8.2 attempts to summarise key elements of the discussion in this chapter in terms of the major themes or characteristics of the value systems of work and consumption.

As we have been discussing in this chapter, one of the major differences between work-based and consumption-based social types is that the activities of consumption offer higher levels of autonomy and novelty than do the activities of work. To the extent that these characteristics are associated with a general preoccupation with the meaning of the things we do (because the meaning of acts of complex consumption cannot so easily be accounted for wholly in terms of practical outcomes), then as the realm in which meanings and values are discussed, the realm of culture assumes a particularly important role. The transition from a work-based to a consumption-based social type creates an especially demanding role for the realm of culture.

Recalling our opening discussion in this chapter however, the fact that this transition from work to consumption has important cultural elements

Value system of	
Work-based society	Consumption-based society
Ethic of production	Ethic of consumption
Survival can never be taken for granted	Consumption is a triumph over survival
Work is sought mainly as a means-to-an-end	Consumption is sought mainly as an-end-in-itself
Positive attitude towards producing things	Positive attitude towards consuming things
Producing more is assumed to be a universal 'good'	Consuming more is assumed to be a universal 'good'
Actions justified because of the inherent need to produce	Actions justified because of the inherent desire to consume
Doubt about meaning of action mostly resolved by reference to material outcomes	Doubt about meaning of action mostly resolved by reference to ideational outcomes
Outcomes assessed in terms of practical utility	Outcomes assessed in terms of symbolic utility
Deferred gratification	Instant gratification
Debt is to be avoided	Debt is a normal practice
Credit is a means of producing more	Credit is a means of consuming more

Figure 8.2   Value systems

to it, does not mean that the transition itself is primarily 'cultural'. 'Culture' remains a key element in the social structure and at times may appear to dominate other key elements of economy and polity, but it can never operate independently of them. Accounts which represent recent social transition as being an essentially cultural transition from modernity to postmodernity, and which follow through with highly detailed and perceptive analyses of changes in the contents of the cultural realm, have much to offer but should not distract us from the fact that change originates in the economic realm. Affluence has profound implications for society and for culture, but it is a condition born of the activities of production.

We should not of course be surprised at reaching this conclusion since all we have really done is identify the same factors and processes which characterised the transition out of pre-modern and into modern society. A transition also gave rise to quite revolutionary changes in culture which again asserted itself as a leading venue for discussing and debating ideas about how people should construct new meanings and values around their activities. Nobody would deny however, that the transition into the modern period was based on revolution in the means of production. Although from our contemporary perspective, the general feel and tone of culture in modern work-based society seems conservative and reactionary when compared with the progressive and revolutionary feel or tone of culture in late-modern consumption-based society, all such comparisons are relative. Compared with the relatively static and mechanical tone of pre-modern agricultural societies, the culture of modernity could certainly not be characterised as conservative.

NOTES

[1]Pakulski and Waters offer the following inclusive definition of culture: 'We take culture to consist of all the meanings, values, norms, preferences, ideas, customs, beliefs, knowledges, lifestyles and symbolic patterns relevant to a given society or social formation ... [customarily] culture is specified as substantively consisting of three value spheres ... of truth or cognition [real versus unreal] ... of beauty or cathais [emotions of love and hate] ... and of morality or judgement [norms]' (Pakulski and Waters, 1996: 115).

[2]It might be possible to experience a sense of value fulfilment as the result of some cognitive or intellectual process which ostensibly lacks 'action' but such performances would have to be defined as a special kind of action. Prayer or meditation for example might fall into the category of activities which enable people to experience a profound sense of value expression or value fulfilment without being ostensibly 'active'.

[3]This author continues: 'Consumer culture is in important respects *the* culture of the modern West – certainly central to the meaningful practice of everyday life in the modern world; and it is more generally bound up with central values, practices and institutions which define western modernity, such as choice, individualism and market relations' (Slater, 1997b: 8). See also Lee, 1994.

[4]'Family values' for example, are an expression of society-wide beliefs about how and why people conduct their familial relationships in particular ways; they are not the unique expression of values of any particular family. The values of a particular family might of course converge with the generally agreed set of 'family values' which is characteristic of that society, and the degree of convergence provides a measure of the social conformity of that particular family.

[5]Glancing back at our discussions of gender-identity in the previous chapter, we can note in passing that in trying to reconcile capitalism and patriarchy as the twin

sources of women's oppression in the modern period, some feminist theorists attributed 'capitalism' to the economic sphere and 'patriarchy' to the cultural sphere. The gender ideology which allegedly preceded capitalism can thus be represented as an ideological/superstructural phenomena as well as an economic/ structural one (Barrett and Phillips (eds), 1992).

[6]The idea of cultural implosion accompanied by a reassertion of basic values is a common motif in so-called 'disaster' movies. Following some natural or other catastrophe – earthquake, volcanic eruption or alien invasion – much of the plot centres around the survival not so much of the people involved but of the collective social values they hold most dear. Many thousands have perished but courage, honour and justice have survived. The considerable popular status of many 'great' actors and actresses derives from the fact that they are so closely associated with the collective social values which the characters they portray typically reassert. Obvious examples would include John Wayne, Charlton Heston, Clint Eastwood, Harrison Ford and Tom Hanks. Leading female sustainers of collective values are currently Jodie Foster, Sigourney Weaver, Julia Roberts and Susan Sarandon.

[7]The coming of industrialism during the nineteenth century for example, triggered a great outpouring of cultural artefacts as artists, composers and writers set about explaining and interpreting what the consequences were of the industrial and urban revolutions (Hughes, 1980; Kumar, 1987; Harrison and Wood (eds), 1992).

[8]As Weber argues, the expression of collective understanding or 'values' is one of the most important constituents of the meaning of action: 'In action is included all human behaviour when and insofar as the acting individual attaches a subjective meaning to it … Action is social insofar as, by virtue of the subjective meaning attached to it by the acting individual, it takes account of the behaviour of others and is thereby oriented in its course' (Weber, *Economy and Society*, 1978: 4, quoted in Morrison, 1995: 274).

[9]The process by which 'meaning' is constructed is extremely complex since (a) there is no way of reconciling differences between one person's subjective interpretation of meaning/value and another person's subjective interpretation, and (b) even if it were, we would then be faced with another series of potential disagreements over the words, pictures, sounds, etc., we might want to use to discuss it. Difficulties over the construction of 'meaning' in sense (a) can however be resolved if one accepts that culture does not really deal with matters of individual interpretation but with shared meanings and values which collectivise people's action. Values, properly speaking, are properties of collectivities not of individuals. As far as the construction of meaning in sense (b) is concerned, the most direct way out of the signifier/signified labyrinth is to recognise that there is an important difference between the attaching of a particular sign to a particular object (the word 'cat' to the object cat), and the attaching of significance to that object (cats signify mystery). An argument for example, over whether cats bring good or bad luck has nothing whatever to do with the attachment of the word 'cat' to the furry creature in question.

[10]The standard point of departure here is Cohen, 1980. He goes on to describe the 'moral panic' caused by emerging youth cultural groups of the 1950s and 1960s as follows:

One of the most recurrent types of moral panic in Britain since the war has been associated with the emergence of various forms of youth culture ... whose behaviour is deviant or delinquent. To a greater or lesser degree, these cultures have been associated with violence. The Teddy Boys, the Mods and Rockers, the Hell's Angels, the skinheads and the hippies have all been phenomena of this kind. These have been parallel reactions to the drug problem, student militancy, political demonstrations, football hooliganism, vandalism of various kinds and crime and violence in general ... In the gallery of types that society erects to show its members which roles should be avoided and which should be emulated, these groups have occupied a constant position as folk devils: visible reminders of what we should not be. (Cohen, 1980: 9)

[11]As Stewart puts it:

[B]y the end of the 1950s an array of goods and services, from fashions and entertainment to food and drink, was specifically aimed at satisfying the needs and aspirations of the youth consumer. Although the overall spending power of the youth population was not that significant in comparison with other consumer groups, young people tended to have a much greater 'discretionary' element in their spending power. Consequently their spending tended to be concentrated in the 'non-essential' sectors and this made them a particularly attractive target to the burgeoning 'leisure' economy. (Stewart, 1992: 203)

[12]These kinds of questions lead us into deep waters because debates about kinds and degrees of satisfaction raise the issue of whether one value is more valuable than another. The short answer is probably that each value system has a relatively small number of core values (the Ten Commandments of Christianity for example) and that other values in the system can be reduced to these. A value which can be traced back in this way is, at least in this sense, less valuable than one that cannot. The core values of a value system are equally valuable and not reducible. This is what makes them core values.

[13]For example: 'Mobile phone ownership nearly quadrupled from 17 per cent of households in the United Kingdom in 1996/97 to 65 per cent in 2001/2, while access to the Internet at home rose at a similar rate between 1998–9 and 2001–02 to reach 40 per cent' (*Social Trends*, 2003: 230).

[14]Referring again to Cohen's analysis of youth culture, he is emphatic that 'personal styles and choice of clothes; selective and active use of music, TV, magazines; decoration of bedrooms; the rituals of romance and subcultural styles; the style, banter and drama of friendship groups; music-making and dance' play an essential role in developing common identity: 'In conditions of late modernisation and the widespread crisis of cultural values [they can be] crucial to the creation and sustenance of individual and group identities, even to cultural survival of identity itself. There is work, even desperate work, in their play' (Willis, 1990: 2).

9

Concluding comments: the affluence hypothesis revisited

Throughout the foregoing discussion, we have been developing the argument that the primary mechanism by which a shift might be occurring away from production and towards consumption is increasing affluence. We have defined affluence as a capacity for most households in contemporary Western society to participate in levels of consumption which routinely exceed those required for basic survival. In moving out of a situation of survival and into one of prosperity, most individuals are able to express historically unprecedented levels of choice and autonomy in what they consume. Evidence of increasing affluence has been obtained by looking at statistical data on average individual and household earnings, and levels of disposable income. If we define affluence in terms of averages and aggregates, it is reasonable to conclude that most people living in Britain today are affluent, and that Britain is an affluent society.

If increasing prosperity (greater efficiency of output combined with rising average wages) was enjoyed in the form of a decisive decrease in the amount of time spent performing paid occupational roles, possibly combined with a levelling-off of incomes and a redistribution of unpaid household tasks, then we might be talking about a shift away from work-based towards leisure-based society. Leisure would be defined as disposable time which is left over after sleeping, working, and necessary household activities have been completed. The evidence we have been looking at however, shows that amongst the affluent populations of the industrialised West, most people actually prefer to spend about the same amount of time working, and to use the similar or gradually increasing amounts of non-work time at their disposal in consumption-type activities. Leisure-consumption, in the form of leisure-oriented goods and services accounts for a higher and increasing proportion of household disposable income than was the case even a few years ago. There has also been a general upgrading of consumption-type activities across the range from relatively mundane consumables which provide simple satisfactions (food and drink, household goods, clothing) as well as intermediate and particularly advanced ones (household services, leisure and recreational goods). It is consumption which is characteristic of modern affluence not just leisure time.

The new consumption

Looking a little more closely at the nature of the new consumption, and particularly at leisure-consumption, we have suggested that the new consumption is liberating in the sense that under conditions of affluence, people are more able to choose for themselves where the balance should lie between work and consumption. If members of the household want to consume more, to enjoy the satisfactions which come from more elaborate and sophisticated kinds of consumption, then they are free to reallocate their spending accordingly. As and when increased income is required, opportunities are generally available to achieve this. If a particular individual craves the highly concentrated excitement which comes from white-water rafting, bungee-jumping or snow-boarding, then they are entirely free to devote their hard-earned cash and leisure-time to it. If they prefer to enjoy their leisure consumption by more sedentary means, then this choice also is easily made. The burgeoning demand for television and satellite channels, computer games and internet access, clearly shows that for the majority of households, 'cost' is no longer a decisive factor in making these choices. If household members decide that they want to reduce to a minimum the amount of time they spend in paid occupational roles (albeit with a corresponding decrease in disposable income), then this too is a legitimate option.

Secondly, whilst choice and autonomy are characteristics of most forms of consumption in the late modern period, activities which take place at the more complex end of the range offer particularly attractive and exciting possibilities for new kinds of satisfactions. As the variety of complex consumption has continued to increase, so also has the desire to gain pleasure and satisfaction from the more symbolic and abstract kinds of enjoyment which are characteristic of it. The capacity to find new ways of enjoying ourselves through these kinds of meaning-laden consumption seems unlimited and forms a very powerful combination with one of our other unlimited capacities which is for producing new means of satisfaction.

Third, the new consumption has been instrumental in stimulating a seemingly limitless enthusiasm for exploring and expressing identity. Although occupational identity provides a generally reliable means of knowing 'who one is' in terms of 'where one stands' in relation to the occupants of other slots in that particular hierarchy, this might be regarded as a fairly narrow and limited basis on which to develop identity. With affluence comes partial liberation from the grind of necessity, and with that, the limitations of the identity-as-occupational-role scenario become more and more obvious. A sense-of-self which is dominated by work and necessity is bound to be less variegated than one that is experienced through leisure, pleasure and enjoyment, and so consumption takes over as the primary field of identity formation. As we have seen, one of the prerequisites of participation in the various hierarchies, codes, fields and experiences of consumption is a preparedness constantly to review one's sense of identity. People continue to relate to others on the basis of work-based identities (the labour process could not function properly unless they did), but identity-relations now extend well beyond this particular, and relatively narrow range of interactions.

Finally, if we accept that part of the satisfaction we seek through our actions comes from the expression of meanings and values – action feeds the spirit and mind as well as the body – the new consumption provides new pathways towards value fulfilment. Established values (for example about provisioning and caring) can be expressed in new ways, and new values, many of which are associated with identity (for example about autonomy and difference) can be explored. Affluence means that we are no longer dominated by the activities of production, and thus we are no longer bound to evaluate our activity mostly in terms of the work-based value system. Over time, this is bound to affect the ways we interpret and express our sense of purpose and creativity.

Getting the fly out of the ointment

Of the fly in the academic ointment we mentioned in our opening chapter, subsequent discussion, and particularly concerning the role of culture in social transition, has emphasised that it is important not to get different kinds of 'change' muddled up with each other. Important developments in academic theory and discourse sometimes prefigure and sometimes follow actual changes in the lives of real people, but the extent to which this happens needs to be explained rather than taken for granted. In the present case, there certainly has been a 'turn to consumption', which can in part be attributed to other academic 'turns' most notably towards linguistics and towards culture. In emphasising the cultural aspects of social change, and in problematising modernist assumptions both about how the various bits of society fit together, and about how meanings and values are arrived at and represented, it is not always necessary to travel to the very end of these projects in order to say interesting things about social change. We have just concluded for example, that the emergence of postmodernist discourses does not automatically render modernist ones obsolete, and nor does the fact that exciting new ways of communicating ideas are available mean that the ideas themselves have necessarily changed very much. Like the advocate who exaggerates in order to establish a more moderate truth, academic commentators sometimes find it difficult not to go 'all the way'.

Almost by definition, one aspect of academic discourse which may be particularly prone to this kind of over enthusiasm is that which concerns social change. As we have found repeatedly in the foregoing discussion, it is not difficult to find clear evidence that actual and important changes have and are taking place in society. If we interpret these as indicating a shift from work- to consumption-based social types, a persuasive if rather crude case can be made that such a shift is occurring. Looking a little more closely however, we also know that much of what constitutes modern industrial society has remained unchanged or at least has only changed a little as we enter a late modern era. The difficult bit, is to assess where the balance lies between continuity and change and to offer explanations as to why some things have changed and others not. What is needed in other words, is a theory of social change which can also explain continuity.

Affluence, continuity and change

One of the reasons why affluence presents itself as such a strong candidate in our analysis of the mechanism of recent social change, is that it does accommodate continuity and change as between production and consumption. The more affluent a household becomes, the more likely it is that its members will be able to indulge in the more exciting and challenging kinds of consumption, and so their lives will be characterised by change. Those who are less affluent will not experience the same degree of change and so their lives will be characterised by continuity. It is also important to recognise however, that within the lives of even moderately affluent household members, a balance of continuity and change is struck because, as we have been arguing, the satisfactions which are sought include the relatively simple satisfaction of basic needs together with the satisfaction of more complex needs. Degree of affluence affects not only the absolute levels at which a household consumes, but also regulates choices between 'cheap' and 'expensive' satisfactions throughout the range. I might not be able to afford an overseas holiday, but I can afford to buy organic vegetables.

A similar combination of continuity and change can be seen as between the activities of production and consumption more generally. For the majority of households, who depend almost entirely on earned income, a balance has to be struck between the production side and the consumption side. In order to sustain and increase their capacity for consumption in general and for complex consumption in particular, household members must continue to discharge paid occupational roles. Even allowing for considerable increases in the technical sophistication and efficiency of key parts of the modern industrial labour process which, together with organisational and managerial innovations have resulted in vastly increased levels of production, affluent consumption presupposes not only continued but often increased participation in paid occupational roles. Unless the kinds of commodities and activities which people consume can be obtained for free, it makes little sense to argue that a preoccupation with consumption will result in a rejection of paid occupational roles. To the extent that many members of affluent households reject increased leisure in favour of more paid work, and/or seek out more expensive (which often means more rewarding and satisfying) forms of consumption, those paid occupational roles become more not less important to them.

Identities

We have also found continuity and change in terms of the kinds of identities which emerge within work- and consumption-based social types. Although the role of affluence in identity-formation is sometimes less obvious than it is when looking at levels of income and expenditure, it does play an important role. For example, a person's capacity to participate in consumption at the identity-laden end of the scale depends in part on their level of disposable income. Although in principle there is no reason why a person who has relatively modest levels of consumption cannot express their identity just as fully as somebody who experiences greater consumption-intensity (a principle which is enthusiastically enacted by all members of low-income sub-cultural groups), in practice, contemporary consumption-based society is a place where the means of expressing identity do have to be paid for. The identity-group hierarchy reflects expectations about a person's capacity to participate in top-end identity-oriented forms of consumption. Morally and ethically this might seem rather objectionable – poor people have less identity than rich people – but it is no more nor less of an imperfect social construction than any other means of registering difference.

Taking a further example, and this time illustrating continuity between the occupational roles and consumption hierarchies, one can observe that a key aspect of the contribution which paid occupational role makes to personal identity, is that it demonstrates an ambitious attitude towards, and capacity to enjoy, advanced forms of consumption. Today, individuals who seek out the highest-paying occupational roles do so because they crave the most demanding kinds of leisure consumption. This craving becomes very much a part of their identity, of who they are and how they engage with the social reality which surrounds them. People become 'affluent' in their expectations and so seek out opportunities to become 'affluent' in their behaviour. From the point of view of somebody who is affluent in their expectations, the other who only engages in modest forms of consumption is demonstrating that they are not affluent, perhaps even 'poor' in this respect. The failure to demonstrate affluence in practice signifies an unwillingness to compass 'affluent' expectations or expectations of affluence. (The person who is apparently non-affluent in their expectations will very likely claim affluence in some other respect. For example being 'rich in spirit'.)

Finally we should say something of continuity and change as between individuals and collectivities. In terms of the balance between social and personal identity, and to the extent that these two aspects can be analysed separately, we can conclude that, what both aspects have in common is the fact that they are profoundly social. Whether they are described as discourses of power, reflexive self-imaginings or subject positions in a structure, the individual and collective aspects of identity are both expressive of a social endowment which is held in common by members of that society. Within that social construction however, it is possible to detect a general movement towards prioritising the individual over the collective. Definitions and expressions of individuality are still bounded by what the social consensus deems them to be, but the consensus now accepts a more autonomous and proactive conception of individuality. Although this continues a well-established historical trend, it may also indicate that whilst we still recognise our dependence on the collective effort for our survival and prosperity, and thus have no difficulty in actively accepting the governorship of the collective will over our production-side activities, in the non-work realm we are less inclined to do so. And here again it is affluence which helps us understand how and why this has come about.

Work or consumption?

Of the three basic conclusions which were mentioned in the opening chapter, we conclude that a full-blown consumption-based social type has not emerged in Britain and elsewhere in the industrialised West at the outset of the twenty-first century. Consumption figures very prominently in people's lives. It is a principal goal to which much activity and resource is directed, but the production side, and particularly of paid occupational roles matters a great deal also. By virtue of the same arguments, it is not realistic to suggest that modern industrial societies, characterised by a general preoccupation with paid occupations and production, have remained untouched by the rise of consumption. To argue this would mean demonstrating that some break occurs in the relationship between production and consumption at the point where consumption is sought for pleasure and enjoyment rather than for survival. Production only gives satisfaction and pleasure at the point of consumption. The rest becomes an argument about where strict necessity ends and indulgence begins. In some important ways the intensity of work has increased. We are even more workerly than we were before, but always in the context of deepening consumption-intensity.

This leaves our third option that a modified social type can be observed, one which is characterised by the coexistence of work and consumption but where the balance between the two has altered. Such alterations do not occur by happenstance and so the question becomes one of understanding what the new balance looks like and how it might develop in the future. Questions of the degree and extent of change depend for their resolution on an understanding of the mechanism of change, and we have suggested affluence as a leading contender. If household disposable incomes continue to increase, if the novelty of consumption-experience is not exhausted, and if people continue to prefer consumption to time away from paid occupational roles, then we would anticipate that the consumption side will continue to grow in importance. If on the other hand, levels of disposable income began to decrease and/or if perceptions of the reliability of the sources of earned income upon which they depend were affected by a downturn in the economic situation, then one would anticipate that consumption would moderate. It must be said however, that the new core values of utility as pleasure and enjoyment, of consumption as an end in itself, and of the right to liberated identity and expression, have become permanent features of the late modern consciousness. If the case for an irreversible shift towards a consumption-based society depended entirely on these kinds of shifts in the underlying value system, then clearly, such a case would be difficult to resist.

Bibliography

Abbott, P. and Wallace, C. (1992) *The Family and the New Right*. London: Pluto.

Abercrombie, N. and Urry, J. (1983) *Capital, Labour and the Middle Classes*. London: Allen and Unwin.

Adorno, T. and Horkheimer, M. (1973) *Dialectics of Enlightenment*. London: Allen Lane.

Aglietta, M. (1979) *A Theory of Capitalist Regulation: The US Experience*. London: New Left Books.

Allen, S. (1997) 'What is work for? The right to work and the right to be idle', in R. Brown (ed.). pp. 540–69.

Alsop, R., Fitzsimons, A. and Lennon, K. (2002) *Theorizing Gender*. Cambridge: Polity Press.

Althusser, L. (1969) *For Marx*. London: Allen Lane.

Amin, A. (ed.) (1994) *Post-Fordsim: A Reader*. Oxford: Basil Blackwell.

Arrighi, G. (1994) *The Long Twentieth Century: Money, Power and the Origins of our Times*. London: Verso.

Bagozzi, R.P., Gurhan-Ganli, Z., and Priester, J.R. (2002) *The Social Psychology of Consumer Behaviour*. Buckingham: Open University Press.

Bahro, R. (1984) *Red and Green*. London: Verso.

Bahro, R. (1985) *The Alternatives in Eastern Europe*. London: Pan Books.

Banks, J. and Johnson, P. (eds) (1998) *How Reliable is the Family Expenditure Survey? Trends in Incomes and Expenditures over Time*. London: Institute for Fiscal Studies.

Barrett, M. and Phillips, A. (eds) (1992) *Destabilizing Theory: Contemporary Feminist Debates*. Cambridge: Polity Press.

Barth, F. (ed.) (1969) *Ethnic groups and Boundaries: The Social Organisation of Cultural Difference*. Oslo: Universitesforlaget.

Barthes, R. (1973) *Mythologies*. London: Paladin.

Baudrillard, J. (1998) *The Consumer Society: Myths and Structures*. London: Sage. First published 1970 as *La Société de Consommation*, Paris: Gallimard.

Baudrillard, J. (2001) *Selected Writings*, edited and introduced by Mark Poster, (second edition). Cambridge: Polity Press (first edition 1988).

Bauman, Z. (1998) *Work, Consumerism and the New Poor*. Buckingham: Open University Press.

Beck, U. (1992) *Risk Society: Towards a New Modernity*. London: Sage.

Becker, G.S. (1965) 'A theory of the allocation of time', *Economic Journal*, 75: 493–517.

Becker, G.S. (1976) *The Economic Approach to Human Behaviour.* Chicago: Chicago University Press.

Becker, G.S. (1981) *A Treatise on the Family.* Cambridge, MA: Harvard University Press.

Becker, G.S. (1985) 'Human capital, effort and the sexual division of labour', *Journal of Labor Economics* 3: S33–S58.

Belk, R.W. (1988) 'Possessions and the extended self', *Journal of Consumer Research*, 15: 139–68. Reproduced in D. Millar (ed.) 2001, Vo. III.

Bell, D. (1974) *The Coming of Post-Industrial Society: A Venture in Social Forecasting.* London: Heinemann Educational.

Bell, D. (1976) *The Cultural Contradictions of Capitalism.* London: Basic Books.

Benwell, B. (ed.) (2003) *Masculinity and Men's Lifestyle Magazines,* (Sociological Review Monographs). Oxford: Blackwell Publishing.

Beynon, H. (ed.) (1985) *Digging Deeper: Issues in the Miners' Strike.* London: Verso.

Bianchi, M. (ed.) (1998) *The Active Consumer: Novelty and Surprise in Consumer Choice.* London: Routledge.

Blauner, R. (1964) *Alienation and Freedom: The Factory Worker and his Industry.* Chicago: University of Chicago Press.

Bly, J. (1992) *Iron John: A Book About Men.* New York: Addison-Wesley.

Bocock, R. (1993) *Consumption.* London: Routledge.

Bomberg, E. (1998) *Green Parties and Politics in the European Union.* London: Routledge.

Bond, I. and Coleman, P. (eds) (1990) *Ageing and Society: An Introduction to Social Gerontology.* London: Sage.

Bourdieu, P. (1984) *Distinction: A Social Critique of the Judgement of Taste,* trans., R. Nice. London: Routledge (originally published 1979, Paris: Les Éditions de Minuit).

Bourdieu, P. (1990) *The Logic of Practice.* Cambridge: Polity Press.

Bradley, H. (1999) *Gender and Power in the Workplace: Analysing the Impact of Economic Change.* Basingstoke: Macmillan.

Bradley, H., Erickson, M., Stephenson, C. and Williams, S. (2000) *Myths at Work.* Cambridge: Polity Press.

Bradley, S. and Greenberg, W.G. (eds) (1991) *Desert Storm and the Mass Media.* Cresskil, NJ: Hampton Press.

Braverman, H. (1974) *Labor and Monopoly Capital: the Degradation of Work in the Twentieth Century.* New York: Monthly Review Press.

Brewer, J. and Porter, R. (eds) (1993) *Consumption and the World of Goods.* New York: Routledge.

Brown, R. (ed.) (1997) *The Changing Shape of Work.* London: Macmillan.

Brubaker, R.L. (1984) *The Limits of Rationality.* Allen and Unwin.

Bryson, C. and Cutrice, J. (1998) 'The end of materialism?, in R. Jowell et al. (eds).

Burrows, R. and Marsh, C. (eds) (1992) *Consumption and Class: Divisions and Change* (Explorations in Sociology, 40, British Sociological Association). London: Macmillan.

Butler, J. (1990) *Gender Trouble: Feminism and the Subversion of Identity*. London: Routledge.

Butler, T. and Savage, M. (eds) (1995) *Social Change and the Middle Classes*. London: University College London Press.

Callinicos, A. (1999) *Social Theory: A Historical Introduction*. Cambridge: Polity Press.

Callinicos, A. (2003) *An Anti-Capitalist Manifesto*. Cambridge: Polity Press.

Campbell, C. (1987) *The Romantic Ethic and the Spirit of Modern Consumerism*. Oxford: Blackwell.

Campbell, C. (1997) 'When the meaning is not a message: A critique of the consumption as communication thesis', in M. Nava et al. (eds).

Castells, M. (1977) *The Urban Question: A Marxist Approach*, (second edition). London: Edward Arnold.

Castells, M. (1996) *The Rise of Network Society*. Oxford: Blackwell.

Charles, N. (1993) *Gender Divisions and Social Change*. Hemel Hempstead: Harvester Wheatsheaf.

Charles, N. (2000) *Feminism, the State and Social Policy*. Basingstoke: Macmillan.

Charles, N. (2002) *Gender in Modern Britain*. Oxford: Oxford University Press.

Charles, N. and James, E. (2003) 'Gender and work orientations in conditions of job insecurity', *British Journal of Sociology*, 54 (2): 239–57.

Charles, N., James, E. and Ransome, P. (Forthcoming 2004), 'Perceptions of job insecurity in a retail sector organisation', in Stewart, P. (ed.), *Globalisation, the Changing Nature of Employment and the Future of work*. Basingstoke: Palgrave Macmillan.

Clark, T., Lipset, S.M. and Rempel, M. (1993) 'The declining political significance of social class', *International Sociology*, 8: 293–316.

Cohen, S. (1980) *Folk Devils and Moral Panics: The Creation of the Mods and Rockers*, (second edition). Oxford: Martin Robertson.

Coleman, J.C. and Warren-Anderson, C. (eds) (1992) *Youth Policy in the 1990s: The Way Forward*. London: Routledge.

Collin, F. (1997) *Social Reality*. London: Routledge.

Compton, M. (1970) *Pop Art: Movements of Modern Art*. London: Hamlyn.

Connell, R.W. (1983) *Which Way is Up?*. Sydney: George Allen and Unwin.

Connell, R.W. (1987) *Gender and Power: Society, the Person and Sexual Politics*. Oxford: Polity Press.

Connell, R.W. (1995) *Masculinities*. Oxford: Polity Press.

Connor, S. (1989) *Postmodernist Culture: An Introduction to Theories of the Contemporary*. Oxford: Blackwell.

Cooley, C.H. (1962) *Social Organization: A Study of the Larger Mind*. New York: Schocken (first published 1909).

Cooley, C.H. (1964) *Human Nature and Social Order*. New York: Schocken (first published 1902).

Craib, I. (1998) *Experiencing Identity*. London: Sage.

Crocker, D.A. and Linden, T. (eds) (1998) *Ethics of Consumption: The Good Life, Justice and Global Stewardship*. Lantham, MD: Rowman and Littlefield.

Crompton, R. (1997) *Women and Work in Modern Britain*. Oxford: Oxford University Press.

Crompton, R. (1998) *Class and Stratification*, (second edition). Cambridge: Polity Press.

Crompton, R. (ed.) (2001) *Restructuring Gender Relations and Employment: The Decline of the Male Breadwinner*. Oxford: Oxford University Press.

Crompton, R. and Harris, F. (1998) 'Explaining women's employment patterns: "orientations" to work revisited', *British Journal of Sociology*, 49 (1): 118–47.

Cross, G. (1993) *Time and Money: The Making of Consumer Culture*. London, Routledge.

Crow, S. (2002) *Social Solidarities: Theories, Identities and Social Change*. Buckingham: Open University Press.

Dalton, R. (1994) *The Green Rainbow: Environmental Interest Groups in Western Europe*. New Haven: Yale University Press.

Dalton, R. and Rohrschneider, R. (1998) 'The greening of europe', in R. Jowell et al. (eds).

Delanty, G. (2000) *Citizenship in a Global Age: Society, Culture, Politics*. Buckingham: Open University Press.

Devor, H. (1989) *Gender Bending: Confronting the Limits of Duality*. Bloomington: Indiana University Press.

Donaldson, N. (1991) *Time of Our Lives: Labour and Love in the Working Class*. Sydney: Allen and Unwin.

Douglas, M. and Isherwood, B. (1979) *The World of Goods*. London: Allen Lane.

Doyal, L. and Gough, I. (1991) *A Theory of Human Needs*. London: Macmillan.

Duffy, R. (2002) *A Trip Too Far: Ecotourism, Politics and Exploitation*. London: Earthscan Publications Limited.

DuGay, P. (1996) *Consumption and Identity at Work*. London: Sage.

Dunford, M. (1989) 'Technologies, politics and markets: the development of electronics in Grenoble and Silicon Glen', in M. Sharp and P. Holmes (eds). pp. 80–118.

Dunne, G. (1997) *Lesbian Lifestyles; Women's Work and the Politics of Sexuality*. Basingstoke: Macmillan.

Durkheim, E. (1933) *The Division of Labour in Society*. New York: Free Press (first published 1893).

Durkheim, E. (1968) *Suicide: A Study in Sociology*, (trans., J.A. Spaulding and G. Simpson. London: Routledge and Kegan Paul (originally published 1897).

Durkheim, E. and Maus, M. (1963) *Primitive Classification*. London: Cohen and West. (first published 1903).

Earl, P.E. (1996) *Lifestyle Economics*. Brighton: Harvester.

Economic Trends: Annual Supplement (2002) No. 28. London: HMSO.

Eder, K. (1993) *The New Politics of Class*. London: Sage.

Elliott, A. (ed.) (1999) *Contemporary Social Theory* (Blackwell Reader). Oxford: Blackwell.

Etzioni, A. (1998) 'Voluntary simplicity: characterization, select psychological implications, and societal consequences', *Journal of Economic Psychology*, 19: 619–43. Reproduced in Millar (ed.) 2001, Vol. I.

Family Spending: A Report on the 2001–2002 Expenditure and Food Survey Bev Botting (ed.) (2003) London: HMSO.

Featherstone, M. (ed.) (1988) *Postmodernism*. London: Sage.

Featherstone, M. (1990) 'Perspectives on consumer culture', *Sociology*, 24 (1): 5–22.

Featherstone, M. (1991) *Consumer Culture and Postmodernism*. London: Sage.

Featherstone, M. (ed.) (1992) *Cultural Theory and Cultural Change*. London: Sage.

Featherstone, M., Lash, S. and Robertson, R. (eds) (1995) *Global Modernities*. London: Sage.

Felstead, A. and Jewson, N. (eds) (1999) *Global Trends in Flexible Labour*. London: Macmillan.

Fine, B. (1992) *Women's Employment and the Capitalist Family*. London: Routledge.

Fine, B. and Leopold, E. (1993) *The World of Consumption*. London: Routledge.

Fineman, S. (ed.) (1987) *Unemployment: Personal and Social Consequences*. London: Tavistock Publications.

Firth, S. (1996) 'Music and identity', in S. Hall and P. Du Gay (eds). pp. 108–27.

Foucault, M. (1972) *The Archaeology of Knowledge*. New York: Pantheon.

Frankel, B. (1987) *The Post Industrial Utopians*. Cambridge: Polity Press.

Freeman, C., Clark, J.A. and Soete, L. (1982) *Unemployment and Technical Innovation: A Study of Long Waves and Economic Development*. London: Frances Pinter.

Fricke, P.H. (ed.) (1973) *Seafarer and Community: Towards a Social Understanding of Seafaring*. London: Croom Helm.

Frisby, D. and Featherstone, M. (eds) (1997) *Simmel on Culture: Selected Writings*. London: Sage.

Fromm, E. (1976) *To Have or To Be*. New York: Harper and Row.

Fukuyama, F. (1992) *The End of History and the Last Man*. Harmondsworth: Penguin.

Gabriel, Y. and Lang, T. (1995) *The Unmanageable Consumer: Contemporary Consumption and its Fragmentation*. London: Sage.

Galbraith, J.K. (1969) *The Affluent Society*, (revised second edition). London: Hamish Hamilton (first published 1962).

Galbraith, J.K. (1972) *The New Industrial State*. London: André Deutsch (first published 1967).

Gallie, D., Marsh, C. and Vogler, C. (eds) (1993) *Social Change and the Experience of Unemployment*. Oxford: Oxford University Press.

Gallie, D., White, M., Cheng, Y. and Tomlinson, M. (1998) *Restructuring the Employment Relationship*. Oxford: Oxford University Press.

Gane, M. (1991a) *Baudrillard: Critical and Fatal Theory*. London: Routledge.

Gane, M. (1991b) *Baudrillard's Bestiary*. London: Routledge.

Gane, M. (ed.) (2000) *Jean Baudrillard* (Sage Masters in Modern Social Thought, four volumes). London: Sage.

Garber, M. (1992) *Vested Interests: Cross-Dressing and Cultural Anxiety*. London: Routledge.

Gardner, C. and Sheppard, J. (1989) *Consuming Passion – The Rise and Fall of Retail Culture*. London: Unwin Hyman.

Gershuny, J. (1983) *Social Innovation and the Division of Labour*. Oxford: Oxford University Press.

Gershuny, J. (1993) 'Post-industrial convergence in time allocation', *Futures*: 578–86.

Gershuny, J. (2000) *Changing Times: Work and Leisure in Postmodern Society*. Oxford: Oxford University Press.

Giddens, A. (1990) *The Consequences of Modernity*. Cambridge: Polity Press.

Giddens, A. (1991) *Modernity and Self-Identity: Self and Society in the Late Modern Period*. Cambridge: Polity Press.

Gilbert, N., Burrows, R. and Pollert, A. (eds) (1992) *Fordism and Flexibility: Divisions and Change*. Basingstoke: Macmillan.

Ginn, J., Arber, S., Brannen, J., Dale, A., Dex, S., Elias, P., Moss, P., Pahl, J., Roberts, C. and Rubery, J. (1996) 'Feminist fallacies: a reply to Hakim on women's employment', *British Journal of Sociology*, 47 (1): 167–74.

Glover, J. (1989) *I: The Philosophy and Psychology of Personal Identity*. London: Routledge.

Glucksmann, M. (2000) *Cottons and Casuals: The Gendered Organisation of Labour in Time and Space*. Durham: (British Sociological Association) Sociologypress.

Godelier, M. (1980) 'Language and history; work and its representations: a Research proposal', *History Workshop Journal*, 10 (Autumn 1980): 164–74.

Goffman, E. (1969) *The Presentation of Self in Everyday Life*. London: Allen Lane (first published 1959).

Goldberg, J. (1993) *Why Men Rule: A Theory of Male Dominance*. Chicago: Open Court.

Goldthorpe, J.H. (1996) 'Class analysis and the reorientation of class theory: the case of persisting differentials in educational attainment', *British Journal of Sociology*, 45: 481–505.

Goldthorpe, J.H. (1998) 'Rational action theory for sociology', *British Journal of Sociology*, 49: 167–92.

Goldthorpe, J.H., Lockwood, D., Bechoffer, E. and Platt, J. (1968a) *The Affluent Worker: Industrial Attitudes and Behaviour*. Cambridge: Cambridge University Press.

Goldthorpe, J.H., Lockwood, D., Bechoffer, E. and Platt, J. (1968b) *The Affluent Worker: Political Attitudes and Behaviour*. Cambridge: Cambridge University Press.

Goldthorpe, J.H., Lockwood, D., Bechoffer, E. and Platt, J. (1969) *The Affluent Worker in the Class Structure*. Cambridge: Cambridge University Press.

Goldthorpe, J.H., Llewellyn, C. and Payne, C. (1987) *Social Mobility and the Class Structure of Modern Britain*, (second edition). Oxford: Clarendon (first edition published 1980).

Goldthorpe, J.H. and Marshall, G. (1992) 'The promising future of class analysis', *Sociology*, 26: 381–400.

Gombrich, E.H. *(1972)* The Story of Art. Oxford: Phaidon Press (first published 1950).

Gorz, A. (1982) *Farewell to the Working Class: An Essay on Post-industrial Socialism*, trans., M. Sonenscher. London: Pluto Press (first published 1980, Paris: Éditions Galilee).

Gorz, A. (1985) *Paths to Paradise: On the Liberation from Work*, trans., M. Imre. London: Pluto Press.

Gorz, A. (1989) *Critique of Economic Reason*, trans., G. Handyside and C. Turner. London: Verso (first published 1988, Paris: Éditions Galilee).

Gottdiener, M. (1994) 'The system of objects and the commodification of everday life: the early Baudrillard', in D. Kellner (ed.). pp. 25–40.

Greenhalgh, P. (1988) *Ephemeral Vistas: The Expositions Universelles, Great Exhibitions and World's Fairs, 1851–1939*. Manchester: Manchester University Press.

Griffiths, M. (1995) *Feminisms and the Self: The Web of Identity*. London: Routledge.

Grint, K. (1998) *The Sociology of Work*, (second edition). Cambridge: Polity Press.

Hakim, C. (1995) 'Five feminist myths about women's employment', *The British Journal of Sociology*, 46 (3): 429–55.

Hakim, C. (1996) *Key Issues in Women's Work: Female Heterogeneity and the Polarisation of Women's Employment*. London: The Athlone Press.

Hakim, C. (2000) *Work-Lifestyle Choices in the 21st Century*. Oxford: Oxford University Press.

Hall, S. and DuGay, P. (eds) (1996) *Questions of Cultural Identity*. London: Sage.

Hamnett, C., McDowell, L., Sarre, P. (eds) (1989) *The Changing Social Structure*. London: Sage.

Hanson, N.R. (1958) *Patterns of Discovery*. Cambridge: Cambridge University Press.

Harris, C.C.H. (1987) *Redundancy and Recession in South Wales*. Oxford: Blackwell.

Harrison, C. and Wood, P. (eds) (1992) *Art in Theory 1900–1990: An Anthology of Changing Ideas*. Oxford: Blackwell.

Harvey, D. (1989) *The Condition of Postmodernity*. Oxford: Oxford University Press.

Hayes, J. and Nutman, P. (1981) *Understanding the Unemployed: The Psychological Effects of Unemployment*. London: Tavistock Publications.

Hebdige, D. (1979) *Subculture: The Meaning of Style*. London: Methuen.

Hebdige, D. (1987) *Cut 'n' Mix*. London: Comedia.

Heelas, P. and Morris (eds) (1992) *The Values of the Enterprise Culture: The Moral Debate*. London: Routledge.

Heery, E. and Salmon, J. (eds) (2000) *The Insecure Workforce*. London: Routledge.

Hermes, J. (1995) *Reading Women's Magazines*. Cambridge: Polity Press.

Herzberg, F. (1968) *Work and the Nature of Man*. New York: Staples Press.

Hills, J. (ed.) (1996) *New Inequalities*. Cambridge: Cambridge University Press.

Hobsbawm, E. (1969) *Industry and Empire*. Harmondsworth: Penguin.

Hoggart, R. (1956) *The Uses of Literacy*. Harmondsworth: Penguin.

Horkheimer, M. and Adorno, T. (1972) *Dialectic of Enlightenment*. New York: Herder and Herder.

Horowitz, D. (1985) *The Morality of Spending: Attitudes to the Consumer Society in America, 1875–1940*. London: Johns Hopkins University Press.

Hudson, K. (1983) *The Archaeology of the Consumer Society: The Second Industrial Revolution in Britain*. London: Heinemann.

Hughes, R. (1980) *The Shock of the New*. London: BBC Publications.

Illich, I. (1971) *De-Schooling Society*. London: Calder and Boyers.

Illich, I. (1973) *Tools for Conviviality*. London: Calder and Boyers.

Illich, I. (1975) *Medical Nemesis: The Expropriation of Health*. London: Calder and Boyers.

Inglehart, R. (1990) *Cultural Shift in Advanced Industrial Society*. Princeton, NJ: Princeton University Press.

Inglehart, R. (1997) *Modernization and Postmodernization: Cultural, Economic and Political Change in 43 Societies*. Princeton, NJ: Princeton University Press.

Isin, E.F. and Wood, P.K. (1999) *Citizenship and Identity*. London: Sage.

Jackson, M. and Marsden, B. (1966) *Education and the Working Class: Some General Themes Raised by a Study of 88 Working-Class Children in a Northern Industrial City*, (revised second edition). Harmondsworth: Penguin Books (first published 1962).

Jackson, R., Stevenson, N. and Brooks, K. (1999) *Making Sense of Men's Magazines*. Cambridge: Polity Press.

Jameson, F. (1991) *Postmodernism, or The Cultural Logic of Capitalism*. London: Verso.

Jameson, F. (1999) 'The cultural logic of capitalism' in A. Elliott (ed.). pp. 338–50.

Jenkins, R. (1996) *Social Identity*. London: Routledge.

Jowell, R., Cutrice, J., Brook, L., Arendht, D. and Park, A. (eds) (1994) *British Social Attitudes: The 11th Report*, SCPR. Aldershot: Dartmouth Publishing.

Jowell, R., Cutrice, J., Park, A., Brook, L., Thompson, K. and Bryson, C. (eds) (1997) *British Social Attitudes: The 14th Report*, SCPR. Aldershot: Gower.

Jowell, R., Cutrice, J., Park, A., Brook, L., Thompson, K. and Bryson, C. (eds) (1998) *British – and European – Social Attitudes: The 15th Report*. Aldershot Gower.

Jowell, R., Cutrice, J., Park, A., Thompson, K., Jarvis, L., Bromley, C. and Strafford, No (eds) (2000) *British Social Attitudes: the 17th Report*, National Centre for Social Research. London: Sage.

Kalvin, P. and Jarrett, J.E. (1985) *Unemployment: Its Social Psychological Effects*. Cambridge: Cambridge University Press.

Katona, G. (1964) *The Mass Consumption Society*. New York: McGraw-Hill.

Keat, R., Whiteley, N. and Abercrombie, N. (eds) (1994) *The Authority of the Consumer*. London: Routledge.

Keefe, T. (1984) 'The stress of unemployment', *Social Work*, 29 (3): 264–68.

Kellner, D. (1989) *Jean Baudrillard: From Marxism to Postmodernism and Beyond*. Cambridge: Polity Press.

Kellner, D. (ed.) (1994) *Baudrillard: A Critical Reader*. Oxford: Basil Blackwell.

Kondratiev, N. (1935) 'The long waves in economic life', *Review of Economic Statistics*, 17: 105–15.

Kriesberg, L. and Misztal, B. (eds) (1988) *Social Movements as a Factor of Change in the Contemporary World, Research in Social Movements, Conflicts and Change*, Vol. 10. Greenwich, CT: JAI Press.

Kumar, K. (1987) *Utopia and Anti-Utopia in Modern Times*. Oxford: Basil Blackwell.

Kumar, K. (1995) *From Post-Industrial to Post-Modern Society: New Theories of the Contemporary World*. Oxford: Blackwell.

Lane, R.E. (1991) *The Market Experience*. Cambridge: Cambridge University Press.

Lancaster, K. *(1971)* Consumer Demand: A New Approach. New York: Columbia University Press.

Langlois, R.N. and Cosgel, M.M. (1998) 'The organization of consumption' in M. Bianchi (ed.).

Lash, S. and Featherstone, M. (eds) (2002) *Recognition and Difference: Politics, Identity, Multiculture*. London: Sage.

Lash, S. and Urry, J. (1987) *The End of Organized Capitalism*. Cambridge: Polity Press.

Lash, S. and Urry, J. (1994) *Economics of Syns and Space*. London: Sage.

Lee, M. (1993) *Consumer Culture Reborn: The Cultural Politics of Consumption*. London: Routledge.

Lee, M. (1994) 'Flights of fancy: academics and consumer culture', *Media Culture and Society*, 16 (3).

Lee, N. and Munro, R. (eds) (2001) *The Consumption of Mass, Sociological Review Monographs*. Oxford: Blackwell Publishers.

Leslie, P. (ed.) (1997) *The Gulf War as Popular Entertainment: An Analysis of the Military-Industrial Media Complex*. Lewiston, NJ: E. Mellen Press.

Lévi-Strauss, C. (1972) *The Savage Mind*. London: Weidenfeld and Nicholson (originally published 1962).

Lewis, J. (1992) *Women in Britain since 1945: Women, Family, Work and the State in the Post-War Years*. Oxford: Blackwell.

Lhamon, W.T. (1998) *Raising Cain: Blackface Performance from Jim Crow to Hip Hop*. Cambridge MA: Harvard University Press.

Sève, L. (1978) *Man in Marxist Theory and the Psychology of Personality*, trans., J. McGreal. Hassocks: Harvester Press (first published 1974).

Shammas, C. (1993) 'Changes in English and Anglo-American consumption from 1550–1800', in J. Brewer and R. Porter (eds).

Sharp, M. and Holmes, P. (eds.) (1989) *Strategies for New Technology: Case Studies from Britain and France*. London: Philip Allan.

Simmel, G. (1904) 'Fashion', *The International Quarterly*, X (1): 130–55.

Simmel, G. (1978) *The Philosophy of Money*. London: Routledge and Kegan Paul.

Slater, D. (1997a) 'Consumer culture and the politics of need', in M. Nava et al. (eds).

Slater, D. (1997b) *Consumer Culture and Modernity*. Cambridge: Polity Press.

Smiles, S. (1958) *Self-Help. With Illustrations of Conduct and Perseverence*. London: John Murray (originally published 1859).

Smith, R. (1987) *Unemployment and Health: A Disaster and a Challenge*. Oxford: Oxford University Press.

Social Trends (2002) No.32, London: HMSO.

Social Trends (2003) No.33, London: HMSO.

Soper, K. (1981) *On Human Needs: Open and Closed Theories in a Marxist Perspective*. Sussex: Harvester Press.

Soper, K. (1990) *Troubled Pleasures: Writings on Politics, Gender and Hedonism*. London: Verso.

Steadman Jones, G. (1984) *Languages of Class*. Cambridge: Cambridge University Press.

Stevenson, N. (2003) *Cultural Citizenship: Cosmopolitan Questions*. Maidenhead: Open University Press.

Stewart, F. (1992) 'The adolescent consumer', in J.C. Coleman and C. Warren-Anderson, (eds). pp. 203–26.

Stratford, N. and Christie, I. (2000) 'Town and country life', in R. Jowell et al. (eds).

Strigler, G., and Becker, G. (1977) 'De gustibus non est disputandum', *American Economic Review* 67: 76–90.

Stuard, S. (1985) 'Medieval workshop: toward a theory of consumption and economic change', *Journal of Economic History*, 45 (2): 447–51.

Swingewood, A. (2000) *A Short History of Sociological Thought* (third edition). London: Macmillan.

Tarrow, S. (1994) *Power in Movement: Social Movements, Collective Action, and Politics*. Cambridge: Cambridge University Press.

Taylor, B. 'Green in word ...', in R. Jowell, et al. (eds).

Taylor, P.M. (ed.) (1988) *Britain and the Cinema in the Second World War*. London: Macmillan Press.

Tawney, R.H. (1960) *Religion and the Rise of Capitalism: An Historical Study*, (Holland Memorial Lectures, 1922). London: John Murray (first published 1926).

Tawney, R.H. (1982) *The Acquisitive Society*. Brighton: Wheatsheaf (first published 1921 by G. Bell & Sons).

Thirsk, J. (1978) *Economic Policy and Projects: The Development of a Consumer Society in Early Modern England.* Oxford: Clarendon.

Thompson, E.P. (1963) *The Making of the English Working Class.* London: Victor Gollancz.

Thornton, S. (1995) *Club Cultures.* Cambridge: Polity.

Tilly, C. (1988) 'Social movements old and new', in L. Kriesberg and B. Misztal (eds). pp. 1–18.

Tilly, L. and Scott, J. (1987) *Women, Work and Family.* London: Methuen.

Toffler, A. (1970) *Future Shock.* New York: Random House.

Toffler, A. (1980) *The Third Wave.* New York: William Morrow.

Tomlinson, A. (1990) *Consumption, Identity and Style: Marketing Meanings and the Packaging of Pleasure.* London: Routledge.

Turner, B.S. (1993) 'Baudrillard for sociologists', in C. Rojek and C. Turner (eds). pp. 70–87.

UK 2000 Time Use Survey, Office for National Statistics. London: HMSO.

Uusitalo, Liisa (1998) 'Consumption and postmodernity: social structuration and the construction of the self', in M. Bianchi (ed.).

van Deth, J. and Scarborough, E. (eds) (1995) *Belief in Government: Volume Four, The Impact of Values.* Oxford: Oxford University Press.

Veblen, T. (1994) *The Theory of the Leisure Class.* Harmondsworth: Penguin Books (first published 1899).

Voth, Hans-Joachim. (1998) 'Work and the sirens of consumption in eighteenth-century London', in M. Bianchi (ed.).

Walby, S. (1986) *Patriarchy at Work.* Oxford: Polity Press.

Walby, S. (1990) *Theorising Patriarchy.* Oxford: Basil Blackwell.

Walby, S. (1997) *Gender Transformations.* London: Routledge.

Wallace, M. and Wallace, W. (eds) (1996) *Policy-Making in the European Union.* Oxford: Oxford University Press.

Wallman, S. (ed.) (1979) *The Social Anthropology of Work.* Association of Social Anthropologists of the Commonwealth (ASA), Monograph No. 19, London: Academic Press.

Warde, A. (1990a) 'Introduction to the sociology of consumption', *Sociology*, 24 (1): 1–4.

Warde, A. (1990b) 'Production, consumption and social change: reservations regarding Peter Saunders' sociology of consumption', *International Journal of Urban and regional Research*, 4 (2).

Waters, M. (1995) *Globalization.* London: Routledge.

Weber, M. (1976) *Protestantism and the Spirit of Capitalism*, trans., T. Parsons. London: Allen and Unwin. (This translation was originally published in 1930.)

Weber, M. (1978) *Economy and Society*, Vols 1 and 2, edited by G. Roth, and C. Wittich. Berkeley, CA: University of California Press.

Westergaard, J., Noble, I. and Walker, A. (1989) *After Redundancy: The Experience of Economic Insecurity.* Cambridge: Polity Press.

Westley, W. and Westley, M. (1971) *The Emerging Worker: Equality and Conflict in the Mass Consumption Society.* Montreal: Queen's-McGill University Press.

Williams, G. (1960) 'The concept of egemonia in the thought of Antonio Gramsci' *Journal of the History of Ideas*, 21: 586–99.

Williams, R. (1985) *Culture and Society: 1780–1950*. Harmondsworth: Penguin.

Willis, P., (1990) *Common Culture: Symbolic work at play in the everyday cultures of the young*. Milton Keynes: Open University Press.

Winter, M.F., and Robert, E.R. (1980) 'Male Dominance, Late Capitalism, and the Growth of Instrumental Reason', *Berkeley Journal of Sociology*, pp. 249–80.

Witherspoon, S. (1994) 'The Greening of Britain: Romance and Rationality', in Jowell, et al. (eds.), 1994.

Wood, S. (ed.) (1982) *The Degradation of Work?: Skill, Deskilling and the Labour Process*. London: Hutchinson.

Worpole, K. (2000) *In Our Own Backyard: The Social Promise of Environmentalism*. London: Green Alliance.

Wright, E.O. (1989) *The Debate on Classes*, London: Verso.

Wright, E.O. (1996) *Class Counts*. Oxford: Oxford University Press.

Zald, M.N. and McCarthy, J.D. (eds) (1987) *Social Movements in an Organizational Society*. Oxford: Transaction Books.

Index